Something to Cry About

• •

An Argument against Corporal Punishment of Children in Canada

Susan M. Turner

Studies in Childhood and Family in Canada

Wilfrid Laurier University Press

WLU

This book has been published with the help of a grant from the Humanities and Social Sciences Federation of Canada, using funds provided by the Social Sciences and Humanities Research Council of Canada. We acknowledge the support of the Canada Council for the Arts for our publishing program. We acknowledge the financial support of the Government of Canada through the Book Publishing Industry Development Program for our publishing activities.

National Library of Canada Cataloguing in Publication Data

Turner, Susan M., 1955–
  Something to cry about : an argument against corporal punishment of children in Canada

(Studies in childhood and family in Canada)
Includes bibliographical references and index.
ISBN 0-88920-382-2

1. Corporal punishment — Canada. 2. Child abuse — Canada.
3. Discipline of children. I. Title. II. Series.

HQ770.4.T87 2002   306.874   C2001-903199-8

Cover design by Leslie Macredie,
using a photograph by Brian Henderson.

The author and publisher have made every reasonable effort to obtain permission to reproduce the secondary material in this book. Any corrections or omissions brought to the attention of the Press will be incorporated in subsequent printings.

Printed in Canada

To Geneva, Katharine and Sean

Love you.

I'll give you something to cry about, Reenie would say. If we'd
been her real children she would have slapped us.
As it was, she never did, so we never found out
what this threatening *something* might be.

— from *The Blind Assassin* by Margaret Atwood

Table of Contents

• • • • • • • • • • •

Preface

• • • • • • • • • • •

In what follows I present a two-part argument designed to rationally persuade readers that, first, all forms of corporal punishment are immoral, and second, that the Canadian law which grants parents and teachers a legal privilege to corporally punish the children in their care ought to be removed from our Criminal Code. I argue for the immorality of all forms of corporal punishment based on its harms to children and the adults they become — harms and risks for harms that have been repeatedly demonstrated in empirical research — and on the absence of evidence that it is effective at improving children's behaviour or character. The most, it seems, that can be said for corporal punishment, based on this evidence, is that it is usually successful at temporarily interrupting specific aversive conduct. But since this can also be said of other disciplinary methods that do not involve the infliction of pain, the interruption of aversive conduct cannot morally justify the use of pain as a disciplinary measure. Contrary to what a long tradition in law of granting parents and teachers the legal privilege of corporal punishment assumes, there is no moral justification for it and indeed, definite reason to morally condemn it.

The law which currently grants Canadian parents and teachers this privilege—Section 43—ought to be removed from the Criminal Code of Canada. There are no grounds for denying that Section 43 violates both the equality guarantee and the right to security of the person enshrined in Canada's Charter of Rights and Freedoms. Can it nevertheless be demonstrated that these violations of children's rights are necessary in a free and democratic society? I argue it cannot. Some of those who think differently argue that a long tradition of leaving the discipline of children entirely up to their parents and teachers is a sufficient reason for preserving the practice. I challenge this reasoning. Others urge that if the autonomy of the family is compromised by the surveillance of the state or of third parties intent on "turning in" parents who spank their children, children will be worse off than they are now. I criticize several of the assumptions required to support this view.

The book begins with introductory material in the area of moral philosophy in order to familiarize the nonphilosopher with the language and context of the discussion that follows. It then circles a number of issues which need to be addressed in order to situate the moral debate over corporal punishment in a specifically Canadian context. I then narrow the terms of the situated debate to those of a particular moral reasoning framework—one described in the introductory material and with which some philosophers will no doubt take issue.

Next I launch a critique of several procorporal punishment arguments which are reconstructed from a variety of sources. Some of you will no doubt find many of these arguments familiar. My criticism of them relies to a large extent on the empirical work of others and raises questions about two unstated assumptions that such arguments appear to make. I thereby invite you to go deeper into your own reasoning on the morality of corporal punishment. On one hand, support of the practice seems to assume that because of the differences between them, children will benefit from being hit for disciplinary reasons even though being treated this way harms adults. On another, resistance to the idea that the practice should not be protected under law seems to assume that children are safe when their parents (and teachers) have complete decision-making autonomy concerning their discipline. Are these assumptions justified? I argue they are not.

After considering the views of three people who have written about the morality of corporal punishment in light of the foregoing analysis, I move on to examine the specific legal questions surrounding the practice in Canada. Without entering too deeply into a discussion of this key issue, I grant that the immorality of a practice may or may not serve as a reason to support its illegality. And so my legal argument proceeds, to a large extent, on separate grounds. However, not on entirely separate grounds. The Charter makes it clear that courts testing the validity of any limit to the individual rights and freedoms of Canadians must make use of the best social science available on the matter. Since my moral argument also depends on the best social science available on the corporal punishment question, the two arguments intersect to some extent.

My conclusion that the law granting parents and teachers the privilege to use corporal punishment against children ought to be repealed by government might be challenged on the grounds it does not apply to spanking or "moderate" corporal punishment. Certain aspects of such a challenge are explored when I consider the views of those who have written on the subject, but a more detailed discussion of spanking in light of both my moral and legal arguments against corporal punishment is presented to show that even moderate punishment practices of this sort ought to be abandoned.

The fashion in twentieth-century philosophy was to move away from these sorts of efforts at moral persuasion and toward the simple presentation of rational options, leaving ultimate conclusions undecided. As we slid from the last years of the century into the new millennium, that fashion slid as well to be replaced, in many quarters, by an even more skeptical agenda. There were no "ultimate conclusions" to be drawn when it came to morality; no rational methods one could use to come to decisions about "what to do."

In spite of this latest trend and its warm reception by those who see strict self-interest as the only justification for all human conduct, there continues, I believe, to be room for philosophers who identify with a social cause. In the eighteenth century, David Hume distinguished between works of moral philosophy and those of metaphysics by noting the former dealt with the practical affairs of living whereas the latter addressed its more abstract and fundamental facets. It was appropriate, he suggested, that works of moral philosophy should exhort the reader; should attempt to persuade as a means of improving character and the conditions of life. This "old-fashioned" way of doing moral philosophy is, in broad outline, my method here.

No one likes to be told that he or she has false beliefs — especially ones that bear on moral matters. This sensitivity to moral criticism is, to some extent, understandable, given the many shameful histories of moral dogmas used to justify extermination, enslavement, oppression or exclusion. From the mouths of those who wield total social, political, legal, economic or military power, moral condemnation is rightly regarded as ominous. But it hardly follows that there is nothing which individuals or institutions should morally condemn. Moral condemnation of slavery in nineteenth-century America met with a great deal of criticism. It was argued that even though the practice should not be allowed to spread to the northern states, people in the southern states who owned slaves ought to be permitted to continue to own them. It was no business of the North's. Yet clearly, the mere fact that slave ownership was widely practised in the south did not morally justify it. The corporal punishment of children may not seem nearly as morally intolerable as slavery to Canadians — may not seem morally intolerable at all — because it is so widely practised. But, as the history of abolition shows, while this fact may explain tolerance or the use of corporal punishment, it does not morally justify the practice. Open-mindedness does not require being silent about one's moral beliefs. Rather, it implies being prepared to engage in rational debate with anyone who thinks differently and is also prepared to argue rationally for his or her position. If my tone seems strident at times, it is because I feel passionate about this issue. And it is, of course, difficult to engage in dialogue with a book.

By the time this one is published, it is possible a constitutional challenge to the law which justifies the corporal punishment of children will be on its way to the Supreme Court of Canada. Such actual events have a way of making arguments of the sort offered here seem beside the point. But whether such a challenge succeeds or fails, the public debate over the corporal punishment of children will just be beginning in our country. In that case, the arguments which I criticize and the ones I advance in what follows might seem more than mere abstractions.

The moral reasoning I use to arrive at my conclusions is conse-quentialist—specifically utilitarian. That is to say that the priciples of morality I employ require that in order for a practice to be considered moral, it must tend to produce a balance of good over harm for most of those affected. This approach is not without its critics in moral philos-ophy. However, in the context of social planning, I assume it will be widely accepted. Nevertheless, I go some way to justifying this approach where appropriate.

The particular route my argument takes has, in part, been deter-mined by expectations about my readers. Mainly, I presuppose a liter-ate readership of Canadians concerned either as parents or profession-ally with the disciplining of children. While the text focuses primarily on the Canadian situation, much of what is discussed here can be applied in other jurisdictions. Overall, I aim to introduce non-philoso-phers to the philosophical dimensions of the issue of corporal punish-ment and to raise the profile of the issue within academic philosophical circles. As with all works that aspire to speak to readers from various backgrounds, some chapters will seem less engaging than others, depending upon your area of interest. For non-philosophers in particu-lar, the discussions of moral and political philosophy may even seem distracting or off-topic. Philosophers are used to this sort of response to their efforts at bringing their subject into the arena of public discourse. But we like to think that becoming familiar with this discourse has tremendous value when it comes to engaging in public debate.

As the manuscript review process unfolded, several basic changes in the original design were made. But as with all such works, a point was reached when further major changes were vetoed. Since that time, the findings of a great deal of additional research into corporal pun-ishment have been published and at least two legal events have occurred which are directly relevant to the topic. I have included refer-ences to the research where possible and in the interest of being on top of the legal issues, I have mentioned recent developments where appropriate.

It is inevitable that over the long course of working on a book like this one, new insights, more succinct arguments and unexpected ver-sions of objections come up. In the interest of putting the overall argu-ment in its best light, I have added a chapter at the end which deals with what I consider the two strongest objections to my thesis. First, that there is insufficient evidence that corporal punishment is part of a continuum of violence which sometimes ends in child abuse. Second, that granting corporal punishment's harms, children would be made even worse off by the erosion of parental autonomy which removing the privilege to use it from the Criminal Code would risk. After having pondered, articulated and critically evaluated other versions of these objections for several years (all of which are included in the book), I present, then critically challenge them in what I think is their strongest and most reasonable form.

It may surprise some philosophers that my discussion does not include a robustly defended theory of punishment. In a work intended for philosophers only, one would rightly expect such a defence. However, I have, for the most part, merely assumed a utilitarian theory of punishment here. That is, I have presupposed that the moral justification of any type of punishment is determined by its tendency to prevent the problem behaviour for which it is administered and, granting it is a harm, by its being less harmful to all affected than the continuation of the problem behaviour would be. There is a considerable amount of significant scholarly work both in moral philosophy and philosophy of law on the punishment question per se. I believe that this work needs to be brought into direct philosophical contact with the social science on corporal punishment of children but have merely gestured in that direction here.

I have no doubt that the *Canadian Incidence Study on Child Neglect and Abuse* (2001), released just this past spring, will provide the basis for a great deal of important future research into the circumstances and rates of the physical abuse of children. The study's results are limited by the fact they only represent cases (dismissed, confirmed and suspected) which come to the attention of and are dealt with by social service agencies. As such, the data do not include cases that are dealt with directly by police. Nor, of course, can they include unreported cases of physical abuse to children. Nevertheless, the study goes a long way to establishing a statistical baseline for how often corporal punishment is implicated in child abuse and for comparison as we strive to improve Canada's record on how our children are treated.

Acknowledgements

Several thanks are in order. I would like to thank Don LePan for suggesting to Sandra Woolfrey, former director of Wilfrid Laurier University Press that I might have something to contribute by way of a manuscript to the Press's series on children and families in Canada. This was not the case at the time but it got me going on this project. Thanks, too, to Sandra for supporting my early work and seeing me through my first round with the Aid to Scholarly Publishing Program at the Canada Council without whom this book could not have been published in Canada. My thanks, of course, to those administering the Program for their encouragement and patience with the manuscript and especially to their reviewers whose criticisms and comments egged me on and made this a better book.

I would like to extend thanks as well to Joan Durrant for her expert advice in the general area of social science research and in the area of research into corporal punishment of children more specifically. And I owe a special thanks to Corinne Robertshaw who reviewed the chapters on legal issues and made many very valuable comments and suggestions.

Thanks also to Elin Edwards, Leslie Macredie and Brian Henderson of Wilfrid Laurier University Press for helping to see the project through.

Finally, thank you to my beautiful children, Geneva, Katharine and Sean. Seeing the way you have grown, the amazingly wise and morally centered young adults you have become has always been the promise motivating me to think hard about the issue of corporal punishment in the context of raising children and to put that reasoning into writing.

And thank you Scot, Liz and the gang for giving me a way out of parenting in a vacuum.

Introduction

• • • • • • • • • • •

The issue of child abuse sits uncomfortably in the background of our awareness, occasionally breaking through to the forefront of our attention. When we witness a child being hit or, less frequently, read sensational news stories in which children were punished to death, our discomfort sharply increases. We are outraged. But this intensity of feeling is usually temporary. And its episodic nature arguably prevents it from instigating sustained public debate on the question of children's "security of the person" rights. Without this sort of ongoing public debate, there is little motivation for the citizenry or government to rethink Canadian law and social policy on the issue of corporal punishment.

As it stands, the rights of Canada's children to security of the person are limited by what the Criminal Law of Canada considers the justified use of reasonable physical force against children by their parents, teachers and other caregivers. History makes it clear that the criminal law in this case is designed to specifically justify corporal punishment. Recent Canadian case law makes it equally clear this is its purpose. All

1

Canadian citizens—including children—have a constitutional right against unwanted hitting and other forms of assault. But in the case of Canadian children, the right does not protect them from being hit by parents or teachers whose intention is to improve children's character or get them to behave or learn a lesson.

There is no question in our society that individual rights such as those to security of the person need to be limited by considerations of welfare to others. Our Criminal Code as well as The Charter of Rights and Freedoms make it clear that since one of the points of such rights is to maximize personal safety and comfort levels for the citizenry, it may, on occasion, be necessary to limit the rights of this or that individual or category of persons to secure them for the rest. So, for example, we grant police the privilege to assault suspects with reasonable force if this is necessary to keep them in custody. We also have laws against the public expression of hate towards groups to ensure that being the member of a minority in Canadian society does not mean having to discount your ethnic origin or conceal your sexual orientation.

The exercise of one's individual rights is therefore (and I would argue, must be) restricted by the ability of most others in society to confidently exercise those same rights. Political philosophers refer to this as "the liberty principle" and it is at the bottom of classical as well as contemporary liberalism. Whether or not one favours liberalism and its emphasis on individual rights over other political theories, it is the guiding ideal of Canada's major political parties on social, legal and political policy. As a general principle, therefore, limiting the security of the person rights of children is neither theoretically nor practically problematic in Canadian society. What is problematic or open to question, however, is the particular manner in which these rights are limited by current law and practice. Whatever limits are accepted, they must directly serve the safety and comfort levels of most Canadians and must minimally limit the rights in question. It is far from clear that hitting children for the purpose of improving their behaviour or learning their lessons is a justified restriction of their security of the person rights on these grounds. Opening up this question to public debate would invite consideration of, among other things, empirical data concerning the effects of corporal punishment on children, their behaviour and learning. I believe, and will argue, that such consideration is to be welcomed by those who doubt corporal punishment is a justified exception to what security of the person rights for children should include. It must also be confronted by those who maintain that corporal punishment is a justified limit to those rights.

In addition to the episodic nature of feelings of outrage over corporal punishment "excesses," confusion and disagreement over the meanings of the terms "child abuse," "corporal punishment," "assault" and "reasonable force" have a tendency to derail attempts at sustained public debate. In the recent past, debates over capital punishment and abortion showed that such attempts all too frequently end in shouting matches as if the most reasonable position to take was the loudest. The speed with which such attempts at discussion descend to raised voices, insult and counter-insult is perhaps a measure of their lack of clarity on key terms.

Everyone agrees that there ought to be laws against child abuse, that these laws ought to be strictly enforced and that those who violate them be severely punished. But there is little agreement on what should be included under the term. Some consider all forms of corporal punishment child abuse and therefore immoral or unlawful. Others regard corporal punishments such as spanking and smacking as not only tolerable and rightly lawful but also morally recommended. In addition to confusion over what the term "child abuse" refers to, there is also confusion over what counts as "corporal punishment." If a teacher physically restrains a violent pupil by knocking him or her to the ground, is this corporal punishment or merely necessary physical interference? If a parent makes a misbehaving child stand in a corner, is this corporal punishment or merely punishment? Finally, there is the question of assault. According to the law, assault is the unwanted application of physical force and is considered a harm even when there is no other damage done. But the ordinary use of the term "assault" implies a much more dramatic and violent act. If our impression of child abuse is informed by images of dramatic violent assault or torture, calls for the legal prohibition of corporal punishment—which may include "light spankings"—sound excessive. If our impression of abuse is instead informed by the view that all hitting of—though not necessarily all physical restraint of—children necessarily involves a serious harm to and a deep disrespect for their persons, the presence of legal justifications and public support for all forms of hitting strikes us as barbaric. The question of whether the use of corporal punishment is a justified limit to the security of the person rights of children requires reference to empirical data. But empirical data will be of limited use in sorting out these definitional problems. This is because no amount of empirical data on its own can help clarify how the terms of this debate ought to be fixed. This is a philosophical issue and one which promises to be ongoing. As such, while I offer certain definitions in what follows, this aspect of the debate will always be open to some extent.

There are many individuals and groups in Canadian society engaged in the work of bringing empirical data to public light and defining the terms noted above in order to heighten the citizenry's indignation towards all forms of punishment which involve the risk of physical or psychological damage — however minor — to the bodies and minds of children. Their purpose is to broaden the public perception of child abuse to include even spanking as part of a continuum of violence which all too frequently ends in the death of a child. On average, fifty children a year die in Canada as a result of injuries sustained in what their assailants believed to be an administration of corporal punishment — a number second only to that from Sudden Infant Death Syndrome [SIDS] as a cause of child fatalities. It is hoped that as hitting children for any reason becomes antisocial, the flow of moral and legal feeling against harming them in the name of "correction" will be unblocked. This book aims to consolidate the voices of those who condemn corporal punishment and assist in the inauguration of sustained and reasoned public argument on this very important social matter.

Two broad supports for the moral legitimacy of corporal punishment occupy my attention. These supports may function together or independently. The first is the set of traditional values implied by corporal punishment as moral practice. These values are rarely examined in bright light. I argue that when they are, they are easily seen to contradict other values we have enshrined as constitutive of Canada's multinational identity. The second support remains even when this first is removed. It is the moral distinction between adults and children where, when all the "every life is priceless" rhetoric is removed, we calculate that a child's life and happiness is worth less than an adult's. If the co-existence of legal permission to assault children and legal prohibition against assaulting persons is rationally defensible, this distinction must be assumed. I argue that on the evidence, it cannot be sustained.

In chapter 1, I present what I will rely on as the definitions of the terms of the debate as they have been worked out by philosophers, sociologists, psychologists and lawmakers. In chapter 2, I introduce a number of moral theories — theories of how we ought to act; of what principles of conduct we ought to embrace and of what values we ought to hold dear — that have attempted to account for and prescribe human conduct through history. I specifically focus on their use in the context of child discipline and punishment. In chapter 3, I consider the matter of what might be called "Canadian moral values" as these are expressed in our constitutional documents and as they reflect the values of individual Canadians who come from a wide variety of cultural backgrounds. I concentrate on the value of "security of the person" and argue that this is a Canadian "super" value. In chapter 3, I also present and criticize two general arguments for the corporal punishment of children: the argument from moral education and the argument from individual welfare. As these and additional arguments are considered, I assume that as the intentional infliction of unwanted pain, a continuum of moral wrong affects all forms of corporal punishment from "nonsevere" ones such as spanking to severe forms such as whipping, punching and kicking. Later in chapter 10, I consider various arguments against classifying nonsevere forms of corporal punishment as in any way morally wrong.

In chapter 4, following from my assumption that any infliction of unwanted pain upon another at least merits moral questioning, I adopt a utilitarian consequentialist approach to the moral assessment of the corporal punishment of children. Utilitarian moral theory states that we ought to promote the greatest happiness for the greatest number affected by our acts or policies and assumes that whether we are successful in doing so is a matter to be decided by their consequences. The theory has been subjected to a great deal of criticism since its initial development in the nineteenth century and was for the most part abandoned in the middle period of the twentieth. However, it continues to be especially powerful when moral questions surrounding the interests and welfare of those not considered competent under law are concerned. As moral concern over nonhuman animals, the mentally chal-

lenged and children have come to the fore in the last part of the twentieth century, utilitarianism has regained a foothold in the minds of
many moral philosophers.

Chapter 4 also introduces seven arguments of varying strength in
favour of corporal punishment which might be advanced on utilitarian
grounds and shows that none of them are persuasive. I conclude that
according to this moral theory, all corporal punishment of children is
immoral. I leave it to the proponents of other moral theories (outlined
in chapter 1) to assess the status of the corporal punishment of children
on their respective preferred views.

Chapters 5 and 6 explore two deep issues which are implied by the
arguments and counterarguments concerning corporally punishing
children. The first is an often unnoticed assumption made by most
arguments in favour of corporal punishment. They assume that human
beings as children are so different from human beings as adults that
equal security of the person protection for children would harm rather
than benefit them. I argue that this assumption is deeply rooted in
poetic fictions and has no rational force nor any empirical basis. I look
at a second deep issue in chapter 6—what I call the paradox of child
protection. This paradox emerges when we put the facts of children's
inescapable vulnerability to—and dependence on—adults, face to face
with the fact that statistically, the adults who care for them pose the
greatest threat to their safety through both action and inaction. I conclude that while the paradox cannot be resolved, the problem it presents can be mitigated by education and community support.

In chapter 7, I present and critically evaluate the work of two writ-
ers who have commented on the corporal punishment of children in
the popular press: Dr. James Dobson, a well known American childcare
authority and Barbara Amiel, a widely read columnist in Canadian
newspapers. I carefully show that their opinions, while popular and
influential, have little to recommend them. I also examine philosopher
David Benatar's comments on corporal punishment and use those
comments to critically analyze the work of Robert Larzelere, an
American child psychologist whose work is frequently cited in the pro-
corporal punishment literature.

In chapters 8, 9 and 10, I shift gears and consider the issue of corporal punishment in legal terms. In chapter 8, I examine the legal sub-

stance of Section 43 — the provision in the Canadian Criminal Code that justifies the use of corporal punishment against children and students — and offer a critique from the perspective of the philosophy of law. I argue that as a "special defense," Section 43 makes assumptions about children, adults and how they relate to one another that cannot be rationally supported. In light of these findings, I show that there can be no intelligible defence of lawful corrective assault and that willful blindness characterizes the courts as well as the government and its agents on this question.

In chapter 9, I challenge the constitutionality of Section 43. Following a walk-through of the Oakes Test (used to determine whether laws which limit individual rights may nevertheless be constitutional), I conclude that while there are strong reasons for believing Section 43 ought not to pass the Oakes Test, given the recent failure of a similar challenge in the Ontario Supreme Court of Justice, it is possible such a challenge at the Supreme Court of Canada level would fail. In chapter 10, I address two lingering questions: 1) Granting that severe forms of corporal punishment are immoral because of the preponderance of harm they cause, is spanking also immoral? and 2) Granting that spanking is immoral for the same reasons more severe forms of corporal punishment are, will the repeal of Section 43 mean that those who spank children could/should be charged with and perhaps even convicted of assault? I conclude that while the law operates under the maxim of *de minimis non curat lex* ("the law does not take account of trifles") — we ought not to think that spanking is therefore "okay." I briefly consider how countries such as Sweden and Italy have dealt with corporal punishment and suggest possibilities for future policy reform in Canada. I consider the situation faced by teachers separately.

In chapter 11, I revisit what I consider to be the two best challenges to the view that corporal punishment is immoral, on the one hand, and that it ought not to come under the protection of the law, on the other. The first challenge is to the claim that corporal punishment is a risk factor for child abuse. Among the harms to children with which corporal punishment is arguably associated, child abuse is regarded with equal moral outrage by both opponents of corporal punishment and its defenders. But its defenders argue the link between corporal punishment and child abuse has not been demonstrated. This argument has some merit but the claims of researchers concerning such links need to be put into context. When we do this, I argue, the immorality of corporal punishment re-emerges.

The second challenge is to the prospect of more state intrusion into families should parents, when they use corporal punishment, no longer enjoy the protection of the law. While some versions of this argument are clearly unacceptable (Barbara Amiel advances one), I propose a version which seems reasonable on its face and argue that it nevertheless makes an assumption which cannot be sustained. Especially given the important role which the "family statism" argument plays in a recent Ontario legal decision which upheld the constitutionality of Section 43, it needs rigorous critical examination.

I have attempted in what follows to present the issues in a manner which will be accessible to a broad, literate audience. Philosophical writing is noted for its density and dryness and cannot help but seem overly abstract to those accustomed to fact-based material or to reading as "sound byte" consumption. I have tried to avoid the excesses of scholarly writing and endless citing of studies (relegating much of it to the footnotes) but some challenges remain. One possible consequence, therefore, of aiming at a broad but not necessarily popular audience is that no reader will be entirely satisfied with the style of the discussion or the coverage his or her field of expertise receives. I apologize in advance to both my philosophy and nonphilosophy readers, but hope that the substance of what follows will nevertheless succeed in its purpose to provoke intelligent debate on this sensitive topic.

1

• • • • • • • • • • •

The Terms of the Corporal
Punishment Debate

I n February of 1998, a couple charged with seventeen counts of assault (including charges of assault with a weapon) against their seven children, ages two to thirteen, was tried in Quebec Superior Court. The Crown's case against the parents relied on the testimony of their children, delivered to judge and jury by video from a secure room outside the courtroom. Amidst claims of accident, magic and reasonable discipline, the defence argued that the Crown had failed to prove a link between the children's obvious injuries and the parents' "corrective" conduct.[1] In this particular case, the issue of "lawful correction" was not itself on trial. What the jury was instructed by Justice Kevin Downs to consider was merely whether they believed the children's story that their injuries were caused by their parents or whether they believed the parents' story that these injuries were the result of accidents and super-natural forces following though not caused by acts of discipline. The jury believed the children and found both parents guilty on all counts.[2]

Notes to chapter 1 are on pp. 237–40.

Other cases of assault against children by their parents, teachers and other caregivers raise the moral issue of corporal punishment directly.[3] Rather than arguing that the incidents did not occur as alleged by the Crown, which is what happened in the Quebec case, defendants charged under similar circumstances plead their innocence on the grounds that their intention was to reasonably improve or correct the child's bad behaviour. According to the law, they argue, their actions were legally justified; the harmful consequences well within the bounds of what one would expect with reasonable discipline. Perhaps in the Quebec case, the defence was less than eager to argue that having one's ears boxed or burned with a hot iron (the child in this case received second degree burns to one ear) is a reasonable punishment for the offence of throwing out some lettuce or that whipping with electrical cord is a reasonable way of correcting children who make errors when reciting the alphabet. Apparently, other defence teams have not been as timid.

In 1995, an Ontario Provincial Court dismissed charges of assault against David Peterson who had been witnessed repeatedly striking his five-year-old daughter's bare buttocks over the hood of his car in a restaurant parking lot. The purpose of the spanking was to punish Rachel for "slamming her little brother's fingers in the car door." This "pants down" corporal punishment episode followed a "pants up" one in the car which Peterson's daughter had physically resisted. Anne McGillivray, quoting from the Court's decision, writes, "Peterson was acquitted of assault on a defense of reasonable correction under s. 43 of the Criminal Code. Rachel was 'hopefully wiser' and 'any physical injury or emotional trauma...transitory.'"[4]

Earlier in 1987, in *R. v. Robinson*, the defendant was charged with common assault for having strapped and bruised his daughter, aged twelve, "with a double leather belt 4 or 5 times 'as was apparently the custom in the house'" because she had "borrowed clothes and money contrary to instructions" and "swore at her mother."[5] The trial judge accepted the accused's defence of "lawful correction" on the grounds that while "bruising a child is 'abhorrent in the general community,'" the law recognizes that parents must be protected from conviction in the execution of their parental duty to educate their children to a societal norm of civil behaviour—"'short term pain' for 'corrective effect.'"[6]

I suspect most Canadians would be shocked to learn of the many persons exonerated and even praised by judges at trial or on appeal who have been tried for assaulting and seriously hurting children just because these persons are their victims' parents and teachers. The main witness in the Peterson case, for example, "told Peterson that 'she as a parent did not believe in the physical punishment of children' and mistakenly added that what he had done was illegal in Canada."[7] Sadly, it also appears as though many of these same Canadians would be equally shocked if the legal defence of lawful correction used so successfully in such cases was removed from the Canadian Criminal Code. What lies at the bottom of these conflicting senses of outrage? How should we deal with the conflict? To begin to answer these questions, we need to define the terms of the discussion.

The Law

While various, sometimes conflicting, definitions of child abuse abound in government policy on a variety of social welfare and health issues, I am going to follow David Archard, a philosopher who has written extensively on children's issues, and avoid the term for the most part. The phrase child abuse has a built-in negative—even horrific—connotation and has come to be used more as a purely emotional rather than reasoned incitement to anger and indignation.[8] Let us begin instead with the term "assault." While this term also has a strongly negative emotive flavour, it has a settled meaning in Canadian law—a meaning which most Canadians are quite happy to accept when it comes to their own protection. The Canadian Criminal Code states that:

265.

(1) a person commits an assault when

   (a) without the consent of another person, he applies force intentionally to that other person, directly or indirectly;

   (b) he attempts or threatens, by an act or gesture, to apply force to another person, if he has, or causes that other person to believe upon reasonable grounds that he has, present ability to effect his purpose; or

   (c) while openly wearing or carrying a weapon or an imitation thereof, he accosts or impedes another person or begs.

(2) This section applies to all forms of assault, including sexual assault, sexual assault with a weapon, threats to third party or causing bodily harm and aggravated sexual assault.

(3) For the purposes of this section, no consent is obtained where the complainant submits or does not resist by reason of
   (a) the application of force to the complainant or to a person other than the complainant;
   (b) threats or fear of the application of force to the complainant or to a person other than the complainant;
   (c) fraud; or
   (d) the exercise of authority

(4) Where an accused alleges that he believed that the complainant consented to the conduct that is the subject-matter of the charge, a judge, if satisfied that there is sufficient evidence and that, if believed by the jury, the evidence would constitute a defence, shall instruct the jury, when reviewing all the evidence relating to the determination of the honesty of the accused's belief, to consider the presence or absence of reasonable grounds for that belief.

The Code also states that:

267.1

(1) Everyone who, in committing an assault,
   (a) carries, uses or threatens to use a weapon or an imitation thereof, or
   (b) causes bodily harm to the complainant, is guilty of an indictable offence and is liable to imprisonment for ten years.

Furthermore, Section 2 of the Criminal Code defines "bodily harm" as "any hurt or injury to a person that interferes with the comfort of the person and that is more than merely transient or trifling in nature."

Next, regarding our "security of the person" rights, Section 7 of *The Canadian Charter of Rights and Freedoms* states that:

7. Everyone has the right to life, liberty and security of the person and the right not to be deprived thereof except in accordance with the principles of fundamental justice.

And Section 15 of the Charter states that:

15. (1) Every individual is equal before the law and under law and has the right to the equal protection and equal benefit of the law without discrimination and, in particular, without discrimination based on race, national or ethnic origin, colour, religion, sex, age or mental or physical disability.

Since no law may discriminate among persons based on their age when it comes to its protections and benefits, we may first assume, on the face of things at least, that provided the victim of an assault is a person under law, the victim's age has no effect whatsoever on the nature of the charge against the alleged assailant or on the alleged assailant's final guilt or innocence. The law against assault is meant, in other words, to protect *every* individual equally from unwanted or unconsented to applications of force, and does this by sanctioning every assailant according to the same principles of guilt regardless of the age (or race or gender or colour or religious beliefs or physical or mental condition, etc.) of his or her victim. Further, since bodily harm is in part constituted by an individual's "comfort," whether or not someone has been harmed in this way is partly a matter of his or her subjective experience. It is reasonable to suppose that what will constitute discomfort for a child might be quite comfortable or trifling for an adult. Nevertheless, the law makes it clear that it is the child's and not an adult's sense of what is uncomfortable that must be consulted when deciding whether or not bodily harm has occurred.

Based on the definition of assault which governs relations between all of Canada's citizens, does corporal punishment count as assault? The Code's definition of the crime of assault includes a material element and a mental element—what are referred to in legal Latin as a crime's *actus reus* (guilty act) and its *mens rea* (guilty mind). The material element of assault or the behaviour which triggers the state's legal mechanism, includes three different sorts of actions: 1) the unconsented to application of force to another person, 2) an act which to any reasonable person would suggest an attempt or threat to apply force to and without the consent of another person and 3) accosting another person or begging while presenting a weapon or facsimile of a weapon. The material element of assault may be defeated or disproved by the defence if it can show that the Crown has failed to establish any one of the number of claims made in these allegations. Is a see-through water pistol really a facsimile of a weapon? Would a reasonable person today and in our culture be threatened by the finger? Isn't the fact that the alleged victim had entered into a bet with the accused over the force in question sufficient to show he had consented to it? When it comes to the issue of consent, the law is clear. If the defendant had, in any context, explicit authority over the victim then whatever the victim said or did to produce the appearance of consent to the application of force, that application of force was not legally consented to.

Assuming that corporal punishment always involves an unwanted or unconsented to application of physical force, all instances of adult administered corporal punishment of children satisfy the material element of the crime of assault. We may now ask whether corporal punishment also satisfies its mental element. In order to answer this question, we need to understand the mental element of the crime of assault and we need a more robust definition of corporal punishment. Firstly, the mental element of criminal assault is one of general intent. In order to be found guilty of assault, the defendant must have freely aimed at doing the action he or she in fact did though not necessarily at the actual consequences of that action. Cr.C.265.1(a) is explicit about this, (b) and (c) are less so. What is required, in any case, for guilt to be proven is that the material element be established, as we have seen, and that it be reasonably inferred from the evidence that the defendant intended to apply force to the victim without the latter's consent.

Defining Corporal Punishment

We must now settle on a more detailed definition of corporal punishment. Once we have done this, we will be able to answer the question of whether corporal punishment satisfies the mental element (having satisfied the material element) of the crime of assault. Such definitions are not hard to come by. What is tricky, however, is settling on just one. I am going to sail over what might be construed as a major philosophical hurdle here—one set up by the worry that one's definition may be too broad or too narrow. Definitions which are too broad apply to instances of the term which common sense dictates are not, in fact, instances of the term. For example, if I define "technology" as "things human beings use to improve their lives," I have defined it too broadly. Religious worship is something humans use to improve their lives, but common sense tells us that it is not technology. Definitions which are too narrow, on the other hand, fail to include instances which common sense says ought to be included under the term. Suppose I define technology as electrical appliances. This definition will exclude things like foot powered pottery wheels from the class of technological things. Yet common sense tells us that many nonelectrical tools should be considered technology. One can expend a lot of philosophical energy sorting out definitions. Typically, the results of such efforts are definitions which of all proposed, offend the least in both directions. For the sake of argument and expedience, then, I propose the following definition of corporal punishment, fully aware that examples may be found of instances which it will problematically include or exclude:

> Corporal punishment is the administration by a recognized authority figure upon a recognized subordinate of some level of physical pain for the purpose of 'causing the latter to suffer for an offense' or 'inflicting a penalty for an offense.'[9] Further, it will be supposed that punishment, in the context of corporal punishment, has a morally, legally and politically acceptable purpose: to get the offender to avoid engaging in 'bad' behaviour.

This definition includes mild spankings but excludes striking children, even severely, out of anger or rage. This does not mean that if a parent is feeling angry when they hit a child that the hitting is not corporal punishment. For the parent may well administer the strike with the clear intention of teaching a lesson. However, parents who hit their children sometimes do so merely because they fail to resist the impulse to strike out which their anger or rage produces. In this case, the hitting is arguably an abreaction or emotional release for the parent rather than a chosen instrument of improving the child's character or behaviour. I am going to assume that the moral wrongness of hitting one's child out of anger or rage is not in question here. And there is clearly no legal defence for this sort of behaviour. The moral and legal question concerning corporal punishment is triggered when it is claimed the action is or was correctional—motivated by the goal of improving the child's character or behaviour. The definition above also excludes most typical uses of physical restraint. The use of restraint, when its goal is to immediately interrupt behaviour which is likely to result in harm to the child or others is better described as an intervention rather than as a punishment. However this does not mean that a physically restraining action cannot be an instance of corporal punishment. If the restraint is effected in a manner intended to cause pain or discomfort and the goal of causing this pain or discomfort is to teach the child a lesson, then a restraining action could be considered corporal punishment. I assume for the sake of my argument that a degree of physical restraint required but not exceeding what is necessary in the circumstances and of the nondisciplinary, interventionist sort would be widely regarded as morally acceptable. And as long as such restraint is deemed necessary in the circumstances, the law allows it.

Distinguishing between physical intervention and physical punishment as I have done above implies the use of an underlying theory of punishment which indeed claims that any action properly classified as punishment must have a reformatory end or intention and must also be reasonably connected to that end. Not all philosophers who concern themselves with theories of punishment agree that this is, in fact, the purpose of punishment. Some argue that its purpose is retributive. According to A.C. Ewing, the retributive position holds that "It is an end in itself that the guilty should suffer pain....The primary justification of punishment is always to be found in the fact that an offense has been committed which deserves the punishment, not in any future advantage to be gained by its infliction."[10] For reasons which I explore in greater detail in chapter 2 and 3, I use the former, outcome oriented theory of punishment in what follows. In this case, punishment of any sort can only be justified by its tendency to prevent behaviour which, understood against a broadly contextualized sense of what human beings individually and collectively require in order to flourish, would inhibit or conflict with those requirements.

Even though the principle goal or intention of corporal punishment, as a particular instance of punishment understood more generally, is to improve someone's character or behaviour, the intention to corporally punish includes the intention to use physical pain or discomfort as a means of achieving that goal. Both intentions are therefore included in the general intent of corporal punishment. Since corporal punishment therefore necessarily involves the intent to cause pain or discomfort to another (as well as other intentions), corporal punishment satisfies not only the material element of the crime of assault, but also its mental element. One would think, given Section 15 of the Charter where every individual is entitled to the equal protection of the law regardless of age, that the corporal punishment of children would always be illegal. It is not. So long as the force used is considered reasonable by the community and the court, is applied by a parent or parental figure and is indeed used for the purpose of correction, corporally punishing children is currently justified by law. The purpose or end of corporal punishment to teach sociable behaviour is compatible with the aims of both the Canadian Criminal Code and The Canadian Charter of Rights and Freedoms and is, I expect, also one which most adults and children would endorse. But when it comes to modifying the antisocial or harmful behaviour of adults, corporal punishment as a means to that end is now regarded by law as unacceptable.

Law and Morality

While the relation between law and morality cannot be fully explored here, we may say that codified law begins in and so expresses those moral values upon which the majority of a citizenry tend to converge over time. While not all such moral values find their way into law (there is no general crime of lying for example), we hope and expect that laws will not specifically justify what most agree is seriously immoral behaviour or specifically prohibit what is morally required or permitted. When it comes to making the distinction between widely agreed-upon moral values which ought to be legally codified and those which should not, we consider issues such as their importance to the common good, general ability to comply as well as the consequences of noncompliance to society as a whole. Opinions on these issues change over time and as such, our laws are under constant scrutiny and are often revised.

The English Common Law tradition, which formed the basis for the earliest Canadian penal code, justified husbands in their use of corporal punishment against wives, masters against their apprentices (and servants), guards against their prisoners, captains against their crew members, and parents and educators against their children and students. By 1892, when the common law pertaining to crimes was first codified in Canada, British society no longer considered the use of corporal punishment against wives to be morally or legally justified. In 1953, Canadian penal law no longer justified the use of corporal punishment against apprentices. In 1972, the code was again amended to remove justification for the corporal punishment of convicts who had, up until that time, been legally subjected to whipping.[11] It might be concluded that the moral value of hitting social subordinates has decreased over time. But this conclusion would be too hasty.

Since a group remains which is legally subject to assault, a more plausible interpretation of the facts is that the class of persons whom anyone can consider a true social subordinate has been reduced to children (along with nonhuman animals) while the value of hitting one's social subordinates has remained the same. Children remain subject to legal corporal punishment, "the common law rule allowing reasonable force in lawful correction" now applying "for all intents and purposes to one category of person only."[12] When it comes to hitting children for the purpose of improving their behaviour or character, the Code retains a defence, located under the title "Protection of Persons in Authority." Section 43 justifies what would otherwise be a criminal assault when the person accused is in a recognized position of parental or school authority and the victim is a child or student of that person. The mere presence of this section in the Criminal Code supports the conclusion that corporal punishment is indeed a violation of the law against assault. Just as long as the physical force used in the assault was reasonable given its purpose, however, the punisher may escape legal sanction. The presence of this section thus converts what would be, in its absence, an illegal act into a legal one. Section 43 states that:

43. Every schoolteacher, parent or person standing in the place of a parent is justified in using force by way of correction toward a pupil or child, as the case may be, who is under his care, if the force does not exceed what is reasonable under the circumstances.[13]

For the sake of argument, assume that to use "force by way of correction" is to apply painful and unwelcome physical pressure to the body of another—to hurt them—in a way which ensures that he, for example, immediately ceases his "bad" behaviour and does not engage in it again. This assumption is consistent with the definition of corporal punishment proposed above and includes what some consider non-severe forms of force such as spanking as well as severe forms such as whipping, punching and kicking.

The idea here that such physical pressure should be sufficient to compel immediate and future compliance relies on a very basic human instinct: the instinct to avoid pain. This instinct is present in almost all persons from birth and is what many philosophers and psychologists argue forms the basis of our moral sentiments.[14] In addition to this very basic instinct to avoid pain, human beings can learn or coax their bodies to endure more and more intense pains, within limits, over time.[15] It is hard to imagine how our species (or any other) could have survived without both of these extremely important traits. In order to be rational and effective, corporal punishment must fit with these basic facts about human beings.

Corporal punishment appears to serve the purpose of correction by causing offenders to associate the idea of engaging in bad behaviour with the memory of their own pain or discomfort causing them to shrink from the former as surely as they shrink from the latter. On the other hand, an individual person may, when recalling the pain which is associated with the behaviour in question, calculate that the pleasure or benefit he or she gets from the behaviour will outweigh the pain caused by the punishment as it is recalled, if, indeed, they are caught and punished a second time. Here, the possibility of escalating corporal punishment enters to give the person good reason to think again.

Where the legal punishment of adults is concerned, it is not unusual to find stiffer and stiffer penalties being administered for repeat offences. There is often public outcry for more severe penalties for certain crimes than the ones we currently have on the grounds "they don't work." Some even argue that capital punishment ought to be reinstated as a penalty of "last resort" for particularly heinous crimes or incorrigible violent offenders. Presumably, the thinking here is that the initial penalty, in the case of repeat offences for example, was not severe enough to provide an adequate disincentive to re-offending. Sentencing guidelines almost always allow for increases in such punishments within prescribed limits and so what is considered a stronger disincentive is sometimes used the second time. The nature of corporal punishment as punishment—as a disincentive to behave badly—makes it open to the same reasoning in the case of repeat behaviour. In addition, when a child re-offends, the parent may believe he or she has a second problem to deal with. The child has not only re-engaged in the prohibited behaviour, the child now appears to have intentionally disobeyed the parent. The merits of such a belief are questionable, especially in the case of very young children. Nevertheless, whatever parental frustration or disappointment the original misbehaviour causes, its repetition has the potential to raise that frustration or disappointment to new levels. The parent may regard not only the fact of re-offending but also the multiplication of offences as justification for increased punishment. Alternatively, due to his or her anger, for example, a parent may deliver a harsher or more severe punishment the second time without meaning to. It is therefore often the case that with the administration of corporal punishment goes an explicit or implicit warning that should punishment be required again, it will become severe or much more severe; something to cry about.[16] As is the case in law, the hope implicit in such a warning is that eventually, even those with very high pain thresholds will come to the conclusion that it simply does not pay to break the rules.

In spite of the promise of success implied in reliance on the corporal punishment strategy for correcting "bad" behaviour, Canadian lawmakers have concluded that it is a morally unacceptable means of correcting the "bad" behaviour of adults. Where once husbands were permitted to beat their wives, masters their apprentices and jailers their prisoners, these "corrective" practices are now not only generally regarded as morally wrong, but are also illegal. This dramatic change in moral attitude towards the corporal punishment of adults has not, however, been seen in attitudes towards the corporal punishment of children. Ongoing debate over the presence of Section 43 in the Code illustrates two still clearly opposed points of view.

Defenders of Section 43 argue that its presence in the Code is required to protect parents, teachers and other caregivers in the execution of their legal duty to raise orderly children. Opponents of Section 43 urge that its presence signals an unconstitutional preparedness on the part of the state to exempt all children from one of the most basic protections in the Charter and in so doing to perpetuate the culture of violence which, at least in part, informs and results from their exclusion. Each side in this debate sees the burden of proof falling to the other. I shall begin by assuming, however, that since the law as it currently stands and customary morality are on the side of those who see the practice of corporally punishing children as justified, the burden of proof falls on those who think otherwise. In what follows, I take up this case.

It is possible that by the time this book is published, an appeal to the Ontario Supreme Court of Justice of a lower Ontario Court's recent ruling upholding Section 43 will have concluded.[17] The outcome of that appeal will probably prompt a trip to the Supreme Court of Canada, regardless of who loses. But unlike the situation with the striking down of Canada's abortion law — a legal change which caused an immediate change in medical practice, a successful anti-Section 43 appeal at the Supreme Court of Canada level would only be the beginning of the end of the practice of corporal punishment of children in this country. In the case of abortion, *Morgentaler, Smoling et al.*[18] succeeded in striking down a law which made certain actions by physicians and anyone assisting in an abortion criminal. In so doing, it made any special defence against the charge of "procuring an abortion" unnecessary. In the absence of any law concerning the matter, physicians and pregnant women are now at liberty to make these important decisions and to act upon them according to the guidance of medical science and personal conscience without any fear of state reprisal.

Should Section 43 be struck down, on the other hand, parents, teachers and other childcare givers would lose rather than acquire a shield against criminal conviction. The removal of Section 43 from the Code would make parents, etc., who strike their children or threaten them with violence for the purpose of correction potentially subject to the same criminal sanctions as a stranger who behaves towards children in this way. While any parent, etc., charged with assaulting his or her child would also have access to the usual common law defences in such cases, anxiety is to be expected among those deemed primarily responsible for childcare. Much work would be needed, in that case, to clarify assault law for parents, teachers and other childcare givers. The moral question, Should Section 43 be replaced by new legislation? would have to be asked. Much work would also be needed, as it is in any case, to persuade everyone of the risks and dangers of corporal punishment especially in light of its potential escalator effect and so its role as a risk factor in much more serious assaults on children. Thorough public education regarding the reasonable alternatives to corporal punishment as a means of dealing with children when they misbehave would also have to be undertaken. In the thoughts and arguments which follow, though I assume that Section 43 remains in force, nothing crucial in the reasoning rides on the success or failure of a constitutional challenge to its validity.

In approaching the question of corporal punishment, first, according to the concerns of moral philosophy and second, to the concerns of law, I presuppose that while the two may be seen as operating independently of one another, they both bear closely on the issue at hand. If one's beliefs are such that the rule of law flows from moral values, then the upshot of the corporal punishment question will be located in the moral arguments for and against it. If one's view of morality and law is such that the rule of law may or must operate independently of this or that system of moral values and with greater authority, then focus will be on the jurisprudential arguments. Finally, you may see each type of argument as potentially relevant. Together, I hope that both prongs of my strategy will make the overall case against the corporal punishment of children philosophically and practically compelling.

Before going on, it is important to address concerns which may be raised about the empirical evidence which will be relied on in what follows. When it comes to empirical evidence for theories and general claims about the way things are (e.g., "if you jump in the lake, you will get wet"), we must be extremely cautious in the language we use to describe the supporting relationship between the two. To avoid controversy, social scientists talk of "risk factors" rather than causes; "strong correlation" rather than causation. Philosophers of science agree we cannot "prove" an empirical theory or generalization the way we can "prove" that the sum of the internal angles of a triangle is 180 degrees. As such, proving is not exactly what we are doing when we are providing convincing support for claims like "cigarette smoking causes cancer"—claims which go beyond what we have observed.

The best we can do is show that two phenomena are frequently correlated or associated with one another in our experience and neither has been as frequently correlated with other factors. Once the statistical frequency of the correlations reaches a certain threshold, we seem prepared to accept the idea that if the first phenomenon occurs either on its own or in combination with certain other factors, the second will (probably) follow. Just what that threshold is might differ slightly from person to person and there may be some individuals whose thresholds are widely off (up or down) the average mark. But though the threshold issue is even further complicated by the value or disvalue of the stakes in being wrong in particular contexts of risk assessment, we are not entirely at sea here. There are many things which we are quite to happy to call "causes" and we are quick to judge those who fail to make the connections we "see" between them and their effects.

Nevertheless, there is plenty of room for safe scholarly and scientific debate over methods, data, interpretation and so on. Such debate is very much like ordinary disagreement about whether it has indeed been proven smoking causes cancer, for example. The tendency among those who have not thought a great deal about reasoning from past and present experience to future experience is to think any number of counterexamples—or even one (Uncle Harry smoked like a chimney and lived to one hundred!)—shows the causal claims of health experts are false. From there it often seems a short step to believing that talk about the dangers of smoking is exaggerated—especially if one is already a frequent user.

While I am not an expert in statistical analysis or empirical testing, I do understand the broad philosophical issues at stake when general empirical claims are made. I expect my treatment and use of empirical evidence in my arguments against corporal punishment will be controversial. I certainly do not expect skeptical readers to be immediately persuaded by the evidence (or my argument) as it stands. I hope, however, that the evidence will not be rejected out of hand. The scholars and researchers involved in the actual testing and interpretation of the data are extremely sensitive and so far very responsive to demands for tighter controls. I refer to the most recent work in the area in order to bring forward the most rigorous analyses conducted so far.

I have attempted to put both the evidence for and against my conclusions in the best light. My argument does indeed rely on the preponderance of studies which support the claim corporal punishment is a risk factor for many serious short- and long-term harms. But my argument also rests on the almost complete absence of data showing corporal punishment is correlated with any benefits or that it is neutral with respect to consequences.

Even if the evidence I rely on is at some point in the future shown to be inaccurate or flawed, the fact is that corporal punishment as a behaviour modification technique necessarily involves the unconsented to infliction of pain or discomfort and, as such, at least merits moral questioning. If your dentist insisted on extracting a decrepit tooth without the use of an anesthetic against your will when such relief was available, you would have good grounds for a moral complaint or legal suit. Regardless of the beneficial consequence whereby the offending tooth was successfully removed, the harmful consequence of the unnecessary pain is seen as outweighing it. Since means are available for achieving the purpose of corporal punishment which do not involve the infliction of physical pain, its use constitutes a morally questionable practice.

Few if any children would survive infancy if we just popped them out and left them to raise themselves. We would soon all be in a world without children—one which P.D. James illustrated with eerie skill in her book *The Children of Men*. So, at a minimum, we raise children to ensure they survive into adulthood and keep things going for us, themselves and the future. Having reared three children as a married then single parent, I know first hand that raising children is an extremely exhausting, often frighteningly frustrating task. Seemingly unending periods of thankless, futile effort frequently punctuate the parent-child relationship. Teachers may be even worse off than parents since they are confined to the education of, for example, group after group after group of six year olds and rarely get to see the fruits of their patient labor. But the work of raising children is unique among all human employments and critical to the success of all other human work. It is the hardest, the costliest of all work; in feeling, in physical and mental stamina. But it can also be the most rewarding. It merits unequivocal social, economic and political respect and at least as much attention from the media and government that banking and cod fishing receive. What is happening to the nation's children should be regarded as a priority of daily news. I hope my words here will play some part in the effort to make it clear that the pressures on this work—poverty, unemployment, isolation, lack of education—must no longer be used as excuses or worse, justifications, for harming the young.

2

• • • • • • • • • • •

A Very Short History of

Moral Philosophy

In this second chapter I introduce the subject of moral philosophy as it has developed throughout the ages on the question of children and punishment. This introduction is necessarily sketchy but this is due as much to the lack of significant scholarship on this question as it is to my interest in getting on with the discussion of it in contemporary terms.[1] Despite its brevity, the discussion will provide an adequate foundation for what follows. In the next chapter, I examine moral values in Canada. Many Canadians consider corporal punishment acceptable and even necessary for passing on their moral values to the next generation or for correcting children's intolerable behaviour — behaviour which endangers them, causes pain or annoyance to others or causes damage to property. The moral argument which I will launch against such views has its origins in the long history of philosophical thought on ideas such as the good life, sin, right and wrong, happiness and pleasure, and misery and pain, and exerts its influence on the

Notes to chapter 2 are on pp. 240–48.

world of Canadian moral values as these are expressed in the various customs of Canadians as well as in The Charter of Rights and Freedoms.

What Is Morality?

The term "morality" refers to the sense of right and wrong or good and bad which human beings use to judge their behaviour towards each other as well as the treatment practices which evolve under those judgements. A moral sense is something we develop as a consequence of living in concert with others under conditions of intimacy, proximity and competition for resources. Given these conditions, everyone's desire to survive and succeed and the realization that we need one another to make the most of life, there are certain ways of treating one another that we come to believe are required or permitted and others that we decide are unacceptable. The works of moral philosophy which this cursory history examines represent a very long struggle by human beings living in a vast array of social, cultural, political and religious circumstances to figure out ways of living together which will secure this or that ideal of human life for as long as possible. I aim here to present a thumbnail sketch of what a more comprehensive survey of Western moral philosophy would involve and allow that as such, this history oversimplifies a very complicated narrative. Also, while I do presuppose familiarity with Western moralities among my readers, I do not presuppose their inherent superiority to any others in using them as the basis of my argument.

Aristotle and the Morality of Ancient Greece

Aristotle lived in Athens, Greece, from 384 BC to 322 BC. He had been a student of Plato who in turn had been a student of Socrates.[2] We know that Aristotle had deep disagreements with many things his teacher, Plato, taught him. He nevertheless expected that when Plato died, he would take over as head of the Academy or school which Plato founded. When Plato named someone else to take his place, Aristotle left Athens but returned many years later at the age of forty-nine to set up his own school of philosophy, the Lyceum.

When it came to their moral beliefs, Plato and probably Socrates believed that one ought to aim at the "good life." Discovering what the "good life" entailed took a careful regime of intellectual digging — a regime which Plato thought few minds were capable of following through to the end. Once human reason revealed the good, it would be impossible for the discoverer of it to do wrong or judge or act badly. In his famous work, *The Republic*, Plato called these great minds "philosopher kings" and argued they and they alone should decide morality in the ideal society. Aristotle could not entirely accept Plato's line. He looked around Athens, a bustling cosmopolitan city, and saw goodness which he believed was diverse and changing, though within limits. The good was not something hidden from all but the most exceptional minds waiting to be discovered for all time. Instead, he wrote, emphasizing the practical nature of goodness, "we must be satisfied with a broad outline of the truth; that is, in arguing about what is for the most part so, from the premises which are for the most part true, we must be content to draw conclusions that are similarly qualified."[3] In a manner of speaking, Aristotle's moral theory changed the idea of good from an absolute to a "more or less" idea.

Aristotle worked out his view of the good life by consulting the wisdom and experience of the oldest Athenians, himself included — the ones who had the greatest experience and recollection of the people's history: its ups and downs, failed and successful political experiments, as well as the longest lives: knowledge of childhood, maturation and great age. Aristotle reckoned that to live a good life, one had to be properly trained in the "virtues." Virtues were learned habitual dispositions or inclinations of character to behave in this or that moderate way rather than in this or that immoderate way. One might act immoderately either by showing too little courage or loyalty, for example, or too much of either. Too little courage would be cowardice: a vice. Too much would be rashness: also a vice. Neither was conducive to living a "good life." If one succeeded in living a virtuous life, however, one would eventually experience *eudaimonia* — the special intellectual happiness that is the good life's crowning achievement.[4]

The emphasis in Aristotle's "virtue ethics" moral theory is on the development of good character.[5] He saw human beings beginning their lives in a state of nervous "incontinence" or inability to direct, control or manage their physical desires. He wrote, for example, that "restraint is necessary for anything that has low appetites and a marked capacity for growth; and these qualities are possessed in the highest degree by the child."[6] He believed that in order to prepare male children for their moral education, teachers had to get them to ignore the promptings of these appetites as quickly as possible.[7] "For children too live as their desires impel them and it is in them that the appetite for pleasant things is strongest; so unless this is rendered docile and submissive to authority it will pass all bounds."[8]

While Aristotle acknowledged that persons in authority over children and other adults were known to act cruelly and even barbarously toward them, and while he condemned such treatment as excessive and so immoral, he endorsed the corrective use of corporal punishment when it came to instilling habits of virtuous behaviour and respect for the law. "If an official strikes someone, it is wrong for him to be struck in return; and if someone strikes an official it is right for him not only to be struck in return but to be punished as well."[9] We know that Aristotle believed that children were naturally disposed to act contrary to the virtues of quiet obedience which were in turn the necessary preconditions for a good life.[10] We also know that he believed it was right for those in authority to beat their subordinates when the latter acted out of turn. We may therefore infer that according to Aristotle's "virtue" moral theory, the use of corporal punishment against children may have been morally required and was, in any case, morally permitted.[11]

St. Thomas Aquinas and the Morality of Medieval Christianity

St. Thomas Aquinas lived in the neighbourhood of Naples, Italy during the thirteenth century. He completed his studies for becoming a Dominican monk in Paris where he began a prodigious literary career.[12] Aquinas greatly admired Aristotle and introduced his teachings into Christian theology. But he had to make certain adjustments to Aristotle's views so that they would not conflict with Roman Catholic dogma which had, up until that point, been heavily influenced by Plato's absolutist moral theory.

Like Aristotle, Aquinas believed that when it came to what morality demanded, the natural appetites of human beings had to be "quieted." Yet Aquinas disagreed with Aristotle that quietude, reason, experience and training were sufficient for morality. He held that the possibility of conquering "sin" or "vice" depended first upon the grace of God. Unless God recognized you as belonging to him, you lacked the spiritual basis of morality and no amount of quietude, reason, experience or training could compensate.

"Both in ethics and moral theology," Vernon Burke writes, "[Aquinas's] position is that morally good action is that which is conducive to man's [sic] attainment of…the everlasting contemplation of the Perfect Good."[13] This may sound closer to Plato than to Aristotle but recall that Christian belief had brought the "perfect good" down to earth where all could experience it. However, when it came to identifying the perfect good in concrete terms, Aquinas departed from Aristotle's conception of *eudaimonia* whose end was the good life. "Now, the end of our desires is God."[14] Unlike Aristotle, Aquinas held that ultimate happiness was fundamentally spiritual in that it culminated in unity with God. If you were in a state of sin, God's interest in uniting with you should not be counted upon. As such, sin was to be avoided at all times.[15]

Aquinas taught that there were two main sorts of sin: original sin and actual sin. Original sin is a corrupted principle of human nature inherited without individual fault from Adam, the "first parent," and its consequence is eventual death. On the basis of Christ's teachings, Aquinas believed that baptism washed away original sin though not the inescapability of its penalty. Actual sin, on the other hand, involves individual fault and so free will, which in turn presupposes an active rational intellect. "Every [actual] sin is traceable to the will as to its cause insofar as every sin is committed with the will's consent."[16] Since Aquinas believed that actual sin presupposed free will and the action of a rational intellect, since he did not believe that very young children had either, he did not believe that very young children were capable of actual sin.

Children, he believed, belonged to their fathers in the same way the family's farm animals and women did. This was part of Aquinas's "natural law theory" of morality.[17] Consider, for instance, Aquinas's view that no child should be baptized (or have its original sin washed away) against its father's wishes. He writes that going against a father's wishes for his child is "opposed to natural justice"[18] and that "indeed, a son is naturally something belonging to the father...he is not distinct in his body from his parents as long as he is contained within his mother's womb."[19] Aquinas continued, "as long as the boy is without the use of reason, he does not differ from an irrational animal."[20]

The Church's views on children as irrational animals and so as categorically opposite to adult human males supported the use of corporal punishment against them as a means of quieting their natural appetites.[21] Curiously, this view of children as irrational is accompanied in Christian thought by a view of them as especially attractive to God. The uneasiness with which these alternative views of children sit in the history of Christian morality would seem to recommend a cautious moral attitude towards the corporal punishment of children. But the tension between the Old Testament view of children in need of "the rod" and the New Testament view that unless we become like little children we will not be able to enter God's kingdom is supposedly resolved by the passion of Christ. According to that passion, suffering is part of what is required to enter the kingdom of God. Corporal punishment is thus regarded by Christian tradition as a necessary and positive means of quieting the natural appetites which thwart our journey towards heaven. If not successfully suppressed, these appetites lead us, as we grow older and acquire the powers of reason, to commit actual sin. Not using corporal punishment in the training of children is therefore considered immoral: "Spare the rod; spoil the child."[22]

Immanuel Kant and the Morality of Duty

In 1517, Martin Luther, a Catholic, publicly disagreed with certain practices of the Roman Catholic Church and the tear in the fabric of Christianity resulted in a deep split between Catholics who continued to follow the principles of natural law and Protestants who adopted a much more practical even democratic approach to religious life.[23] In the eighteenth century, Immanuel Kant, a German Lutheran and a philosopher by profession, set out to formulate a theory of morality which would transcend the religious differences which had emerged partly as a consequence of the Reformation. Kant firmly believed in the possibility of individual moral authority. This was not the view, so popular now, that each individual had his or her own unique morality.

Rather, Kant believed that every rational person could arrive at the same single universally authoritative moral law—one which objectively justified various religious moralities—through the use of reason.[24] What would such moral authority depend on? It would be grounded, Kant thought, in something which no rational person could dispute but it must also tell us how to act in novel situations. The propositions of geometry and arithmetic seemed indubitable. The claim "2+2=4," for instance, was clearly true whatever your particular religious beliefs were. Kant also argued that contrary to what many theorists believed, the claims of mathematics told us something about the world.[25] Could a formula for a "transcendental" or contextless morality be found which also had both of these properties?[26]

Kant's answer was yes. The moral law or categorical imperative, he argued, could tell us what we ought to do and could do so "categorically"—no room for doubt. Applied in particular circumstances, the moral law therefore determined what Kant regarded as our moral duties. One version of it (there were three) reads "Act as if the maxim [or policy] of your act were to become by your will a universal law of nature."[27] Reason dictated that the maxim or policy under which an action is performed must be "universalizable" or applicable to all rational beings in similar circumstances if the action is to be considered moral. The categorical imperative is like a mathematical formula where letters stand for values to be filled in later. You must fill in your "maxim" when using the categorical imperative and see if you can consistently act upon it when everyone else has to act upon it as well.

In order to fill in your "maxim," you must first identify it. Identifying your maxim means figuring out what policy you are intending to follow when you act. For example, suppose your three-year-old daughter has just tried to poke out her baby brother's eyes for the fifth time, after you have warned her over and over not to. Morally speaking, what should you do? Should you take her hand away and warn her that if she does it again she will be put to bed or grab her hand away from baby's eyes and give it a smart slap? There may be other options but for the sake of argument, let's consider these two and look at the second option first. What policy would acting in such a manner express? Based on our definition of corporal punishment, the policy here would be: "Whenever children behave in a manner harmful to others and have not responded to verbal commands, administer some level of physical pain to them for the offense."[28] Could you act on this policy when everyone else has to act on it as well? Say that every time a child behaves intolerably, a nearby authority figure will be irresistibly compelled by a law of nature (in the same way "what goes up must come down" for example) to strike it in order to correct the behaviour. Could you continue to act under the same policy in such a world? Of course you could. The fact that every authority figure treated children in this way would not interfere with or contradict your aims in doing so.

If we tested the alternative nonviolent option in similar fashion, we would also find that it passes the categorical imperative test.[29] So while according to Kant, morality permits corporal punishment, it does not require it. In his writings on education, Kant distinguishes between "moral" and "physical punishment." The latter, he says,

> ...consists either in refusing a child's requests or in the infliction of pain. [Refusing a child's requests] is akin to moral punishment [or appeal to the child's sympathies] and is of a negative kind. The second form [infliction of pain] must be used with caution, lest an *indoles servilus* [slavish character] should be the result. It is of no use to give children rewards; this makes them selfish, and gives rise to an *indoles mercenaria* [mercenary character].[30]

Kant's test for morality clearly imposes limits on the use of corporal punishment. Since your intention is to improve your daughter's behaviour and not eliminate her ability to behave altogether, the use of corporal punishment must not, among other things, be used too frequently, or when used, result in permanent damage or death to her. An act of corporal punishment which intended this result or was reckless or negligent with respect to it would fail Kant's moral test. This is because an act of corporal punishment which was carried out with the intention of disabling your child or without intending to avoid causing her serious injury would contradict the educative purpose of the act. Also, Kant tells us, "physical punishments must merely supplement the insufficiency of moral punishment. If moral punishment have no effect at all, and we have last resort to physical punishment, we shall find after all that no good character is formed in this way. At the beginning, however, physical restraint may serve to take the place of reflection."[31] We might assume here that by physical restraint Kant meant to exclude the infliction of physical pain; exclude hitting, for example. In this case it would seem Kant vacillated on his endorsement of corporal punishment as a disciplinary strategy of last resort. What he clearly tells us is that while repeated use of physical punishment or reliance upon it may affect behaviour, it cannot contribute to the formation of good character. Whether he believed this because he also believed that "where moral punishment has no effect at all" there is a so-called congenitally bad child or that physical punishment itself was causal with respect to the formation of bad character is somewhat unclear. This ambiguity surfaces repeatedly in contemporary debates over the causal direction between corporal punishment and defiant children, as we will see later when these empirical issues are discussed.

In any event, under Kant's moral system, it is no longer clear that corporal punishment is required by the ends of morality and as such morality may conflict with certain religious beliefs and cultural practices which claim it is. Morality, under Kant, was philosophical. That is, it took a step back from particular cultural and religious moral practices and set up a more authoritative rule — one with which those other practices should conform. Also, since Kant's moral system seemed to place a constraint on the use of corporal punishment, it was no longer clear that parents, fathers in particular, owned their children in the same way they owned their other "beasts of burden." One serious practical problem for Kant's moral theory, however, was inaccessibility. Few but the university educated learned of it, much less understood it.[32] While his comments on child education are very readable, much of what he argues there is based on consideration of the consequences to children and society which the use and non-use of corporal punishment had — particularly in the area of character formation. It may therefore be argued that to whatever extent Kant's moral theorizing on child discipline is accessible to most readers, he has, to that same extent, departed from his own rational moral method. Moral judgement based on the consideration of consequences will be discussed later.

Basic to Kant's moral view then is the notion of moral duty — that there are things we ought or ought not to do, regardless of the feelings we have about them or the feelings they might produce in ourselves or others. Morality, for Kant, is therefore a matter of absolute requirements and prohibitions. Conduct which is neither required by the categorical imperative nor prohibited by it—for example, using corporal punishment as a last resort—falls into the class of actions which are, depending on the circumstances, permitted.

Jeremy Bentham, John Stuart Mill and the Morality of Utility

While the Germans were following Kant to one degree or another, eighteenth and nineteenth century British thinkers and social reformers such as Jeremy Bentham and John Stuart Mill were working out an alternative moral theory for a religiously and culturally diverse society.[33] This theory held that consequences were what morality was ultimately all about—that mental states such as intentions, while relevant, did not determine the morality of actions. These thinkers and social reformers were the utilitarians or, as they referred to themselves, the Radical Philosophers. They considered themselves radical because they were politically active dissidents very much focused on improving the living conditions of the poor, women and children. Many of them were deeply involved in the abolition movement as well. They were also skeptics about absolute truth.[34] As empiricists or philosophers who held that everything we know is based on observation and experience, they did not think that "2+2=4" was absolutely true because they did not think that there was observational or experiential evidence for believing that anything was.

According to Kant's "morality of duty," the logic of intentions was key; feelings and consequences were at best indirectly relevant. Indeed, regardless of its outcome, Kant argued that we could know that a philanthropic act by a misanthrope had moral worth but could never know whether a philanthropic act by a philanthropist did.[35] Utilitarians, on the other hand, considered feelings and consequences all important. Whatever the moral relevance of the intentions and policies behind it, the actual moral worth of an act was based on the feelings it produced. Utilitarians believed that for an act to be moral it had to produce the greatest amount of happiness for the greatest number of people (or sentient creatures) affected by it.

It must be the aim, the utilitarians argued, of all human conduct and policy to secure those conditions of life for everyone which their happiness requires and this aim must be approached through means which are reasonably expected to achieve it. To secure these conditions was always to make people happier over their whole lives and although the notion of happiness was a difficult one to clarify, utilitarians argued that broad agreement was possible and adequate.[36] They believed that the feeling of happiness is identified primarily with the experience of what most human beings term "pleasure." The reverse of happiness — misery — is identified with what we term "pain." As Jeremy Bentham, the "father" of classical utilitarianism, put it, "the [moral] question is not, Can they *reason*? nor Can they *talk* but, Can they *suffer*?"[37]

It is clear from Bentham's remark that according to his utilitarian moral theory, human children (as well as non-human animals) were morally on par with human adults. But the fact that children suffered, indeed the fact that anyone did, was not sufficient to show that the acts which caused their suffering were immoral. For recall that the mark of the moral according to utilitarianism is the production of "the greatest happiness for the greatest number." If an act or policy of causing suffering to children had the result of causing happiness to many more others or simply causing everyone less misery than some other policy, it may be moral to punish children by making them suffer. Utilitarians faced serious objections due to what appeared to be many unacceptable implications of their moral theory.

The fact that utilitarians could not absolutely rule out the corporal punishment of children does not imply that they could not rule it out as a matter of policy. If it could be shown that the use of such punishment consistently tended towards the violation of the greatest happiness principle, a moral rule against it would be called for.[38] Thus, utilitarianism endorsed a consequentialist theory of punishment. One had to predict the widespread and short- and long-term consequences of its use before deciding whether any particular punishment was moral. In the nineteenth century, there was little debate on corporal punishment though, as we will see later on, John Stuart Mill, a student of Jeremy Bentham's, was a rare male opponent of the corporal punishment of both women and children.

Today, in Canada, experts in the fields of justice, social service, sociology, developmental psychology and law enforcement are virtually unanimous in the view that corporal punishment is a factor in many of our social ills.[39] But this view does not yet have the official support of the nation's teachers nor the general population. Many parents and teachers argue that without the permission to administer corporal punishment, they would be unable to pass on important values to the children they care for, teach them to look out for themselves or to behave in a sociable manner. If these parents and teachers are right, the consequences of prohibiting corporal punishment would be socially disastrous.

On each side of this question, a number of empirical claims are made which require scrutiny. Since the utilitarian refuses to acknowledge the existence of absolute truths, the logical uncertainty of any conclusion reached about those claims poses no theoretical threat.[40] Nevertheless, it must turn out that one set of claims is clearly more probable than the other if the moral question of corporal punishment is to be resolved according to utilitarian moral theory. Should it turn out that there is no clear balance of probability here, this result would strongly suggest that the issue of corporal punishment is, at least for the present, morally neutral for the utilitarian.

Morality in the Postmodern Era

At the end of the nineteenth century, Henry Sidgwick tried but failed to correct utilitarianism's perceived flaws by rooting it in the theoretical ground of Kant's "transcendental" morality of duty.[41] The result of his failure was deepening skepticism among philosophers concerning the very possibility of moral theorizing. Under the electric light of their skepticism, we enter the twentieth century gateway to the postmodern era. The soon-to-be "parents" of postmodernism say they have discovered a disturbing paradox: as we pursue the task of philosophically justifying our moral intuitions, the force of logic generates implications which lead us further and further away from those intuitions. For example, take the moral intuition that we should not kill other humans beings for our own pleasure. In seeking a justification for this intuition, we ask "Why shouldn't we do this"?

If we lived in Plato's *Republic*, the answer could be "because the philosopher king says it is wrong." In medieval Italy, we would answer, "Because the priest tells us that God says it is wrong." If we were Kantians, we might respond by saying that the intention behind the act is self-contradictory. And a utilitarian might answer that killing other human beings for our own pleasure would decrease the general happiness. In pursuing this last philosophical justification, for example, we might explain further that the harm to the humans we kill outweighs the pleasure we get from killing them and when this is added to the anxiety which our behaviour would cause everyone else, it is clear that such an act would produce a considerable net balance of unhappiness. Our pleasure, then, is not a good reason for killing human beings. It follows from what we have offered by way of justifying the intuition against killing others that if we got a lot more pleasure from killing them than we do, and could keep our behaviour a secret, it may be moral according to utilitarianism to kill humans. In which case, our pleasure would be a good reason for killing them, at which point we have contradicted the moral intuition with which we began.

While this chain of reasoning appears to impugn utilitarianism specifically, postmodernists argue that it could be cited in any case of moral justification.[42] The strong form of the postmodern thesis asserts that opposition between the traditional goals and results of rational justification is ineliminable regardless of what methods are used. As such, the postmodernist concludes that philosophical prescriptions for proper human conduct and moral theories are just not possible.

In the middle of the twentieth century, John Rawls, a political philosopher at Harvard University, proposed a method of rational justification in the domain of human conduct and policy which he believed circumvented the paradox just described. The goal of rational justification in the area of human conduct was to support principles of human living by which people with a wide variety of goals would agree to abide, and which would in fact advance those goals. Rawls illustrated his method of rational justification with the help of a thought experiment. Suppose that you and all those seeking principles upon which to base your society convene a meeting for working them out. Rawls called this meeting "the original position."[43] Next, suppose that in order to sit at the "table," you and every other participant must wear a sort of cloaking device—Rawls called this the "veil of igno-rance." The veil of ignorance temporarily erases everything you know about your biographical particulars and anything else which might give clues to others about your identity. No one at the table knows whether he or she or anyone else there is male or female, rich or poor, black or white, young or old, etc. Yet everyone is rational and is aware that they must reach unanimous agreement on principles for living.[44]

What principles, if any, would be reached under such circum-stances? The trick is that once the meeting is over, everyone must remove their veils of ignorance, be restored to their normal identity and live in the society they have just founded, according to its rules. Rawls concluded that under these conditions, any rational person would insist on a principle of maximum individual liberty consistent with the same amount for every other individual and on a principle of redistributing surplus individual goods so as to benefit the most dis-advantaged members of society. Rawls concluded, in effect, that while principles of morality might indeed be subject to the postmodern par-adox, principles of justice were not. In detaching justice from morality, he had made a move not unlike Kant's in the eighteenth century when morality was detached from virtue, religion and culture.[45] Rawls's the-ory of justice has encountered a great deal of criticism. Foremost among those criticisms is the complaint that detaching justice from morality (or morality from feeling, as Kant had done) simply cannot be done without doing conceptual violence to some of our deepest human values. The long and short of this is that Rawls's theory of justice may have failed to slip the net of the postmodern paradox after all.

The postmodern paradox may be felt at the practical as well as the-oretical level. If we consider corporal punishment, we have a very good example of how it works in "the real world." Recall what the par-adox predicts: the goals and results of rational justification will always be at odds with one another. If we consider the goals and results of practice rather than theory, and consider corporal punishment as such a practice, we would say that the goal or purpose of corporal punish-ment will always be at odds with its results. Is this true? One goal of corporal punishment is to prevent children from behaving unsociably: from indefensibly causing pain to themselves, pain or annoyance to others or damaging property. The method used to achieve this goal is causing children pain. The result of using this method is to teach children that it is acceptable to hurt others in order to get them to do what you want them to do or not to hurt others. But, as the Peterson example in chapter 1 illustrated, this is the sort of thinking that parents punish their children for through the use of corporal punishment. The postmodernist may therefore argue that the goal and result of the pain lesson contradict one another. The possibility that corporal punishment is philosophically problematic or practically contradictory, however, need not trouble every postmodernist. In its strongest versions, postmodernism rejects the tyranny of logical and practical consistency.

In spite of many criticisms against it and its vulnerability to the postmodern paradox, Rawls's work nevertheless inspired a generation of moral theorists to pick up Kant's "morality of duty" thread.[46] These neo-Kantians are largely responsible for the recent trend towards "rights talk" which has come to dominate professional moral discourse. According to the deontological (or duty-based) rights theorist, it is contrary to moral rationality to even suggest that the murder of one innocent human being in order to prevent the deaths of many others may be moral. Yet, utilitarianism allows that this might be the case depending upon the circumstances. As such, the rights theorist continues, utilitarian moral theory is wrong. The reason why murdering the innocent person in the above example must be morally wrong according to the deontologist is that since he or she is innocent, he or she has a right to life and if it is taken, that right is clearly violated. It can never be moral to violate an individual's rights and therefore, it can never be morally right to kill an innocent person despite what is allowed in principle by utilitarianism.

Utilitarian responses to this very strong criticism have varied from theorist to theorist. But in the end, a true utilitarian must admit that his or her moral theory does not provide the same sorts of absolute, utterly inviolable protections which a deontological theory might. Nevertheless, to argue that because it cannot offer such protections, it therefore offers none at all is unfair. Utilitarians have generated rights theories which place extremely high value on things like security of the person and promise-keeping. Mill, for example, argued in the nineteenth century that "To have a right then, is, I conceive, to have something which society ought to defend me in the possession of....The interest involved is that of security, to everyone's feelings the most vital of all interests."[47] The utilitarian's conception of the way in which such rights are arrived at appeals to certain widely agreed-upon ideas of what human beings require to be happy (or for their well-being) rather than upon what human rationality and the logic of duty entail. All told, it may be that in spite of such defences, utilitarianism still suffers from vulnerability to the postmodern paradox, but then, if we accept the force of the paradox, so do all moral theories.

Postmodernism seems as repulsed by the notion that an empirical fact can serve to justify a normative or moral claim as deontologists are. It is also as critical of the role of formal logic and "pure" reason in this regard as empiricists, like the utilitarians, are. Postmodernism tends to be especially suspicious of "rights talk." But while the postmodern critique of "the cult of rationalism" (of both the Kantian and the Rawlsian sort) continues, it is not yet clear that logic and science have been driven out. Once again, the choices are not only between rationalism or scientism on the one hand and absurdism or atavism on the other. Furthermore, not all postmodernisms are equally intolerant of the goals and methods of rational and empirical justification. The postmodern turn is arguably the peak of a comprehensive attack on all dogmatism which took off in the eighteenth century — it prides itself on never being one single thing; on never being entirely reconciled with itself.

The moral question of corporal punishment is now at least an open one. The view of children as irrational or animal-like central to traditional religions such as Christianity still holds considerable sway even among adults who do not consider themselves particularly religious. On the other hand, the twentieth century has seen an advancing tide of liberation knocking down wall after wall of insupportable prejudice against members of groups historically seen in a similar light. In the next chapter, I turn to the issue raised by morality in the postmodern "splintered" era — an issue which dominates many of the central concerns of morality in Canada: cultural and religious pluralism. You will see how the value of security of the person consistently floats to the surface and as such provides us with a postmodern "anchor" in choppy moral waters.

3

· · · · · · · · · · ·

Morality and Culture:

When Values Collide

We have now briefly surveyed the Western European philosophical influences on Canada's present moral environment. It is clear from this survey that the demands of politics, morality, culture and religion have interacted in various ways over history. There have been times and places where all of these demands were understood "under one roof," where some were understood together and separately from others and where each was understood independently. The postmodern era is predominantly characterized by this last understanding—by the idea that one really can be a liberal utilitarian Catholic Native or a Quebecois conservative Kantian atheist, an East Indian maritimer or just an Albertan.

In a country like Canada, where maximum tolerance for different conceptions of the good life is desired, the established governing and social order is clearly informed, at least to some extent, by the postmodern "end of dogma" ethos. Note that the legitimacy of an open

---

Notes to chapter 3 are on pp. 248–54.

(though not necessarily wide open) attitude towards values does not exclude the legitimacy of politics, moralities, cultures or religions which disagree with it. But as we will see, it does place limits on the legitimacy of attempts to put certain aspects of such disagreement into moral, social or political action.[1] Those who try to do so often find themselves in conflict with Canada's Constitution Act, Charter or Criminal Code. Such conflict is often regrettable but ultimately unavoidable in a politically, morally, culturally and religiously free society.

Despite a great amount of variety among Canadians when it comes to their concrete moral commitments, I believe that we can make some sense of the notion of "Canadian moral values." This idea may be understood in two ways: as the *de re* or officially inscribed set of moral values which our nation upholds at the foundation of its laws and policies or as the *de facto* set of all the actual moral values which individual Canadians hold personally or in groups. The official values contained in the first set need not be affirmed by all Canadians and the second *de facto* set may contain values which do not appear in the first. However, regardless of the extent to which an individual's or cultural community's concrete moral values depart from those in the official set, all members of Canadian society are obliged to obey the entirety of laws and policies based upon it. From this point forward I will use the notion of Canadian moral values in its official sense. As we begin to examine the moral question concerning corporal punishment, the character of our nation as an open and multicultural liberal democratic society will be studied. I also look at the "culture of individualism" as characteristic of our liberal ethos. In the course of these discussions, I introduce the first and second of several moral arguments advanced in favour of the practice of corporal punishment: the moral education argument and the individual welfare argument. I show that both arguments assume values which fall afoul of the official set of moral values at the core of Canadian identity (understood multinationally) expressed in our governing documents. In so doing, I argue that to the extent these values issue in practices which violate Canadian law, they ought not to be officially tolerated.

Escaping Oppression and Seeking Opportunity

The postmodern turn against dogmatism makes holding older traditional moralities such as those of Plato or Aquinas difficult. Why is this? Two features of traditional moralities make them difficult (though not impossible) to hold. The first is their normative absolutism. They each tend to claim that all human beings must accept them because these moralities command moral truth. When these theories were first shaped, ideas of individual liberty, freedom of thought and expression and freedom of religion had neither the support of the people, governing authorities nor the intellectual elite. The moral legitimacy of individual dissent could only emerge when the grounds for dogmatic belief in a single "absolute truth" had been dislodged. The second feature of these moralities which makes them problematic today is their exclusionism. This implicates them in an *ad hominem* fallacy. They say, "if you are a moral human being then you must believe that (for example) not attending mass on Sunday is a grievous sin." If you do not see the connection between being a moral human being and attending mass on Sundays, then these moralities may say that you are not a moral human being and as such, not properly entitled to moral respect. In a tolerant society such as ours, any morality which suggests that persons who for any reason do not agree with it are not moral human beings is considered narrow-minded at best. Based on the widespread acceptance of the legitimacy of individual dissent and the values of personal freedom, we no longer accept that decisions about personal moral worth based on, among other things, religious belief are ever politically justified.

These changes in our deep understanding of morality have introduced a difficulty in our ability to get along with one another. In a religious context where the fulfillment of one's moral duty demanded traveling over long distances to where the "pagans" dwelled to convert them, not doing so was to act immorally.[2] As time passed, being moral no longer required the missionary zeal it once did. "Pagans" and dissenters could dwell where they dwelled and the morally upright could dwell where they dwelled and they all could live apart from one another in relative peace. However, as the grip of the idea of a single absolute morality continued to weaken and as there were fewer and

fewer livable unpopulated places left to go, the conditions for moral
tension actually increased. Having different moral groups in any single
society — any territory where its inhabitants must do business with one
another in order to survive or flourish — meant that all of its members
were going to have to exercise a great deal of tact if peace was to be
maintained. This requirement for peaceable enjoyment often conflicted
with the new value of freedom of speech.[3] Serious problems could be
avoided as long as the differences between the "one truth" dogmatists
and the "personal freedom" fighters were not too dramatic. Where differences were dramatic, more and more serious tensions developed
between various groups and individuals. Tolerance for difference
within such societies often reached a breaking point.

This scenario may be said to loosely resemble a large number of
intolerance episodes in the history of humankind as well as a number
of current ones. Emigration waves frequently originate in countries
where for this reason or that, a significant segment of the population is
penalized by another group's political power and intolerance.
Members of the target group might be harassed, imprisoned, tortured
or killed just for their religious beliefs or ethnic origin. Their family
members might be threatened or systematically starved, kept out of
jobs, exposed to disease and illness, refused education, and so on. What
the emigrant is sometimes — and the refugee always — trying to do is
escape oppression, persecution and the threat of poverty and bodily
harm in his or her homeland in the hope of better life opportunities
elsewhere.[4] The promise of personal freedom and safety which Canada
offers beckons. And so it may come as a surprise to learn that the promise is limited by a very complex, largely implicit morality or set of rules
for everyone living under it. In Canada, some argue, this morality is the
morality of liberalism.

Gift Shop v. Fish Tank Liberalism: Bodily Harm and the Limits of Tolerance

Liberalism is usually understood as a political commitment to a set of
institutional arrangements understood to maximize individual freedom, promote individual welfare and maintain representative government. But it can be understood in moral terms as well. Liberal moral-

ity refers to those values which support the political commitment noted above. Those values speak to what liberal moralists believe are necessary conditions for human flourishing. Personal equality, freedom, publicly funded health and education are some of these values. Many people have come to Canada to escape illiberal oppression, persecution, poverty and the bodily harm which comes of these dangers in their homelands. Canadians by birth overwhelmingly choose to remain partly because of the opportunities for happiness which their personal freedom and sense of security offers them. Their choices imply something substantive about the moral commitments people in Canada have. They imply that like all human beings, Canadians new and old place high value on living in safety and according to their deepest convictions. A prime consideration in the emigrant's mind may be the fact that Canada is a country where state authority is committed to liberal moral values and as such to remaining neutral on concrete questions of the good life. When acting legitimately, the Canadian government promises to never sanction any of its citizens unless it can be shown that their acts violate the rights and freedoms of others in a way proscribed by law.[5] Understanding what those fundamental rights and freedoms include raises the question of morality and liberalism in greater detail.

What follows are two fanciful models of liberal morality. In essence, both models hold that diversity in society is desirable. A society operates most freely, peacefully and prosperously when its members differ on their personal or cultural conceptions of the good life provided that no single conception is given exclusive official preference and the realization of all such conceptions are subject to the same regulations. The two models compete in the popular imagination for the right to represent what liberal morality is all about. Since there are important differences between them, we need to decide which one best describes Canadian liberalism. First, what is *gift shop* liberalism?

Gift shop liberalism affirms the values of freedom and equality in difference stated above.[6] Say you are erecting a six-foot-high realistic sculpture of the crucified figure of Jesus Christ on your front lawn and your neighbour comes over and pulls it down because it upsets her. That is illegitimate interference with your personal freedom and it triggers the protection of the state. The state may, in protecting you and your lawn art from further interference, legitimately interfere with your neighbour. Now say that your neighbours go to the police to complain about the crucifix instead of confronting you on the lawn. Unless they can show the police that your lawn art is "obscene," hate propaganda or interferes with someone's "negative liberty"[7] or physical freedom to go about their business, the police, as representatives of the state, cannot legitimately interfere with your lawn art. But nor can they interfere with your neighbours for complaining as long as this is done lawfully.

What does gift shop liberalism say in addition to this? It says that there is absolutely no limit to the amount or type of value diversity a morally liberal society can accommodate. Picture a gift shop. There may be statues of Elvis nestled alongside of Buddha key rings; there may be veggie burgers sitting on a rack in a deep freeze next to a slab of back-bacon; there may be Ouija boards, tarot cards and crystals sharing counter space with Virgin Mary wall plaques and the *Globe and Mail*. Neither the statues nor the key rings nor the veggie burgers nor the bacon nor the boards, cards and crystals nor the wall plaques nor even *the Globe and Mail* seem to mind the company at all. And it does not appear that bringing in a number of maquettes of the Shah of Iran or even an Adolf Hitler whoopee cushion will have any effect whatsoever on the other gift shop items. In fact, there is no limit to the diversity among those items that the shop could accommodate. Just what gets in might largely be a matter of the preferences of the marketplace but then again, not necessarily.

There is another model of liberalism — fish tank liberalism. Everything about the values of equality and diversity continues to hold on this second liberal model. However, unlike gift shop liberalism, fish tank liberalism believes that there are limits to the amount or type of moral diversity a liberal society can tolerate. Picture a fish tank. Plants from the tropics, fish from Spain and Australia, snails from the local riverbed, a little stone castle ruin made in Hong Kong, a miniature deep sea diver from *20,000 Leagues Under the Sea* copyrighted by Walt Disney, maybe baby's soother. So far so good for liberalism. But let's look at the fish a little closer. You want to add some variety. A friend (who as it turns out doesn't know very much about fish) suggests a piranha. So you buy one of those at the local pet shop and introduce it to your tank. Soon there is little organic material left but the new arrival. If only you had known that there are certain breeds of fish which simply cannot occupy the same tank with others — that certain breeds of fish cannot tolerate certain plants and vice versa. And then there's temperature. Different plants and fish have different tolerance levels when it comes to the temperature of the tank water so, just on that basis alone, you cannot put them in the same tank. The most beautiful and healthy aquarium environments may indeed be chock-a-block with diversity. But no environment should be required to sacrifice itself for the sake of diversity per se.

Gift shop liberalism, even in caricature, does not describe the sort of liberal morality which has prevailed in this country since its inception. To believe this would be to deny that Native Canadians have been subjected to racist and intolerant treatment in their own land; that Japanese Canadians were unjustly incarcerated during WW II. The problem with gift shop liberalism is that it describes an inert world. It presumes that the units of diversity in question are not organic, that they never change, do not interact with one another or their environment beyond taking up space within it. It fails to represent a "life-world"[8] and we will make the wrong predictions about how a living society will respond to changes in its make-up if we assume it.

I think that fish tank liberalism, while still a caricature, best describes Canadian liberalism and further, since it describes a living environment, I think it is a model of liberal morality which we ought to cautiously endorse. This model is not free of problems. It appears, for instance, that assuming it might lead us to endorse policies like the internment of Japanese Canadians during WW II; something I do not want it to do. It is true that fish tank liberalism allows limits on what sort and how much variety may be tolerated in a given society. The ultimate criterion by which these limits are motivated, determined and justified, however, is the survival of the society. Where limits on toleration are instead motivated, determined or justified by racism, they are not endorsed by fish tank liberalism.[9]

Prohibiting unjustified and harmful interference with others thus functions as an internal limit on how far fish tank liberalism can go to protect a morally diverse society. We ought to tolerate anything that does not involve, support or encourage such harm and interfere with anything that does. The prevention of such harm also functions as a limit on individual rights and freedoms — freedom of religion for example. It is not necessary, according to this model, to tolerate violent practices simply because they are based on unique cultural or religious values which might wither in their absence. The practice of performing clitorechtomies on young females may be seen as such a violent practice. The fact it is a highly integrated element in a specific culture with significant religious overtones may shape the way in which our society decides to implement a prohibition against it, but does not stand in the way of such a prohibition. The challenge is to interpret or apply this limit on religious freedom (or other freedoms) in a way which affords the greatest exercise of the freedom consistent with the least amount of protection necessary to prevent the harm in question.

Moral Dogmatism

The problems with moral dogmatism are well documented both in the general history of humankind as well as in the particular history of Canada. Moral dogmatism refers to the view that whatever one's moral commitments, those commitments are the only true, the only right commitments for anyone to have and that there they are complete. Given the sort of moral diversity sanctioned by fish tank liberalism, moral dogmatism is problematic. One of the theoretical weaknesses of moral dogmatism is that the grounds for dogmatically holding to one's moral principles are epistemically weak. How can anyone know for sure that there are no more things to be said about morality than have been said by a minority — sometimes a very small minority — of human beings, many of whom are long dead? To have such knowledge presumes impossible access to all of human experience, past, present and future.

Moral dogmatism may be practically hazardous as well. When a moral dogmatist confronts someone whose moral principles do not fit with his or hers, the dogmatist is apt to regard the other as in some state of moral deficiency. Their moral deficiency may be regarded as grounds for treating others as less than human or as less deserving of moral respect than those whose principles fit with the dogmatist's. It is not necessary to assume that the moral dogmatist is otherwise in a position of authority over the "moral deficient" to see that the deficient may be in danger. However, where there is an inequality of this sort, the risk of harm to the "deficient" is great.

Moral dogmatism may be considered problematic in another practical sense. It assumes that a given set of moral principles is infallible. If, on the contrary, there is no infallible set of moral principles and one has closed oneself to this possibility, then a great deal of time and energy may be wasted protecting false beliefs. It may be that the narrowing of the imagination and atrophying of one's sympathies as a result of protecting a falsely restricted view of the moral life is itself a factor in the intensification of one's intolerance for alternative moral values — values which just might be better at solving the problems the dogmatist has. Instead of seeking new ways to improve social conditions, he or she may blame others. As history shows, it is often a short step from taking up this blaming attitude to embracing xenophobia.

Moral dogmatism would be less troubling if it restricted itself to situations where those who hold to it had no interaction with people who held different moral values. But such interaction is very difficult to avoid in Canadian society — in fact we embrace it. Still, when the survival of a morality is the primary value, moral dogmatism appears to be a good defence strategy. Sets of moral principles historically attached to extremely dogmatic religious codes or to extremely xenophobic cultural practices are very durable and have survived a great deal of external threat. By contrast the secular humanist values of liberalism and individual happiness, equality and freedom may be seen as historically fragile. Nevertheless, the cost of moral dogmatism is high for those coerced or excluded by it as well as increasingly costly for the dogmatists themselves. Complete moral isolationism is no longer possible.[10] There are no more new lands to go to and increasingly fewer opportunities for noninteraction with people who hold different moral views from your own. If you agree that morality is important yet reject moral dogmatism, then you may be a moral pluralist.

Moral Pluralism and Moral Relativism

One is a moral pluralist if, according to Lawrence M. Hinman, one believes that, "the truth, at least in moral life, is not singular or unitary. There are many truths, sometimes partial and sometimes conflicting" and that, "disagreement and difference...can be sources of moral strength."[11] Here one may hold to a set of moral principles — even the same set the moral dogmatist holds to — and yet allow that any of the principles it contains may be incorrect or that the whole thing may be completely off track.[12]

Moral pluralism has the ring of moral relativism. Moral relativism says that whatever a people think is right, is indeed right for them even if it is wrong for — or according to — others. It also says that since there are no higher or overarching moral principles to appeal to, we are no more in a position to correct them than they are in to correct us. Live and let live. Polygamy is morally acceptable to certain peoples. The moral relativist says that polygamy is therefore right for that people wherever they are. The moral pluralist, on the other hand, may allow that according to that people's own moral code, polygamy may be right but insists that since their moral code cannot be considered the only or last word on morality, they may be prohibited from practicing it on other grounds. If they are in a society such as ours, for example, which may be said to reject polygamy on equality grounds (polygamous cultures rarely allow women to have multiple spouses) among others, then their polygamous practices need not be tolerated.

Moral pluralism represents a position opposed to both moral dogmatism and moral relativism. The dangers of moral relativism may not be as clear to most people as those of moral dogmatism but they cannot be ignored. Moral relativism, philosophers generally argue, cannot help but slide to extreme moral subjectivism — what they call "solipsism."[13] Extreme moral subjectivism says that no one — no person or group of persons — can possibly know what is right or wrong for any other person or persons since such knowledge is based on the contents of private mental states and these cannot be accessed by anyone other than the subject him or herself. This is alleged to describe a state of affairs in which no one has the right to judge anyone else on moral grounds. Without such a right, we are rationally prohibited from morally condemning the conduct of others. Surely there are many examples, in particular those involving harm to children, where such condemnation would be rational according to most people. Also, it is unclear, given the ultimate logic of moral relativism, what grounds can be used to justify educating children in those moral virtues which their society endorses. If it is all just up to the individual, then no child should be influenced to behave this way rather than that. In fact, a society dominated by the logic of moral relativism would probably not be a society at all.

Good Fences Make Good Neighbours: Diversity and Separation

Moral pluralism, like moral dogmatism and moral relativism, is a "meta" moral position—a theory about substantive moral views. It is taken up alongside the observance of any one of a variety of substantive moral positions which are consistent with it, but not necessarily with one another. For instance, Jehovah's Witnesses have long imposed a no blood transfusion rule on themselves. From the point of view of an atheist, however, morality may require blood transfusions in certain circumstances. Alongside this deep moral difference between them, a moral pluralist atheist and a moral pluralist Witness could still both agree that each's moral commitments might be based on certain errors or be open to revision. Like moral dogmatism and moral relativism, moral pluralism does not eliminate the problem of clashing moral values. It merely affirms that under the condition of lively interaction, it is better at reducing tension and keeping the lines of communication open than other metamoral positions.

Moral pluralism, as noted above, is a theory about attitudes towards moral beliefs. It may be used to describe, as in "most Canadians are moral pluralists" or to recommend, as in "we ought to be moral pluralists." It may also be used to describe other theories, as in "liberalism is a moral pluralist political theory." Finally, we may use the term "moral pluralist" to describe societies which endorse moral pluralism in its normative sense. A moral pluralist society needs to be distinguished from one which is "morally pluralistic." A society may be described as morally pluralistic if, for example, it is characterized through its members by commitments to more than one particular set of moral beliefs and especially where no one set dominates. Societies may be morally pluralistic yet not be moral pluralist. That is, despite the fact a society may contain members with various and sometimes opposing moral viewpoints, it is possible that all of them hold to these

moral viewpoints dogmatically and that tolerance of moral disagreement is not collectively endorsed. It is not likely that such societies
would enjoy much civil peace. Most societies in the West are best
described as morally pluralistic but their members also collectively
endorse moral pluralism.

Ours is one such society. Yet, where opposing moral points of view
are officially tolerated (and even celebrated), their adherents tend to
freely develop value-homogenous neighbourhoods or communities in
order to reduce, in a practical way, the sorts of tensions which might
arise as a result of clashing. A certain amount of local homogenization
helps preserve global moral peace and diversity. But homogeneous
neighbourhoods may experience their own internal tensions. A moderate process of rising and decaying dissent might occur between individuals in the most Irish, Italian or Sikh areas never quite reaching
open hostility on the one hand or cultural stasis on the other. This state
of affairs is captured by Robert Frost's adage "good fences make good
neighbours." Good fences are borders that provide privacy but do not
isolate. It must be born in mind, however, that this state of affairs can
only help preserve diversity and peace when the neighbours are moral
pluralists.[14] Where this is not the case, tensions often escalate into
open hostilities.

Passing Moral Culture on to the Young

There may be much that a random sampling of moral pluralists would
disagree on when it comes to substantive moral matters. But given
their commitment to tolerance and their willingness to leave answers
to most questions about the good life ultimately open, they would
agree that security of the person must be respected by all acceptable
personal or cultural moralities within the society they share with others. Moral pluralists might be uncomfortable with the implication that
living by moral codes which reject the primary importance of security
of the person should not be tolerated. But this discomfort, if it cannot
be eased, would likely be born since unlimited tolerance could make
any sort of broader, collective moral life virtually impossible. For the
most part, I expect that what I have argued so far will not oppose the
views of most readers regardless of your own concrete moralities. But
consensus here depends on a bit of vagueness left untidied throughout

the previous discussion. As long as terms such as people, individuals, citizens, landed immigrants, those who choose to live in this land and so on are understood to refer to adults, the argument may proceed more or less smoothly. But if we open up the reference of such terms to include children, the argument for toleration is likely to hit opposition.

In our historical survey, we learned of what many argued was a necessary condition of moral education and character. To be properly prepared for your moral lessons on many traditional moral views, be they in education to the virtues, the perils of sin or the rigors of moral logic, you have to be conditioned against your natural impulses, appetites and passions. As infants and young children, these moralities caution, human beings are born unable to respond to anything except the administration of pleasure and pain. Pain, in particular, is a powerful tool in domesticating a child's early behaviour. Given the supreme importance to morality of controlling all natural impulses, appetites and passions, pain must therefore be used — even if only as a last resort. Here, the emphasis is on the distinctiveness of human reason or spirit in the animal kingdom and the view that to be moral, you have to have unfettered use of your rational or spiritual faculties. To have that, you must be liberated from the pull of natural instinct — something which takes time and the use of physical force to achieve.

Agreeing with the opposing view that trying to deny or destroy our "primitive nature" is a bad idea for human morality does not commit you to rejecting moral education or the idea that certain preparations must be made before any human being can begin such an education. After all, not even nature agrees that every impulse we are born with should remain operative throughout our lives.[15] And so traditional moralities are not completely wrong-headed about the necessary conditions for moral education. The problem is in what they think those conditions include and how they think it best to establish them.

Moral diversity, which must include room for traditional as well as nontraditional moralities, is considered a positive and not a negative feature of Canadian society. As Section 27 of The Charter of Rights and Freedoms states: "This Charter shall be interpreted in a manner consistent with the preservation and enhancement of the multicultural heritage of Canadians."[16] A diversity of cultures implies a diversity of substantive moral criteria or values by which conduct is judged. In a moral pluralist society, this diversity is seen to contribute to the over-all menu of moral options available to all of its members. To aim at or maintain this moral diversity, it is necessary to transmit these diverse moral values from one generation to the next. In ours as well as in most other societies, this transmission occurs between parent and child and we must accept that children will be trained according to moral beliefs with which not all agree. We must also expect children to resist such training, at least on occasion. Hardening calls for learning and obedience with the threat of or actual bodily harm is an accepted pedagogical approach in many cultures, including ones which follow the Christian religion. Such hardening appears to many parents and educators as expedient at least in the short term or necessary as a last resort. Here, we face the first in a series of arguments advanced in favour of the use of corporal punishment. Given the moral pluralist aim of preserving and enhancing moral diversity, may we violate the "super" value of security of the person in order to morally educate children?

The Argument from Moral Education

The argument from moral education runs roughly as follows. The Canadian commitment to the attitude of moral pluralism is expressed in our positive valuing of different conceptions of the good life. This valuing is expressed in, among other places, our laws prohibiting the use of physical force and interference when it comes to persuading others that they ought to act one way rather than another. One may nevertheless claim that the corporal punishment of children is required for passing on this or that conception of the good life and so preserving and enhancing Canada's diverse moral heritage. In which case, the moral pluralist prohibition on the use of bodily harm as a means of moral suasion must itself be limited by the higher purpose of maintaining Canada's actual moral diversity.

Does this argument have merit?

In order to answer this question we need to get clearer on the threat which prohibiting the corporal punishment of children allegedly poses to Canada's diverse moral identity. As the piranha problem for fish tank liberalism showed, a morally diverse society might be threatened if one morality in particular becomes dominant—and may be destroyed if that one morality is aggressive and dogmatic. While one may argue that morality per se remains, the diversity does not. But a unimoral state is not really what the threat to morality noted above is about. The concern above is over the perceived threat to the possibility of morality itself. If no moral values and practices are transmitted to the next generation, morality will not survive. Given the "primitive" nature of children, they will not adopt the values and practices of their elders unless commands to do so from their parents or other caregivers are backed up by force. Threats of force, the worry continues, are rarely sufficient incentives to obey parental commands and so actual force must be used at least on occasion.

The main concern here is that if parents and other caregivers are not permitted these shows and uses of force, the next generation will fritter away their moral heritages. The worry continues that whatever rights children may have, such rights must be interpreted in a way that makes their possession consistent with the preservation and enhancement of Canada's morally pluralistic heritage. Even if the bodily harm limit on tolerance for moral practices describes an individual right to security of the person, the exercise or protection of that right should not be allowed to threaten the existence of Canada's morally pluralistic identity or the passing on of moral values from one generation to the next. It would seem that the case of morally educating children provides an example of why and how the bodily security limit could itself be limited. As I noted earlier, when it comes to placing limits on the exercise of individual rights, it is crucial that those limits not be interpreted or applied in ways which overprotect one side at the cost of underprotecting the other. Such balances are admittedly hard to achieve and maintain. I assume in what follows that children, like their adult caregivers, actually have a right to security of the person. The questions we must ask are first, whether the value of multiculturalism and its implications for moral education ought to figure at all in the limiting of children's right to security of the person. Second, if it ought to, does the argument from moral education strike the right balance between over-and underprotection of the value we place on children's right to security of the person and the value we place on moral diversity?

Children are in a very special situation according to the argument from moral education. They are "precivilized" and the receivers and future transmitters of all of our values and practices—a peculiarly onerous obligation given their inexperience and immaturity. It is the responsibility of their parents and teachers to prepare them for this task. Two preliminary questions arise. The first is empirical. Does getting children "ready" to receive the moralities of their parents ever require the use of painful physical force against them? That is, do we really have a conflict of values here? The second is philosophical. Is the value of Canada's pluralistic heritage less, as or more authoritative than the value of the bodily security of its children?[17] With respect to the first empirical question, the answer in the past was clear. The view of children we find in Aristotle and Aquinas, for example, has had a long reach: getting them ready for their moral education meant training them to control their bodily movements (to "sit still"), suppress their natural appetites ("not before dinner"), and "quiet" their natural passions ("don't be a sissy"). Learning to obey is effected by pain and fear, leading children away from their desire for pleasure and their independent and unruly identities and bringing them under the firm identity of authoritative adults.[18] As Aristotle put it, when it comes to their natural wildness, "unless this is rendered docile and submissive to authority it will pass all bounds."[19]

With respect to the philosophical issue, since our valuing of security of the person expresses itself as a legal right and our commitment to moral pluralism and our valuing of a morally diverse society may be said to express itself in terms of freedom of religion, there is initial reason to conclude that the latter value is less authoritative than the former. However, it could be argued that since protecting moral diversity is one of the guiding purposes of protecting individual rights, it is, for that reason, as or more authoritative than those rights.

Rejecting the Argument from Moral Education

Based on the above, there are two reasons for calling the argument from moral education for corporal punishment into question. With respect to the empirical issue, a leap is made from the idea that children must be trained to some measure of self-control to the idea that they must be made "docile and submissive." Philosophically speaking, the leap is invalid. Docility and submissiveness to the ruling order were once considered the primary virtues of all political subjects—adults as well as children.[20] Under such conditions, it made perfect sense to train children to these virtues. But human beings yearning for individual freedom eventually realized that docility and submissiveness were distinct from self-control.

While we may grant that self-control is a necessary condition of moral training, we may not, on those grounds, say that docility and submissiveness are as well. On balance, docility and submissiveness to authority or the ruling order are no longer unproblematically regarded as desirable attributes of childhood any more than they are of adult women, the poor or blacks.[21] Children are often encouraged by their parents and teachers to ask questions, to be creative, to "not do things just because everyone else is doing them" though all in a self-controlled way.[22] The empirical question is then whether corporal punishment is required for teaching children self-control. Since many parents and teachers have successfully prepared a wide variety of children for their moral education without the use of corporal punishment, it is reasonable to conclude that it is not.[23] It is therefore not necessary to administer corporal punishment to children in order to ensure the intergenerational transmission of moral values unless one of those values is the value of corporal punishment itself. But in that case, the argument from moral education begs the question—that is, it assumes that corporal punishment is valuable rather than shows it is. As such, the aim of passing on moral values and preserving and enhancing Canada's multicultural and morally pluralistic heritage should fail to persuade us that the bodily harm limit in the case of morally educating individual children must be violated. There is therefore no conflict of values here which requires balancing.

The second and philosophical reason for calling the argument from moral education into question has to do with its assumption that moral pluralism is as or more valuable or important than security of the person. The Charter of Rights and Freedoms makes individual human beings and not groups or ideas the sole bearers of rights and freedoms. This means that while Canadians may talk about the rights of Native Peoples or the disabled or of gays and lesbians or of women and children, what they mean is that individual members of one or another of these groups have the rights in question.[24] The language of individual rights is a relatively new one for human beings in the history of moral philosophy and one which is not universal. What Western history tells us is that over time and as the consequence of much painful trial and error, a growing number of human beings have concluded that, when they conflict, individual welfare must always take precedence over the welfare of this or that group or idea. Moralities, in other words, have no right in themselves to survive.

This individualistic attitude has faced criticism from those who worry that the traditional liberal picture of the individual is unrealistic or worse, pathological. Their main concern is that the notion of individual welfare is unintelligible when separated from its roots in socialized morality. Recall John Rawls's original position.[25] Some of Rawls's critics have voiced serious concern with the idea that a human being could continue to be a person when all "personal" characteristics are concealed by the veil of ignorance. The welfare of human beings is so intimately connected to their identity as "Native," "able-bodied," "gay," "female," etc., they argue that to conceal personal characteristics is to erase the person.

I think that there are at least two responses individualists can make to this criticism. Firstly, it is possible to understand aspects of individual well-being independently of their roots in ethnic origin, gender or other institutions of socialized morality.[26] When we consider an individual's need for a certain quantity or quality of oxygen, for fluids, for a certain level of nourishment as well as his or her requirements for a certain minimum level of physical safety, it is possible to evaluate these needs without checking biographical credentials. This is not to say, for example, that all adults have identical needs for their physical safety as all children or that all women have identical nourishment needs as all men but only that there is such a thing as a basic human need. We know, for example, that repeatedly beating any human being over the back with a leather belt will cause painful welts—we don't need to know whether or not they have two arms, are over eighteen years of age or male or Native or heterosexual or what have you to draw this conclusion.[27] Fulfilling all of a person's basic human needs will usually not, however, guarantee him or her a happy or even decent human life.

The Nazis experimented on human beings to determine what they actually required to be able to keep working. Needless to say, their findings should not be used to guide policy on social assistance. Basic human needs should therefore be distinguished into "basic biological needs" and "basic social needs."

Objections to individualism which take the form of rejecting basic biological needs as the sole basis for social assistance policies, for example, have philosophical merit. But few individualist moral theories imply such restrictions. Bentham's may have been a notable exception though Mill revised utilitarianism to include basic social needs as part of basic human goods. Clearly, the individualism of documents such as The Charter of Rights and Freedoms is also inclusive in this way. Nevertheless, we must not lose sight of the notion of basic biological needs. Arguably, security of the person is one such need.

Second, there are cases of individual human beings who, for one reason or another apart from serious impairment of their faculties, never identify with any socialized morality. Such cases may be exceptional. But I do not grant, as some moral theorists do, that such persons are not "normal" human beings at all and that as such might not merit the moral respect of others.[28] While some such persons may be psychopathic, I do not agree that psychopathology is the same thing as even extreme eccentricity.[29] In any event, we do not allow that psychopaths have no basic individual welfare interests, so even if all eccentrics were psycho- or sociopathic, it would not follow that individual well-being cannot be assessed independently of its roots in socialized morality. Children, because of their newness, may also fall into this category of persons who do not identify with a particular socialized morality. But if they do fall into it, this is not because they choose not to identify with a particular morality or are congenitally incapable of doing so but rather because they have not yet developed this sort of identification. However it happens, simply falling into this category does not diminish or weaken one's right to security of the person.

For these two reasons, one, that is it possible to assess individual welfare independently of its roots in socialized morality and two, that this must be done in certain cases, we have additional reason to be wary of those who argue that our commitment to transmitting a variety of moralities must be placed above or even alongside of the value to individuals of their security of the person. While moral pluralism ought to include tolerance of amoralism, our commitment to an open attitude towards moral variety must not include tolerance for the practice of inflicting physical pain on others against their will for the purpose of their moral education. Further, our desire for moral diversity in and of itself ought not to be more authoritative than our desire to ensure the physical safety and security of all Canadian citizens and residents. Nevertheless, proponents of corporal punishment argue that it must continue to be a morally and legally permitted practice in Canada. This may be urged on the grounds that it is necessary for children's moral education, which is in turn necessary for the survival of socialized morality and the preservation and enhancement of Canada's pluralistic heritage. I have argued that the "necessity" linchpin of this argument is decrepit and also that while the value of multiculturalism is held high by Canadians, it is not and ought not to be held above or in contest with the value of individual bodily security for children.

There is another group of arguments for the corporal punishment of children which this treatment does not capture. For some argue that the corporal punishment of children has nothing to do with socialized morality, moral diversity or moral education at all. Instead, they argue, it has to do with teaching children to look out for their individual well-being — their physical safety.

The Argument from Individual Welfare

The world is a dangerous place: sharp edges, steep inclines, deep waters, irresistible forces, immovable objects. There is a lot to learn about safely navigating it. When we are very young, we know little about these dangers and must learn from those who have been here longer. As it happens, most of us have the instinct necessary to pick up what we first need to know — we seek pleasure and avoid pain. Without the use of language and given that we are occasionally unobserved, having this instinct is crucial to our safety and survival. In teaching us, adults are initially limited to exploiting this instinct in the execution of their task. "Don't wait until your daughter is trying to poke out her baby brother's eyes for the fifth time. Just give her a good sharp smack the first time she does it" and "Don't try and explain to a two year old why the stove element is very bad to touch. If he tries to do it, give his bottom a whack." A little soreness, feelings hurt but then no eyes poked out; no burnt fingers. Or so the argument from individual welfare goes.

Like the argument from moral education, the argument from individual welfare depends for its force on the truth of the claim that children cannot be reasoned with. In its strongest terms, it says that children necessarily lack the mental "equipment" and/or experience they need to be compelled by warnings such as "It will burn you" to avoid hot stoves and the like. In order to get children to avoid these dangers, the promise of pain they already understand — that of a spanking for example — is required. Even though it might be extremely effective, it would be wrong to put their hands on a live element to prevent them from putting their hands on a live element again. The undesired effect here is not merely pain, it is the severe pain (and subsequent threat of infection and death) that burns cause. As such, we must inflict a less serious pain to prevent it.

As we have seen, our tolerance for different conceptions of the good life is limited by the view that one cannot use bodily harm against someone's will in order to morally educate her. But while an individual's security of the person cannot be compromised for this purpose, there are nevertheless situations in which we believe that her short-term safety may be sacrificed for her survival or for her long-term safety. The use of corporal punishment in such cases represents the sacrifice of the child's short-term security of the person for her long-term security. Surely, the argument might go, ensuring the long-term safety and survival of our children is required from us all regardless of our substantive moral commitments, and ought to override a child's short-term personal security in some cases.

Rejecting the Argument from Individual Welfare

Individual safety and survival is an instrumental "super" value. Without a sense of personal security, nothing else would mean very much to us at all. As such, I cannot criticize the argument from individual welfare for corporal punishment on the grounds that the end or value aimed at violates the value of security of the person. Regardless, the argument must be rejected. In claiming that children cannot be compelled to avoid danger by verbal warnings, this argument rests on the view that no children understand the verbal language of their care-givers. This view is, of course, false. Perhaps the argument can be strengthened by noting that understanding the language of their care-givers does not mean that children will understand every word used by them. So, for example, a child may understand "NO" but not know what the word "burn" means or just how bad a pain a burn is. The claim would then be that when "NO" is insufficient and "burn" is unintelligible, a smack or spanking is required. As we saw in the eye-poking case, it is true that "NO" is frequently if not almost always insufficient in the case of very young children for immediate compli-ance. And based on their inexperience, "burn" may indeed be a new word. Therefore, for the argument to have the greatest credence, it must be about very young or pre-school children — say from birth to four years old. The question now is whether it follows that corporal punishment of very young children is required by the super value of their individual safety and survival.

It follows from this value that in keeping children safe, adults must avoid violating it whenever possible. As such, if corporal punishment is to be used at all, since it does violate the value, it should only be used when all non-violent means of protecting children have been exhausted or when no such means are available and the harm which the punishment is intended to prevent is greater than the harm it involves. Furthermore, the argument might then conclude that in either of these situations, corporal punishment *must* be used. In both cases described above — the eye-poking and finger burning cases — however, there are many nonviolent ways of preventing the dangerous behaviour. Some may seem unacceptable: send your daughter to live with Grandma; get rid of the stove. But they ought not to be rejected out of hand. In any case, there are more moderate responses available in both cases which work with time. It may be, however, that especially in cases where serious bodily harm is threatened, that expedience is required.

Say you have warned your three year old not to climb up on the kitchen counter and removed her over and over again with no effect. Say you have tried sending her to her room, canceling her various privileges and even shouting at her that it is simply not permitted — "Do you see Mommy climbing up on the counters?" And she's at it again. The question before you now is whether spanking her will achieve the desired result. When all else has failed, surely it must be a last resort given your obligation to protect her from serious harm. If you are in a position to spank her, then you are also in a position to remove her from the danger and give her a strong verbal command to stop the behaviour. If this strategy has not worked so far to prevent her dangerous behaviour, then you have not used it often enough. You may have a child who is determined to be adventurous, one who is slow to learn or one who needs extra attention from you. None of these dispositions warrants the violation of her bodily security. Increased supervision is always an option. My recollections as a mother of active young children as well as of the stories of other mothers include many instances of "I just can't take my eyes off him for a second!" We must be cautious regarding our frustration when nonviolent methods of educating our children don't work. We should not fall into the trap of concluding something has not worked just because it has not worked right away. Many behaviours with some children will require months, sometimes years of patient teaching and reminding to instill. Parenting is hard work and it should not surprise us that it requires as much deeply internalized self-control and perseverance as we expect our children to develop as a result of our efforts.

The argument from individual welfare for the corporal punishment of very young children fails first for logical reasons. The argument might support the use of forced physical removal from a scene of danger but never supports the use of corporal punishment since whenever this is an option, so is removal or restraint. But even in this case and except in an emergency, forced physical interference may only be used when all else has failed to bring the point of their safety and survival home and only in the case of very young children who at times will explore the world on their own.[30] To support such intervention is not to support corporal punishment. Furthermore, in emergency cases, the minimum intervention necessary to bring the point home or avoid the harm is the maximum that should be allowed.[31] We are talking about very young children who, according to the argument from individual welfare, have little experience of the world and who have not yet developed a tough skin when it comes to its "abrasive beatings."[32] The time element in this rejection of the argument from individual welfare is key. In the past, parents may have believed in the use of corporal punishment for traditional reasons. Today, even though such reasons may not have as much force as they once did, it may be that due to chronically lacking enough time to adequately watch over our children that we believe corporal punishment is a natural means of protecting them. In this case, it must be emphasized that adults choose to place their obligations to others ahead of those to their children and demand that their children pay for this choice with their bodies.

Every morality is someone's morality. For our moral values to survive through time, human beings must pass them on to their children. Socializing morality through family practice, organized religion and private and public education has proved a very effective way of transmitting it from one generation to the next. I have argued that Canadian moral pluralism upholds the aim of moral diversity and so endorses moral education, but only so long as it does not involve violating the security of children's persons. If their moral education required the violation of Canada's super-value, then that value would be worthless. Thankfully, it does not. Furthermore, their individual safety and survival cannot be used as a general reason for ignoring children's need for and violating their entitlement to security of the person. This would only be the case if hitting a child was the sole method available for preventing them from harming themselves or others. Since, if you are close enough to hit, you are close enough to remove or restrain, there always is a humane option however time consuming it may seem.

4

• • • • • • • • • • •

Philosophical Morality:

Happiness and Harm

either the argument from moral education nor the argument from individual welfare supports the conclusion that the corporal punishment of children is required or ought to be permitted. Neither argument appears to commit itself to any particular moral theory in its effort to persuade. In what follows, I will introduce what I take to be the implicit moral commitment of a number of other arguments for corporal punishment. In the final stages of the historical survey presented in chapter 1, one of the modern theories of morality, utilitarianism, occupied our attention.[1] Utilitarianism holds that in order for an act, practice or policy to be moral, it must promote social utility or "the greatest happiness for the greatest number" affected by it. If you follow utilitarian moral reasoning, social utility is the test of an act's, practice's or policy's morality. This philosophical moral theory boasts the capacity to render moral judgements accessible and practical in contexts where people may disagree about the details of what

Notes to chapter 4 are on pp. 254–63.

65

constitutes the good life and has a long tradition of compatibility with the ideals of liberalism.

As moral theories go, utilitarianism competes mainly with deontology which makes the logical consistency with rationally determined individual rights and duties the test of morality. However, this debate among moral philosophers between the moral ultimacy of general welfare concerns versus individual rights and duties will not be settled here. Utilitarians like John Stuart Mill argued that while individual rights concerns were of the utmost importance in the realm of moral theory, such concerns were themselves ultimately based on welfarist considerations. Why, Mill asked, emphasize the rights and duties of individual actors when morally evaluating their actions? If it ever makes moral sense to do this, he answered, it is because it has a tendency to produce the greatest happiness for the greatest number.

Deontologists like John Rawls, on the other hand, have argued that welfarist considerations only make sense when derived from conceptions of what individual human beings are ultimately entitled to regardless of how the realization of these entitlements affects others. This is not to say that effects on others are irrelevant to every aspect of moral decision-making but only to say that they cannot trump the basic entitlements of individuals.

Each camp in this debate argues that theirs is the more fundamental basis of moral judgement. Currently, there is no point of view from which the question can be settled once and for all and may never be. In the end, preferring one over the other may just be a matter of taste. Or it may be that some situations seem to call for the use of one rather than the other. Perhaps a new moral perspective is yet to be formulated from which the debate would be resolvable. I do not think that choosing utilitarian over deontology is merely a matter of taste. To justify my preference for utilitarian moral reasoning in the current context, I propose the following. Over intergenerational time and based on much transregional and transcultural discussion, the people of Canada and their representatives decided that no one in Canadian society should have an inviolable legal right to anything including security of the person. The Charter allows that any right or freedom outlined in it may be violated by law—that is, by the state, if doing so can be clearly demonstrated as in the best interests of Canadian democracy and freedom. The test for that allowance is ultimately consequentialist. Now, you might argue that while it is consequentialist, it is not utilitarian because the criteria are "democracy" and "freedom" rather than happiness. But here you must ask Mill's question: Why are democracy and freedom as features of our society as a whole considered so important that the rights of certain individuals might be sacrificed to it? It is because democracy and freedom have come to be regarded by most people as necessary conditions of the well-being of the majority of society's members and that it may—on occasion—be necessary to curtail the rights and so the well-being of some so that most may enjoy it. Morally speaking, the ultimate consideration here is the wellbeing of most individuals and that, I would argue, involves a utilitarian rather than a deontological approach.

In appealing to the Charter, I am not suggesting that its existence settles the philosophical debate between utilitarianism and deontology. I am instead suggesting that the Charter provides a powerful justification for using utilitarian moral reasoning to sort out and assess the issues involved in what I take to be a serious Canadian social and moral matter—one that stands in urgent need of reform. This is not to say that this moral theory has no flaws. Like all such theories, it does. Yet, while having flaws is indeed a reason to proceed with a certain humility concerning the conclusions which follow from any moral theory's use, it is no reason to reject that theory when all other theories also have flaws. Depending on your sense of the overall number of flaws in utilitarianism, consider my use of it proportionately humble.

Where your substantive moral commitments are concerned, you might be a utilitarian or might look to utilitarianism to further justify for example, a religious moral code. In chapter 3, we discussed various attitudes which might be taken up towards one's moral beliefs. One could be either a dogmatist, a relativist or a pluralist when it comes to how convinced one is of their truth and breadth. We are going to examine the issue of corporal punishment in specifically utilitarian terms. But before doing so, we need a handy way of categorizing all of these various types of moral commitments. Then we will examine and criticize seven utilitarian arguments in favour of corporal punishment.

Customary Morality, Philosophical Morality and Metamorality

Let us say that one's customary morality refers to one's ethnic, cultural
or religious moral commitments. Customary morality is handed down
generation after generation in the form of celebratory (birth, death,
coupling, religious), eating, dressing and etiquette values and practices
among others. Next, let us say that one's philosophical morality refers
to one's considered beliefs about the conceptual foundations of one's
customary morality. Few people ever formally identify their philosophical morality. But that does not mean they do not implicitly operate with one. Whatever principled reasons people might give in
defence of their customary moral practices or judgements would begin
to reveal or shape their philosophical moralities. To complete this
process, they would have to examine those reasons in many different
sorts of situations to harmonize them as a whole or at least reduce the
amount of tension between them. It may turn out that their customary
moralities are justified on the basis of their ability to promote the greatest happiness for the greatest number or because the intentions behind
their rules and practices are logically coherent. Philosophical morality
justifies customary morality — purports to give it a firm basis which
most other people — especially those who have different customary
moralities — can acknowledge as legitimate. Philosophical morality
may also function on its own as a moral code.

Finally, let us say that one's metamoral position refers to one's
epistemic attitude either towards one's customary or philosophical
morality. Moral pluralism is one such metamoral position. Moral dogmatism and moral relativism are two others. I have argued that moral
pluralism is the official metamoral position taken up by Canadians.
This is not to argue that every Canadian is a moral pluralist but rather
to note that Canada's democratically devised constitutional and political commitments are — that moral pluralism is held up as that attitude
towards their moral beliefs which Canadians ought to adopt.[2] It is
extremely important to see that in upholding moral pluralism, the
government is not telling Canadians what philosophical or customary
morality to follow. It is, however, telling us what metamoral position
we should have. Liberals are sometimes uncomfortable with this fact.
But, as I have argued, officially abandoning this normative commit-

ment would have terrible consequences for personal freedom in our country.

In chapter 3, I discussed corporal punishment in the context of customary morality as well as in the context of individualism as it is understood in our moral pluralist society. I argued that the two grounds for corporally punishing children that were advanced from within each of these contexts fail to support the conclusion that children ought to or may be hit in order to promote their interests as moral, or simply, human beings. Let us now consider in greater detail the matter of philosophical morality and its potential contribution to the corporal punishment debate. In the course of this discussion, four arguments on behalf of corporal punishment firmly based in utilitarian moral reasoning as well as three arguments which may or may not be based in it are critically examined.

Corporal Punishment and Securing the Greatest Happiness for the Greatest Number

Utilitarian moral theory claims that whatever its ethnic or religious credentials, for an act (or rule or practice) to be considered moral, its execution must promote the greatest happiness for the greatest number affected by it. In using the term "happiness" in this context, Mill meant something more than the temporary sense of physical satisfaction one gets, for instance, from a good meal or on hearing a wonderful piece of music. The terms "well-being" and "welfare" are often used in place of "happiness" to avoid confusion with fleeting or strictly sensual pleasures. Indeed, it may be argued that the term happiness has been so overused since Mill wrote in the nineteenth century that it no longer conveys the depth and breadth of meaning it once did. While I agree that broad notions of well-being and welfare must be included in what utilitarianism aims at, I believe that narrower ones such as "felt satisfactions" must also be considered. Geoffrey Scarre, for example, has argued that "an inclusive-end view of happiness singles out neither pleasure nor any other individual element as the whole of happiness, but sees happy existence as a coherent construction out of a variety of complementary parts—a construction on which the subject can look with satisfaction."[3] Further, he states that "at the social level, the best way to assist individuals to be happy is to create the basic political, economic and educational conditions which permit their chosen lifestyles to be realized."[4] I will therefore continue to use the term happiness (rather than well-being or welfare or desire satisfaction) and do so in Mill's "inclusive-end" sense.

It is possible that of all the options for action available in the circumstances, none will promote any happiness for anyone at all. In that case, utilitarian moral theory tells us to choose, as far as is possible, that act which will produce the least amount of unhappiness for the least number of all affected. Acts which do not produce happiness or unhappiness for others may be judged morally neutral. For example, if, as I am typing, completely alone in the building where I live, I rock back and forth in my creaky chair, this act has no utilitarian moral significance. If, however, in doing so, my chair makes a noise which keeps a downstairs neighbour awake all night, my act takes on moral significance whether or not I am aware of its effects. There may also be acts which all have the same overall utility. They may, as far as anyone can see, all produce the same net amount of happiness or unhappiness.[5] In such cases, which are presumably very rare, utilitarian moral theory says we may "toss a coin" if acting is indeed called for.

In our historical survey, according to utilitarian moral theory, "if an act or policy of causing suffering to children had the result of causing the greatest happiness overall, it may be moral to cause children to suffer" but "if it could be shown that its use as a practice violated the greatest happiness principle, a moral rule against it would be called for."[6] Utilitarians, I noted, do not accept that any moral rule (be it customary or philosophical) applies absolutely or universally — that is without regard to the particular circumstances which seem to call for its application (though they may accept that such rules apply generally). They do not accept universal moral rules because they do not accept that moral rules exist independently of human experience and observation. Moral rules, according to the utilitarian, do not determine us, we determine them. As such, a utilitarian analysis of the use of corporal punishment will depend for its conclusions on empirical claims about what is going on in the world, with children and the adults who care for them and with all those who are affected by the use or non-use of corporal punishment.

In the end, the data must be submitted to the greatest happiness principle. If you ask a utilitarian, "Should we ever use corporal punishment on children and if so when?" the first step in responding will be to identify the individuals or groups who are affected by its use and non-use and consult studies and reports concerning the tendency of either to promote the happiness or unhappiness of all those affected. A utilitarian will then compare the bottom lines of both use and nonuse to arrive at a conclusion about which policy will likely promote the greatest happiness for the greatest number.[7]

To consider utilitarian moral theory on the topic of corporal punishment in greater detail, let us begin by looking at what John Stuart Mill had to say about it in the middle of the nineteenth century.[8] Both Mill and his wife, Harriet Taylor, were utilitarians, social reformers and active contributors to the daily newspapers and popular magazines of the day on subjects of controversy and public interest. Commenting in their pamphlet *Remarks on Mr. Fitzroy's Bill for the More Effectual Prevention of Assaults on Women and Children*[9] in 1853, Mill and Taylor write:

> Overwhelming as are the objections to corporal punishment except in cases of personal outrage, it is peculiarly fitted for such cases. The repulsiveness to standers by, and the degradation to the culprit, which make corporal maltreatment so justly odious as a punishment, would cease to adhere to it, if it were exclusively reserved as a retribution to those guilty of personal violence....It is the moral medicine needed for the domineering arrogance of brute power. After one or two cases of flogging for this description of crime, we should hear no more of outrages upon women or children for a long time to come.[10]

While rejecting corporal punishment as a moral sanction against women and children as well as against convicted persons in general, Mill was so incensed by its use against the young (and women) that he seemed prepared to make an exception of those who harm children in this way.[11] "Those who presume on their consciousness of animal strength to brutally ill-treat those who are physically weaker should be made to know what it is to be in the hands of a physical strength as much greater than their own, as theirs is than that of the subjects of their tyranny."[12] Mill's optimism here regarding the eventual outcome of the use of corporal punishment in this special case was, however, clearly ignorant of the problem he was addressing. Such ignorance is in less evidence elsewhere in his writings on the subject. In a stinging editorial comment *Punishment of Children*, Mill writes:

> It is assumed and goes uncontradicted that a punishment which is brutalizing and degrading to grown men is quite fit and proper for helpless infancy; unfit to be inflicted, according to prescribed rules, by men called judges, after solemn enquiry and in the full light of publicity, but, "by the law of nature" (as Lord Campbell says) quite proper to be administered at discretion by men called fathers in the secrecy of their own houses, subject, when some peculiarly atrocious case accidentally comes to light, to a gentle admonition....Take any naturally sensitive boy, who has been habitually flogged, and one who has never suffered that indignity, compare them, observe the difference in self-respect and in all that depends on self-respect, which will mark those two human beings throughout life. On a boy of a dull, hard nature, its effect is to render him ten times harder than he would be without it — to qualify him for being a bully and a tyrant....The object of his respect will be power.[13]

In this instance, Mill appeals to the idea that human character is shaped by external forces from the time of its earliest development well into adulthood. Implicit in his argument is his rejection of the so-called "law of nature" according to which children are the private property of their fathers. The law implies that since they are not "self-owning" — not real persons — children cannot suffer the serious harm of personal indignity caused by the painful and humiliating effects of corporal punishment. Since only adults or true persons are subject to such pains or humiliation, this "law of nature" implies only adults need protection from them. In rejecting appeal to such a law, Mill is relying on the authority of human experience which to him says otherwise.

In concert with the principle of utility, the facts as Mill saw them recommended that we beat those who use corporal punishment against children. From a utilitarian point of view, would an eye for an eye in this sort of case be morally acceptable? Mill's suggestion that it would implies, in concert with his later remarks about the effects on children of corporal punishment, that once a brutalized child has become a brutalizing adult, he or she no longer recalls the experience of being corporally punished at the hands of caregivers. If the impression of this experience is refreshed, the adult would not treat children in this manner.[14] Further, Mill's call for the corporal punishment of those who corporally punish children implies that there is no better way of getting them either to recall those experiences or to stop harming children in this way. Since many other options were available even in Mill's time, we may conclude that his call for the corporal punishment of such "brutes" was largely rhetorical. In any case, for today's utilitarian, there would be no social utility whatsoever to such a policy. We know from the considerable testimony of psychologists, social workers and law enforcement officials that it is impossible to teach anyone — child or adult — to be non-violent by being violent towards them and that there are non-violent ways of both preventing and correcting violent behaviour.[15]

Mill's point in the end is, nevertheless, straightforward and consistent with what is argued today (though now from the vantage point of social science), concerning the effects of corporal punishment on children. Taking a philosophically utilitarian moral position on this issue therefore demands that no children be subjected to such treatment. As such, when it comes to justifying one's customary morality, its rules and practices should be consistent with this philosophical moral principle. However, being a utilitarian in this case does not demand that children never be interfered with in a physical way as a means of regulating their behaviour or protecting them from harm. Mill recognized that physical interference is sometimes morally necessary. In his famous "decrepit bridge" thought experiment, he illustrates this point:

> Again, it is the proper office of a public authority to guard against accidents. If either a public officer or anyone else saw a person attempting to cross a bridge which had been ascertained to be unsafe, and there were no time to warn him of the danger, they might seize him and turn him back, without any real infringement of his liberty; for liberty consists in doing what one desires, and he does not desire to fall into the river. Nevertheless, when there is not a certainty, but only a danger of mischief, no one but the person himself can judge of the sufficiency of the motive which may prompt him to incur the risk: in this case, therefore (unless he is a child, or delirious, or in some state of excitement or absorption incompatible with the full use of his reflecting faculty) he ought, I conceive, to be only warned of the danger; not forcibly prevented from exposing himself to it.[16]

In the case of clear and present serious danger, physical interference may be employed against adults as well as children whenever verbal interference or reasoning is likely to be ineffective. In the case of uncertain danger, adults must be left to their own judgement of the risks. Children, however, may be physically interfered with in this circumstance along the same lines allowed in the case of clear danger for both adults and children. We may presume that Mill draws the distinction in the latter case between adults and children on the grounds that adults are, generally speaking, competent judges of dangerous situations and children are not. Given the constraints on what such physical interference could involve however — "might seize him and turn him back" — it would be inappropriate to refer to such interference as "punishment." Punishment of one sort or another might follow such interference as means of getting the child or even adult to be more careful in the future but again, the choice of punishment would be constrained by the utilitarian moral rule against corporal punishment.

This moral rule against corporal punishment relies on the claim that violence towards anyone — but especially children — is an ineffective and harmful method of deterring intolerable (including dangerous) behaviour and has a strong tendency to instill the value of violence deep in the child's mind, risking an eventual influence on his adult sensibilities. The risk of a violent or latently violent society is thus courted. Everyone's security of the person is potentially threatened.

There is no denying that, based on the evidence, some sort of causal relationship between the use of corporal punishment and the existence of social and domestic violence is assumed here. This is not to say that corporal punishment alone is responsible for the risk of such violence but only that it has a significant role. As such, the counterargument that since corporal punishment rates have been historically steady, variations in levels of social and domestic violence challenge the causal assumption of their relationship is not persuasive. Also, it is sometimes urged by well-intentioned relatives and hard on crime advocates that given what they perceive to be problem children or increases in youth crime, more not less corporal punishment is in order. Such urgings presuppose that there is less corporal punishment now than in the past and that it is the failure to corporally punish, not its use that causes violence. As we will see later, this theory has no basis in fact.

While there are always calls to "bring back the lash" and so on, such calls for highly-punitive state authoritarianism come from a disgruntled minority of Canadian citizens.[17] A dangerous, violent world is morally unacceptable from the utilitarian point of view and so granting the risks noted above, utilitarianism tells us we should morally condemn corporal punishment. Several features of this position rely on empirical claims about the world, about children and about the adults who care for them, which are denied by those who support corporal punishment on what appear to also be utilitarian grounds. A critical analysis of four arguments defending the use of corporal punishment based on the philosophical morality of utilitarianism follows.

The Utilitarian Argument from Efficiency

The utilitarian moral argument against corporal punishment states that violence towards anyone—but especially children—is ineffective in managing their behaviour. Despite numerous studies which come to this conclusion, many parents and adult caregivers disagree with it.[18] They argue, for instance, that spankings are very efficient in interrupting their children's intolerable behaviour. It seems hard to reject this claim as it stands. Nothing like a swift swat to the back of his head to make Mickie stop playing with his food at the dinner table. Then there is the shrieking, collapsible child in the supermarket checkout line. Squeezing her arm harder and harder until she stops then quietly telling her "It will be worse when we get home if you start up again" works wonders. Supporters of corporal punishment assert that since moderate physical violence has the immediate effect of stopping a time-and place-specific intolerable behaviour, when expediency is called for, it ought to be used. They also assert that no other method of external discipline is as efficient. And so from the point of view of utilitarian philosophical morality, it would appear that under certain circumstances, corporal punishment of children may be morally required.

The problem with the efficiency argument is that while it does address the interruption of a specific instance of bad behaviour, it does not speak to the improvement of behaviour at all. Behaviour such as bad table manners and temper tantrums simply cannot be improved in a one shot way. In the first case, we know that at the root of bad table

manners are either deeper emotional issues for the child or simple physical immaturity. Temper tantrums are most often the consequence of
tiredness and while giving in to the child may indeed reinforce the
behaviour, it is not the only nonviolent way of responding to it. When it
comes to what is perhaps perceived as the moral necessity of just stopping the behaviour in question, this argument also fails to persuade.
The effect on, for example, many bystanders of listening to a child
scream for five minutes in a checkout line must be weighed against the
effect on the child of being assaulted by someone whom he or she loves.
Since avoiding the circumstances which bring such behaviour on is
always the most effective way of preventing it, this strategy is morally
preferable from a utilitarian point of view. When the behaviour could
not have been predicted, it is tempting but morally wrong to discount
the child's distress and overestimate the annoyance to adults or its
moral importance. Ignoring the child's tantrum might seem an embar-
rassing approach. But if the value of multiculturalism enshrined in the
Charter is not sufficient to defeat any child's right to security of the person, neither is one parent's momentary embarrassment.

The Utilitarian Argument from Genetics

The second empirical claim upon which the utilitarian moral judgement
against corporally punishing children rests is that the use of corporal
punishment instills the value of violence deep in the child's mind where
it grows and eventually influences their adult sensibilities and behaviour. This claim is often disputed by adults who, recalling their own
experience of being corporally punished, insist that neither they nor anyone they know were affected by it in this way. Implicit in such claims is
the belief that if it is not true that most adults who were corporally punished as children are violent, then the empirical claim that such punishment has a tendency to cause violent adult character is false.

It must be said up front that the truth of the empirical claim does
not require that the majority of children who are corporally punished
will become violent adults.[19] All that is required to establish the claim
is that significantly more children who are corporally punished
become violent adults than children who are not. Many studies show
that this correlation does exist. But such studies often go further and

argue that corporal punishment is therefore a strong risk factor for violent character.[20] Many supporters of corporal punishment reject the implied conclusion that being corporally punished causes children to become antisocial—or worse—assaulters in their adult lives arguing that the causal connection goes the other way: some persons are genetically disposed towards violence. Even as infants, their behaviour is defiant and calls for extreme measures including the administration of physical pain. In this case, corporal punishment is not the cause of or a risk factor for a violent character but merely a necessary response to it. In adulthood, such persons may be very violent and dangerous not because they were beaten or spanked as children but because they were genetically destined to become so.

The facts that a majority of violent adults were corporally punished as children and that more corporally punished children become violent adults than children who were not punished in this way are consistent with the genetic theory. As such, these facts do not automatically support the conclusion that corporal punishment is a risk factor for violent character or a dangerous society. However, to establish the claim put forth by the genetic argument that corporal punishment is not a contributing factor to violence in adulthood, one would have to show that eliminating corporal punishment in the case of aggressive children has no reductive effect on their bad behaviour. Studies show the reverse.[21]

In most anecdotal testimonials to the efficacy and acceptability of corporal punishment, one is often told of the existence of persons who were corporally punished "for good reasons" and who went on to become peaceful, caring, successful and happy adults.[22] Whether the momentum of such testimonials is in the direction of showing that corporal punishment is therefore a good thing or less controversially, that it is not a bad thing, their point is simply not supported by the evidence adduced in their favour. First, the existence of such persons does not establish that there is no tendency to produce the reverse. Second, even if the majority of corporally punished children go on to live peacefully, the fact that almost all persons who become violent in adulthood were corporally punished as children, that corporal punishment tends to increase aggression in children and that its cessation tends to decrease it tell us that the causal theory of corporal punishment and violence ought to be preferred over the genetic theory. For if the genetic theory were true, the cessation of corporal punishment in the case of these "naturally bad" children would have no beneficial effect on their behaviour. It must also be noted that while not all children who are corporally punished will develop violent characters as adults, many of them will nevertheless be affected in ways which make their lives and the lives of those around them unbearable. Adult depression and anxiety, for example, are now believed to be symptomatic of the repression of the rage which often follows a corporal punishment episode.[23] Finally, according to the genetic argument itself, corporal punishment has no improvement value—that is it has no lasting benefit regarding the child's behaviour. Given the risk of harms with which so many studies show it is correlated, the argument therefore fails to support the normative conclusion that such punishment ought to be used or permitted against children.

The Utilitarian Argument from the Greatest Good

Next, assuming that some defenders of corporal punishment may be persuaded that its use is inefficient and tends to contribute to violence in adulthood, would they accept this as sufficient reason to consider it morally unacceptable? What if, due to some other confounding variable, societies in which corporal punishment was not used or permitted actually had worse levels of violence? We need evidence here that this is not the case before we morally judge parents who corporally punish their children. Once again, however, studies show that prohibiting the use of corporal punishment does not have this result.[24] Continuing to claim, in the face of this evidence, that not using corporal punishment would still produce a worse society implies the belief that violence and aggression between adults and children is not the worst thing that can happen to a society. Perhaps the worst thing that can happen is a large-scale loss of freedom. Here, one may prefer a society fraught with domestic and social violence to one less violent though highly controlled by state, propaganda- or drug-induced compliance. Cautiously granting the reasonableness of this preference, for it to morally justify the use of corporal punishment, it would have to be shown that failing to use it would indeed result in such an unfree society. Whatever the difficulties of establishing the claim that the use of corporal punishment is causally implicated in adult violence, the claim that the use of nonviolent discipline would cause a large-scale loss of individual freedom is simply a nonstarter.[25]

The Utilitarian Argument from Forgiveness

To establish a utilitarian moral claim in favour of corporal punishment, one must present evidence acceptable according to the methods of social science that it produces more good than harm to those affected by its use. Since the most current evidence shows the contrary, utilitarian moral theory tells us that the corporal punishment of children is immoral and ought, therefore, to be condemned. But what might the theory say to someone who wants to argue that parents, for example, usually strike children in situations where they have "lost it"—have been pushed beyond endurance? Morally condemning or punishing them would have no positive effect and would simply cause families pain. From a utilitarian point of view it might be argued that those who use painful physical force in this way ought to be forgiven not condemned.

I have already argued that striking a child out of anger or rage is not to corporally punish that child. As such, the argument from forgiveness is not an argument defending corporal punishment. Instead, it is an argument for clemency towards those who wrongfully fail to resist the impulse to hit which their anger or rage produces in them. Where forgiveness is called for, a moral wrong has been admitted. If offering forgiveness to those who are truly sorry for behaving in this way promotes the greatest happiness for the greatest number, then utilitarian moral theory tells us we ought to forgive them. But this endorsement would be limited by the effect of repeatedly forgiving those who behave in this manner. If doing so interfered with the cessation of the behaviour, then forgiveness would have to be withheld on moral grounds. For the utilitarian, the overall consequences to the happiness of most of those concerned is the final judge of the morality of the act. Forgiveness may be morally permitted, even in some cases, required. But this judgement must always be made on the basis of actual consequences. If one's concern for overtaxed parents and caregivers demands that morality endorse forgiveness no matter what the consequences of doing so, then one's morality cannot be utilitarian.

However, this criticism of the forgiveness argument might not be to the point. If the loss of control is naturally unavoidable, then it will not matter that repeatedly forgiving it fails to stop the behaviour and results in more and more pain to children. This consequence to children might just be an unavoidable social evil. What might be said in response to this countermove? What must be said is much the same thing said in response to one of the arguments in favour of legalizing prostitution. This argument states that since prostitutes draw the most harmful yet completely natural impulses of many males away from respectable women and children, their profession ought to be morally permitted if not required. In response, feminists have pointed out the dubious science behind such a claim.

The commercial language of "service provider" insidiously neutralizes the facts of victimization which characterize prostitution. Any being who feels left without any work option but to become the servicer of impulses which men ought otherwise to resist, for example, is indeed a victim of those impulses. In forcing or even allowing someone to end up this way, we *create* or sustain the impression that the impulses are "normal" or at least to be expected from males, for example, when they live in society with females. But impulses towards sexual violence are, generally speaking, no less irremediable than other sorts of violent impulses. While we may say that such impulses are to be expected, this in no way warrants the normative inference that there should be a group of persons set aside to service them. What it does warrant are serious and ongoing social efforts to see to it that the impulses are suppressed or kept in check by education and legal sanction.

If the anger an adult experiences when dealing with a misbehaving child and the impulse to strike that child which might accompany it are sufficiently different from other anger responses and violent impulses — that is, stronger than those other impulses — then we are left with the conclusion that no degree of abreactive parental violence towards children can be morally condemned or legally punished. If we want to block the further conclusion that parents must therefore simply be left to act on these impulses, then we might suggest that they be ordered restrained, on medical grounds, from seeing their children unsupervised. Such restraint does not imply wrongdoing, yet it takes into account dangers to others. But routinely restraining parents who hit their children in rage from being with them as a family is obviously no solution to the childcare problem which corporal punishment poses. We are thus forced back to the conclusion that the impulse to strike children who misbehave, however strong, has to be controlled and that in order to achieve this, it must be suppressed or kept in check by education and law.

The Question of Harm

With its moral focus on the greatest happiness, utilitarianism has frequently been criticized as upholding an impossibly vague moral standard. Geoffrey Scarre explores this worry in his book *Utilitarianism*[26] and concludes that this criticism is unwarranted. As I noted earlier, John Stuart Mill argued that for the purposes of utilitarian moral theory, the greatest happiness is a complex and comprehensive state of individual well-being and satisfaction for all, importantly grounded in each's empirical sense of the general welfare of one's "fellow creatures,"[27] in the empirical and subjective sense of the specific welfare of one's intimates and familiars[28] and in the subjective sense of or satisfaction with oneself as an intellectually independent, creative and growing individual.[29] In addition, one's sense of oneself as happy must be carefully informed by facts about the natural, historical and conventional world. There is, of course, a lot of room for disagreement on the details of this notion and what it takes to achieve happiness. But such disagreement cannot be taken as evidence that the notion is impossibly vague unless a criterion of mathematical precision is imposed — something most theorists consider inappropriate in the domain of moral reasoning.

Anything that interferes with the attainment of happiness at the individual, family or social level should attract our moral attention. In the final analysis such interferences need not be considered immoral however. As we have seen, for such judgements to follow, it has to be shown that in the presence of a harm, no weightier consideration of overall or longer-term benefit applies. More needs to be said now concerning the harms with which corporal punishment is correlated. A harm, let us say, occurs whenever damage occurs to a living thing. We confine ourselves here to the case of living human beings (though this is not to say harm cannot occur to nonhuman animals). Damage occurs whenever the health or normal function of a human being is impaired. While our definition of corporal punishment does imply the infliction of pain or suffering — what the Law Reform Commission of Canada has called "hurting" a child[30] — this need not imply that the child has been harmed. I might stub my toe on the coffee table but unless I limp around as a result and my limping disables me in a more serious fashion, I have not been harmed. "It's nothing," I might say even though it hurts. It might also be argued that even if this sort of damage occurs, since the table could not have intended or avoided its role in my pain, I am not in fact harmed by it at all. Harm to a living human being is therefore understood here as occurring whenever its health or normal function is impaired by the action of another human being.

The action in question is the action of corporally punishing a child. Corporal punishment may harm children in three general ways, two of which may be referred to as traumatic. First, the act itself may result in physical trauma or damage which immediately impairs the child's health or normal function. The terms health and normal function are characteristically vague. I will not spend a lot of time trying to make them less so. Let us say that both include reference to states of the body easily ascertained through the immediate visual or tactile examination of physical evidence — skin, hair, nails, organs, muscles and bones. If the ordinarily intact state and so function of any of these is obviously traumatized or damaged, then harm of this first sort has occurred. Bruising counts here, as do welts and other more serious effects to the skin.

The second way in which children may be harmed by corporal punishment is less obvious than the first and involves damage to aspects of the child's health and normal function which may not be easily ascertained by a direct visual or tactile examination of physical evidence. On the one hand, it may include states of the body only ascertainable through the use of sophisticated diagnostic technology. This sort of harm may also be included in the first sort and as such is "penumbral."[31] On the other, this second sort of trauma may involve the child's immediate psychological or emotional state.[32] A child may be severely frightened by a corporal punishment episode and as a result enter a state of emotional distress, shock or disassociation. This may occur whether or not physical trauma has occurred. It would be unreasonable to argue that such hurting does not impair the normal function or health of an individual given our obvious preparedness to acknowledge mental or emotional incapacity as such an impairment even in the absence of physical disability or damage.

It is crucial to note that evidence of this latter sort of trauma may be latent for long after the corporal punishment episode. And it may be due to this latency that parents who use corporal punishment are unwilling to believe social scientists who, having tracked large numbers of children over long periods of time, claim it is a demonstrated risk factor for problems such as undue aggression. While parents may notice increasingly distant and rejecting behaviour from their children as they become adolescents, these phenomena are more often attributed to "normal" teenage behaviour than to poor parent behaviour. Yet, of thirteen controlled studies (involving a total of 2497 participants) conducted to examine the correlation between corporal punishment and parent-child relationship deterioration, all showed a marked association between the two factors.[33]

Nevertheless, while often grounds for tort liability, Canadians have generally declined to consider the infliction of just any psychological or emotional trauma as so seriously immoral that it must be made criminal.[34] In addition, since the aim of corporal punishment is often to "put the fear of God" into a child, it would seem that emotional harms are acceptable as long as only children sustain them. But there is little doubt that such harms can be extremely serious and that their signs can be detected. The human body is organized to respond to many types of pain and threats of pain or damage—through the release of adrenaline for example. But even if it is true that as we mature, our bodies can be coaxed to respond in nondamaging ways to more and more intense dangers, the bodies of children are extremely sensitive to them. Even if obvious physical trauma has not occurred, the use or threat of corporal punishment is morally problematic given the likelihood that it is implicated in psychological or emotional harm to children.

Imagine your own reaction to a much larger angry person raising an arm to strike you. You would no doubt experience an intense adrenaline rush and the "fight, freeze or flight" response. Now imagine being confined to an environment where this person was in control of what was right and wrong and also made it clear that hitting you whenever you made errors was an ongoing possibility. Next, imagine that person has a gun and has said they will use it if necessary. Such images are the stuff of what most adults consider torture (and some consider entertainment). I expect that the intensity of what especially young children feel as a consequence of living in a corporal punishment environment is comparable to what an adult would feel in this "torture chamber." Indeed, torture chamber is a term children sometimes euphemistically use to describe their home lives.

There is a third sort of harm which children suffer as a consequence of corporal punishment, a nontraumatic sort. Long-term studies following children who are corporally punished support the claim that corporal punishment is a strong risk factor for aggression, below-average academic performance and, as we have seen, adult violent behaviour.[35] The character described here is that of a person who is generally unhappy and unable to resolve his or her more serious problems without resort to physical violence either to themselves or to others. Such consequences are often disastrously harmful to these persons and others over the long run as well as extremely costly to society. Permanent disability, death or incarceration are commonly regarded as the worst things that can happen to anyone. To the extent that the use of corporal punishment is a risk factor, however low, for these outcomes, it is morally problematic to use it against any child.

The incidence of such harms makes corporal punishment a moral issue from the point of view of utilitarian philosophical morality. But the existence of such harms is not enough to support the claim corporal punishment is immoral. To do this, it is also necessary to consider the general happiness. It may be that the unhappiness of children caused by corporal punishment promotes the happiness of the greatest number and in that case, as I have stated before, it may be moral to cause that unhappiness. Assuming that there are more adults than children in Canada, the unhappiness of children subjected to corporal punishment might be outweighed by the happiness of all adults produced by the practice of corporal punishment. However, the happiness at issue here is "a complex and comprehensive state of individual well-being grounded in though not exhausted by the general welfare of one's fellow creatures and carefully informed by facts about the natural, historical and conventional world." It seems to me highly unlikely that all or even many adults are made happy in this sense by the practice of corporal punishment. Perhaps further research is required on this question.

In order to make a utilitarian determination of the moral status of corporal punishment, one must include all children harmed by corporal punishment in the class of one's "fellow creatures." And the happiness of adults must be informed by facts about the natural, historical and conventional world. Social scientists have argued that one can indeed conclude from the studies that have addressed the issue that corporal punishment is a risk factor and in some cases a very strong one for a variety of harmful outcomes for children. And while the possibility of immediate harm to children caused by corporal punishment is of crucial moral concern, its long-term and wide-spread effects make the overall harm of corporal punishment almost incalculable.

Morally speaking, our treatment of one another, including children, should not interfere with the realization of happiness for individuals, unless that realization, in particular cases, interferes with the same for most others. This does not mean that we must never do anything to someone else which causes them sadness or pain. Rather, it means that acting in this way requires a well thought-out and strongly established moral accounting of our reasons for doing so. If we cause another pain or sadness, our act can only be morally justified if it is likely, on the evidence, to contribute to rather than detract from the overall happiness of everyone affected.

In spite of the fact that many Canadians believe that corporally punishing children may be justified on these grounds, there is, despite many attempts to produce it, no empirical evidence which supports the belief and plenty which contradicts it.[36] Since utilitarian philosophical morality presumes that the act of corporally punishing a child is morally wrong, it places the burden of proof on those who defend its use. In relying on this moral theory, I have, in effect, turned the tables on the defenders of corporal punishment. Morally speaking, it is they and not those who find the practice morally objectionable who must now justify their position.

The Argument from Social Order: "Personal Security" and "Last Resort"

From the point of view of utilitarian philosophical morality, while not sufficient, it is necessary that in order to have a happy life a person must feel secure both physically and emotionally. Without this sense of security of the person, human beings will be unable to think beyond the next moment; unable to plan, unable to develop or ever fully exercise their especially human faculties. How, you might ask, can a human being focus on the joys of living and attend to the training and practice so many of life's joys require, if that human being is afraid of being physically attacked for no obvious reason or for making a mistake? Such fear puts the individual on constant, even if low level, adrenaline alert and especially in the case of extreme fear, takes up all of one's mental and physical energy. As Mill wrote, the reason we have rights is to protect our interest in,

> Security, to every one's feelings the most vital of all interests. All other earthly benefits are needed by one person, not needed by another, and many of them can, if necessary, be cheerfully foregone, or replaced by something else; but security no human being can do without; on it we depend for all our immunity from evil and for the whole value of all and every good, beyond the passing moment, since nothing but the gratification of the instant could be of any worth to us, if we could be deprived of anything the next instant by whoever was momentarily stronger than ourselves. Now this most indispensable of all necessaries after physical nutriment, cannot be had, unless the machinery for providing it is kept unintermittently in active play.[37]

Whether one prefers social and political disorder to unthinking social conformity or the reverse, a vibrant and peaceful social order is surely preferable to either from a moral point of view. A key part of maintaining such order is, as Mill says, keeping "the machinery for providing" a sense of personal security "in active play." Another way of describing the play of this machinery is to say that social order is necessary for the preservation of a reality based sense of personal security. Social order may be realized in many ways—through political process, law, formal education and the passing on of cultural traditions. Each institution or agency of social order sets up rules for individual behaviour which realize, among other values, the value of personal security. Whether they are legal rules or rules of customary morality, all ought to work to instill this value in each and every person affected by them and aim at making individual conduct in keeping with the value habitual. The end then, of the best social order is the greatest happiness for the greatest number and one necessary aspect of it is the preservation of a sense of security of the person against the harmful acts of other persons or the state.

On this personal security reading of the argument from social order, instilling a sense of insecurity of the person in the minds of those we wish to bring into line by referring to the importance of social order could not be justified. We may not, according to utilitarian philosophical morality, endorse, enact or adopt practices or rules which call for or permit the use of sanctions which are reputed to serve social order in this way. It would bring about precisely the bad consequences we are trying to avoid—it would deny certain or many human beings what they require for "immunity from evil and for the whole value of all and every good, beyond the passing moment."[38]

The view that the social fabric would unravel if children, among others, were officially freed from this sort of tyranny is an old one. In 1850, Mill wrote an anonymous letter to the editor of the *Leader* in which he rejected the fears of those who sensed that allowing women to dissolve their marriage contracts would lead to the imminent collapse of civilized society:

> I am the more desirous to be enlightened on this matter as I cannot call to mind any great improvement in human affairs, or the eradication of any deep-rooted and long-standing evil, which was not, at the time it happened, represented as subverting the foundations of society. The abolition of slavery; what a laying prostrate of the whole fabric of society was there! There was a time when even the boldest speculators were afraid to entertain such an idea....The Reformation! another dreadful blow to the stability of society. The Revolution of 1688...nay, the Reform Bill, and even Catholic emancipation, all made society crack and totter. Cheap newspapers, teaching people to read; this last was a thing after which, we were told by many people, society could not much longer exist. A Turk thinks, or used to think (for even Turks are wiser now-a-days), that society would be on a

sandbank if women were suffered to walk about in the streets
with their faces uncovered. I look upon this expression of loos-
ening the foundations of society, unless a person tell in unambiguous terms what he means by it, as a mere bugbear to
frighten imbeciles with.[39]

The personal security version of the social order argument
founders on its vagueness. This charge may also be laid against a contemporary version of this argument: the "last resort" version. It says
that unless parents and teachers are permitted by law to strike their
children—even if this strategy for compelling obedience and responsible behaviour is not recommended—and children know this, these
adults might lose control of them in which case the possibility of a
peaceful, progressive society would be seriously undermined. This second version of the social order argument implies that the emancipation
of adult women is one thing; that of children another. For Mill also
wrote in his *Principles of Political Economy* that "women are not children
or animals."[40] "Children below a certain age," Mill says, "*cannot* judge
or act for themselves."[41] Even if we grant this difference between adults
and children, is it sufficient to warrant the belief that the social order
will collapse if children are not aware that their insistence on rebelliousness will be met with pain? The idea here is that if children are not
instilled with a sense of their insecurity of the person, they will not
learn to be civil. Unable to observe those rules and practices which
secure the peaceable enjoyment of life for all, this emergent wild adult
class will shape a society in which no one is safe from wanton threat
and attack—the social fabric carefully woven at great cost over history
will unravel.

The last resort version of the social order argument depends upon
the claim that children will not learn to behave in a civil manner unless
they are legally threatened with and sometimes even legally subjected
to corporal punishment; unless they are violently coerced into behaving. As we have seen, when children are no longer corporally punished, so long as they are not neglected, their ability to control themselves improves rather than deteriorates, so this claim is simply false.[42]
As such, even though as children, human beings may not be left as free
to pursue their impulses as they may be as adults, there are simply no
grounds for thinking that "the stability of society"—whatever that is

exactly — depends upon their exemption from full protection under a right to security of the person.

The Argument from Divine Command

What rationale could a person give who still insisted upon the accept-ability of corporal punishment for children which did not appeal to the need for moral education, individual welfare, efficiency, genetics, the greater good, forgiveness or social order? Only two arguments remain as far as I can see. The first is the argument from divine command. As the Old Testament story of Abraham shows, a father may be convinced that God has commanded that he subject his children to violent treat-ment and just because God has commanded it, it must be done.[43] While a person offering this reason may be perfectly rational, I assume that on moral grounds and in spite of every Canadian's right to freedom of religion, this reason does not justify the use of corporal punishment in our society any more than it would infanticide.[44]

The Argument from Strict Self-Interest

The only argument remaining is what I call the argument from strict self-interest. An individual parent may argue that deep down inside just like everyone else, he or she is someone whose sense of personal security depends on expressing the natural desire to control the behaviour of others, regardless of how those others feel about such control. The society in which such a person lives may not permit adults to control other adults or other people's children. Yet, this need must have an outlet. Since the role of the state is to protect individual adults in pursuit of their interests, it ought to reserve a certain seg-ment of the population for this purpose. Since achieving that purpose is exclusively in the interest of the adult who seeks such control and not in the interest any of the controlled or of society in general, the fact that corporal punishment is not needed for transmitting or is anath-emic to moral values, securing the greater good, maintaining social order or protecting children from themselves, is not an efficient cor-rective, and is a risk factor for increased aggression and numerous other harms to children is irrelevant.[45]

This extreme libertarian[46] argument for the corporal punishment of children may seem bizarre — a red herring. But since it has been and is still used to defend certain practices which are clearly harmful to women, it might be used here. As such, it must be faced again. While such defences may never, in the end, win the day, history shows that they exert sufficient pressure to delay reforms. Clearly such an argument depends on making a distinction between adults and children which justifies not only different treatment but also the full-blown exploitation of children by adults. If the harmful effects on children of their exploitation could be restricted to them as children and if the supply of children could be maintained with relative ease then this libertarian argument for corporal punishment would insist that children be regarded as fair game.

There are societies in the world where the economic and sexual exploitation of children flourish. But the effects of the maltreatment of children cannot, as we have seen, be restricted to children. Maltreated children often become angry or depressed adults. Also, maintaining the supply of children is no easy matter. Even if the process could be detached from its present biological circumstances, there is little doubt that it would be exorbitantly expensive. In short, even on this most bizarre of libertarian arguments for corporal punishment, it is highly unlikely that any of its supporters would agree to accept the practical costs of its realization.

The rare, very hard-core libertarian could argue that he or she would, as an individual, happily take on the entire cost of supplying the children needed by finding a partner of like mind and that the children's transformation into problem adults would be prevented by killing them or forcing them to remain in the family. On extreme libertarian grounds which deny children much semblance with adult human beings and discount the interests of future generations, this argument would be difficult if not impossible to refute. Nevertheless, it represents thinking few would hesitate to regard as abhorrent. For one thing, it completely discounts what most would consider natural feelings of sympathy and affection toward children. Even if these feelings fail to secure the ultimate safety of all children, they do exert some benevolent force on how we treat them. Again, if one is tempted to dismiss this scenario as ridiculous or fantastic, one needs reminding that much of the multibillion dollar international pornography and prostitution industry sometimes justifies itself in this way. By the time we get to this extreme libertarian argument, however, we have left morality far behind.

In addition to the arguments from moral education and individual welfare, the specifically utilitarian arguments from efficiency, genetics and the greatest good, we have added three others which might be raised in favour of the corporal punishment of children. The social order argument may be understood in utilitarian terms but need not be. The arguments from divine command and strict self-interest appeal to putatively nonphilosophical and nonmoral considerations respectively. The only one of these arguments which works to support its conclusion is the last from which we may infer that the corporal punishment of children can only be justified if we abandon moral consideration of children altogether.

As each argument in support of the corporal punishment of children has been presented, one theme in particular has come up: granting that human beings as children are importantly different from human beings as adults, does that difference warrant extreme moral differences in our conduct towards members of these two groups?

5

. . . .

Human Adults and

Human Children

C entral to virtually all moral arguments offered today in favour of permitting or requiring the corporal punishment of children is the belief that the way in which children are different from adults warrants dramatic differences in the way we value and treat members of each group. This belief is based on the empirical claim that children's minds and bodies are very different from those of adults. The empirical claim is then used to support the normative view that these differences make it wrong to afford children the same protection from assault that adults have. Given their differences from adults, this position says that if we did give children the same protection, children and society would be the worse and not the better for it.

It would be foolish to reject the empirical claim that children and adults are different from one another in mind and body. Nevertheless, in most of the world's liberal societies, age figures in the prohibited grounds of discrimination found in their various constitutional docu-

Notes to chapter 5 are on pp. 263–68.

ments suggesting that these differences are not sufficient on their own to warrant the unequal treatment of children before the law. For the sake of argument, I suppose that such prohibitions rest on the belief that an individual suffers a harm from an assault, for example, regardless of how old or young that individual is. I also assume such prohibitions are grounded in a commitment to the moral equality of persons. The moral equality of persons while modern, is hardly a new idea. However, it is important to note that just who counts as a person may not include children. As historian Neil Sutherland states, "English Canadians [in the late nineteenth century] showed little awareness of children as individual persons...saw nothing of the inner, emotional life of youngsters."[1] As we will see, even though we are now more aware of children's personhood and even though our law reflects this, echoes of the older view continue to exert some moral and legal influence.

Their age or immaturity insofar as it is correlated with less capacity is commonly accepted as a moral justification for giving children fewer rights than adults. In particular, children have fewer rights of self-determination and citizenship than do adults. In order to be truly self-determining agents, human beings require a certain amount of legal space in which to pursue their personal interests without forcible even if corrective interference from others and a safe way of expressing their political interests in public forums. Where children are not regarded as self-determining agents, these principles operate to justify denying them the right to vote, for example. They also operate to justify a parent's submitting a child for a surgical procedure in the face of the child's resistance. Justifying the restriction of children's rights in these ways rests not only on the fact that they are physically and cognitively different from adults. Adults, after all, are physically and cognitively different from each other. More importantly, it rests on the belief that children as a group are physically and cognitively weaker and less experienced than adults.

Especially in the case of the very young, children will not survive in the world unless the adults who care for them are allowed to physically interfere with children's potentially dangerous behaviour. In Canada, parents and other caregivers, in addition to having this permission also have a legal privilege to hit children for the purpose of correcting their behaviour. In legal terms, this means that under certain conditions, caregivers are free to assault children in their care. I will discuss this legal issue more in later chapters. We may assume that the provision of these permissions and privileges is ultimately based on their moral credentials. Given the demands of survival in our society, the physical and cognitive immaturity of children morally justifies denying them certain self-determination and citizenship rights. While a child's immaturity is no longer seen as grounds for denying them the right to security of the person, should their weakness and inexperience nevertheless limit this right in ways in which it is not limited for adults? If it should, then it follows that, like self-determination and full civic rights, security of the person is something which, if children had an equal right to it, they would tend not to survive or flourish. This implication raises serious philosophical concerns.

In general terms, the implication that a right to security of the person would be a harm and not a benefit contradicts just about everything that has been discovered, written and accepted in the Western tradition and beyond about its importance to human flourishing. But then, the implication in this case addresses children and almost everything that has been said upholding the principle of security of the person has been said about adults. Could it be that the physical and cognitive deficiencies of children compared to adults are so drastic that the principle applies in reverse in their case? What sort or degree of difference would cause the application of the principle of security of the person in the case of children to produce an effect opposite to the one it produces in the case of its application to adults? The assumptions lying in wait when one picks at the view that the immaturity of children warrants treating them according to principles which are opposed to those according to which adults are treated, are based on poetic fictions.

Difference as Opposition

We need some assistance in making sense of the view that if children were given the same right to security of the person adults enjoy, their ability to flourish would be compromised. A similar problem arises when it comes to applying the principle of equality — the principle which tells us that we must treat everyone with the same consideration. If this principle is applied to a level playing field, it produces equality. Presuming that everyone affected by policies based on the principle of equality starts off on more or less the same footing, the effects of those policies should be more or less the same for everyone which is good enough under the principle. One may ask "why apply a principle of equality to an already equal social situation?" The point would be to enshrine the value of equality and back up its application with force to stabilize the existing equalities. Where the principle is applied to a level playing field and there are nevertheless drastic differences in effect (and so where the result of applying the principle of equality appears to be its reverse), we may infer that unforeseen, uncontrollable external factors have been at work. And in that case, it could still be argued that the policies or the principle of equality were themselves fair — that in the absence of such factors, the result would have been the maintenance of the original equalities.

If, however, the principle is applied to a very uneven playing field, assuming no compensating external variables, it will produce inequalities — more than their fair share of this or that good for some, enough for many and not nearly enough for others. As long as rough equality of outcomes is what we are after, we may conclude, in this case, that applying the principle of equality is unfair. For the imposition of the principle of equality and policies based on it to make sense, controlling for unforeseen external factors, its application must produce results which do not violate the point of their application. That point has always been to see to it that everyone has more or less the same amount of basic goods and hopefully somewhat more than enough of what they need.[2]

The application of a straightforward principle of equality may bring about fairness as far as outcomes are concerned where everyone starts off on a more or less equal footing. So one could argue that before any such principle is imposed, existing inequalities must be remedied. But since there are certain inequalities that cannot be eliminated, it makes more sense, for this reason among others, to devise and apply a less straightforward principle of equality — one that takes into account a very uneven playing field. Given various ineliminable inequalities that exist in our society, we need a principle of equality that will level things out in terms of outcomes and not build up the hills at the cost of deepening the valleys.

How might this discussion assist us in understanding the claim that applying the principle of security of the person in full when it comes to the treatment of children would fail to benefit them and even cause them harm, even though when applied to adults, it is clearly beneficial to, even necessary, for their well-being? If we regard the presence of both children and adults in our society as an instance of an uneven playing field, then we could say that the universal application of the principle of security of the person should result in the same inequality between children and adults with which we began. We could therefore morally justify the corporal punishment of children on the grounds that this different treatment under law would ameliorate and not preserve or worsen the ways in and extent to which children are weaker and less experienced than adults. At a minimum, this amounts to claiming that limiting children's right to security of the person—allowing them to be assaulted under certain circumstances— would have no detrimental effect on their ability to flourish and indeed may be required for that flourishing.

But are children sufficiently different from adults in the relevant respects to warrant this reasoning about their treatment? When it comes to their capacity for self-determination or their ability to exercise citizenship, children lack many if not all of what is presumed necessary for responsible action in either sphere. They may indeed lack the sense of self usually required for forming rational life plans, experience of the common good and the long-term foresight that generally comes with living a certain length of time.[3] Due to the particular way and extent to which children are different from adults in these respects, we can say that applying the principles of self-determination or citizenship to children would not benefit and may even harm them even though they benefit adults. In what precise way must children be different from adults if full protection under the principle of the security of the person also works on them in reverse?

Security of the person, as we have seen, is intended to give human beings a sense of freedom from physical attack or interference so that they do not have to live in fear or anxiety. This sense of physical safety or absence of fear, it is argued, is necessary for a human being to flourish and enjoy the sense of self required for rational life plans, concern for the common good and long term foresight needed for a successful adult life. This then is the benefit to adults of full security of the person rights. If it is true that full rights to security of the person do not benefit children, then it must also be true that either their ability to flourish is not adversely affected by fear for their person or that they simply do not experience such fear. Since, on either theory, there would be no benefit to full protection and possibly even harm, there is no compelling moral reason to extend full security of the person rights to children.

Is it plausible to claim that children's ability to flourish is not compromised by fear for their person, regardless of its intensity or that they do not experience such fear? It may be argued that a child's sense of his or her self (both physical and psychological) is weak or insubstantial compared to that of an adult's and is not as negatively affected as an adult's would be — or not at all — by assaults upon it. It may also be argued that since children know little of the dangers that the world poses, they experience much less fear than adults do concerning their safety. The first argument that since children have a weaker sense of self than adults do, what sense they do have is less adversely affected by violence than an adult's is a non sequitur. The sense of "weak" traded on here must refer to what we customarily think in the case of young children — that they are not as strong, durable or tough as adults and as such must be treated and handled with extra care and gentleness. It follows instead that a child's sense of self is as if not more — and not less — affected by threats and violence than an adult's.[4] So while there is a difference between children and adults in this case, that difference does not support the conclusion that children would be harmed by or not benefit from full security of the person rights.

As for the second theory that children do not experience the fear associated with a lack of security of the person and as such would not benefit from full protection, the argument in support of it misses a crucial point. While it may be true that young children might not know that people could hit them and as such, not fear this, once hit, that naïveté vanishes and the same anxiety any adult experiences at the prospect or threat appears. Further, since children are less able to defend themselves and may be more prone than adults to overgeneralize, their lack of full protection from assault would arguably have a worse affect on their sense of security than it would on an adult's. Children are therefore as, if not more, in need of full security of the person protection than adults. Why then does the belief that they will not benefit from or be harmed by full security of the person protection persist? To justify this belief, we must believe in turn that children are somehow immune or less sensitive to the pains and indignities of corporal punishment than adults. There is good evidence from writings and commentary on children that this belief has had considerable influence on our views of corporal punishment. Yet it stands in sharp contrast to other views of childhood, including those we tend to profess today.

Savagery, Civility and the Recapitulation Theory of Childhood

In *The Philosophy of Childhood*,[5] Gareth B. Matthews considers the work of Dr. Benjamin Spock in his famous book *Baby and Child Care*.[6] In response to Spock's view that the tentatively exploring infant "is probably reliving that stage of human history when our wild ancestors found it was better not to roam the forest in independent family groups but to form larger communities,"[7] Matthews writes:

> Here Dr. Spock draws on something well beyond his own clinical experience, indeed well beyond the clinical experience of any other physician, to present a theory of childhood. His theory is the recapitulation theory. It is captured in the slogan "Ontogeny recapitulates phylogeny," that is, the development of the individual repeats the development of the race or species.[8]

While Matthews acknowledges the poetic usefulness of the recapitulation theory of childhood as well as its power to help explain various phenomena observed in the field, he cautions that the theory, like others[9] "may dehumanize [children] and encourage inappropriately condescending attitudes towards them."[10] In particular, he worries that the recapitulation theory of childhood implies "that children live in a pre-rational, pre-scientific world."[11] Like the myth of the contented cow on its way to slaughter, it is surmised that since they lack a strong conception of themselves as "selves," they do not fear for themselves. If this implication is correct, then we cannot be expected to teach children how to manage themselves. At most, we can teach them to behave in the same way we teach our pet dogs to do so: by exploiting their desire to seek pleasure and avoid pain. In doing so, we do not cause them debilitating anxiety or fear since these states of mind imply foresight and rationality.

The recapitulation theory encourages the view that the world of childhood is categorically separate from the world of adulthood. It does this by appealing to, on the one hand, an impression of our microbial, aquatic and mammalian ancestors and on the other, to the modern human. When these two worlds are juxtaposed in the minds of those who are not anthropologists or biologists, there is a tendency to ignore the middle. Whatever happened in between the time when all life was noncognitive and the present where human life is civilized and intelligent is lost sight of and the two worlds settle themselves in the popular imagination separated by a bottomless chasm. For some, the fact of modern human beings is even seen as something on the order of a miracle.[12] This theory of childhood as free from debilitating anxiety due to its savagery or primitiveness is latent in much unreflective thinking on the differences between children and adults. It has, as Matthews notes, a certain aesthetic attraction.[13] But this hardly justifies it as empirical fact. And empirical fact is required to justify the claim that applying the principle of security of the person to children will fail to benefit them or cause them harm that they would not suffer otherwise.

Guilt, Innocence and the Separation Thesis

There is a second theory of childhood which relies on a different categorical difference between children and adults. In his extremely influential 1960 work *L'Enfant et la vie familiale sous l'ancien regime*,[14] Philippe Ariès argued that the tendency to view childhood as a completely separate world from that of adulthood first developed late in the seventeenth century. He based his conclusions on a study of medieval representations of children, the childhood of Louis XIII as it had been documented by his physician Heroard and his own common knowledge of modern attitudes towards childhood. Finding, for example, that the future King Louis had been treated by the adults who cared for him in the most "adult" of ways, Ariès concluded that prior to the late seventeenth century, the world of childhood and adulthood was one world.

Proceeding with the view that to treat children in an adult way was to treat them cruelly due to their immaturity, Ariès considered the theoretical and practical separation of the worlds of childhood and adulthood to have been a good thing for children. It acknowledged differences in physical, cognitive and moral development between children and adults—differences which called for the segregation of children from the world of adults and which subjected adults to a different set of obligations when it came to their dealings with children when compared to their dealings with other adults. When children are faced with adult demands, one must expect them to exhibit anxiety and fear. Children must be protected from these states of mind. Their resulting segregation keeps these disturbing mental states at bay. The assumption here is that since the child's mind is completely innocent, there is nothing native to it which resembles the anxiety or fear an adult feels at the prospect of impending harm.

Ariès's thesis has been sharply criticized on several grounds. In *Children: Rights and Childhood*,[15] David Archard argues that as a descriptive claim about the Middle Ages and Early Modern period, the thesis is at best an armchair hypothesis based on inadequate data.[16] Archard complains that Ariès mistook a different view of childhood prior to the seventeenth century for "no view" of it and mistook a different sentiment toward children than the one his separation thesis models as necessarily hostile towards them. Neither judgement of the facts is fair according to Archard who is as dubious about the moral benefits to children of the separation thesis as Matthews is about the moral merits of the recapitulation theory. Both the separation thesis and the recapitulation theory involve, according to these thinkers, problematic empirical and normative beliefs about children and adults.

Stereotyping Children: The Worlds of Innocence and Experience

In his famous collection of poems *Songs of Innocence and Experience*,[17] William Blake played a discordant theme long resonant in his adult culture's attitudes towards children. Ruth Everett writes that, "in contemplating the pain and evil of the world, Blake reached a state of disillusionment. This resulted in a series of poems paralleling the *Songs of*

Innocence but, in a more realistic mood, describing symbolically the travail which separates the human soul from the ideal State of Innocence, of which it has momentary visions."[18] Children were, according to this theme, perfectly innocent creatures and (second perhaps only to women) primitive, diabolical beings.[19] As such, the world of childhood was seen as good: a world of purity, a world which was bereft of duplicity and most importantly, a world of sexual naiveté and inexperience.[20] But it was also seen as bad: a messy, disingenuous, impulsive world; a world permanently vulnerable to the dictates of Satan — the Arch-deceiver — and a world lacking all sexual inhibition.[21] Both are, in some sense, naive worlds — worlds where civilized or sophisticated anxieties and fears about non-being and offence or harm to others do not apply.

Ariès's separation thesis exploits the good (innocent) view of childhood and the view of adulthood as bad (experienced) for its normative force while the recapitulation theory exploits the bad (savage or primitive) view of children and a view of adulthood as good (civilized) for its. According to the separation thesis, the world of childhood must be kept separate from the world of adulthood because the innocence of children must be protected from the shameful experience and knowledge of adults. According to the recapitulation theory, child nature as prerational and prescientific ought to be regarded as analogous to the primitive and savage nature of the protohuman. In comparison, modern adult humans viewed as rational and scientific may be regarded as sophisticated and civilized. Failing to uphold the superiority of the modern adult human risks demeaning the *telos*[22] (purpose) of and undoing the achievements of the species.

According to the separation thesis, adults must do everything in their power to discourage children, naturally free from anxiety, from acting like independent adults. According to the recapitulation theory, adults must do everything in their power to bring children to adulthood and out of their savage state which may be characterized as either free from anxiety or as relatively impervious to its effects. In both cases, children are regarded as guiltless — in the first because they have no reason to feel guilt and in the second because they do not have the capacity to do so. The discordant theme at the core of the conjunction of these normative beliefs as well as at the base of the empirical belief that children do not experience debilitating anxiety — do not suffer the way adults do when their security of the person is violated — involves a contradiction. Thinkers like Archard argue that this contradiction — that children are naturally good and naturally evil — is rampant, irrational and is what keeps children of both genders and all colours the most endangered class of human beings. Theoretically, contradictory reasons are useless for supporting claims and justifying acts since it is in the nature of a contradiction that it has no logical meaning.[23] Even if, as Blake and other artists have demonstrated, such contradictions are aesthetically or spiritually evocative, they must be denied any role in the support of public policy or moral judgements. Neil Sutherland has pointed out that for the most part, prior to the turn of twentieth century, the predominant view of children in English Canada presented them as "tough matter" though this view shifted to seeing them as "a seed of divine life" sometime in the 1890s. The seed view did not entirely replace the tough matter view, however, and the two continue to vie for attention in the formation of public policy on child welfare.[24]

It may be argued that current defences of the corporal punishment of children which rely on children's differences from adults do not make the mistake of basing themselves on this contradiction nor of assuming that children are not affected by the anxiety being corporally punished by adults produces. Except perhaps for the youngest of infants, academic (though not all popular) views of children seem to have abandoned the innocent strain found at the bottom of the separation thesis. Furthermore, the impression we have of primitive peoples is no longer one of the "moral blank"[25] or reprobate. Even if we identify childhood with primitiveness, we may accept that they are affected by anxiety in the same way as adults. Children, on a more scientifically sophisticated view of them, are neither naturally good nor bad. Nevertheless, while we may have abandoned the view of children implied by the separation thesis as well as the view that the primitive is morally empty or threatening, the normative shadow cast by the recapitulation thesis continues to darken the popular imagination when it comes to theorizing about childhood.

However interesting the lives of primitives or children seem to us from the point of view of wondering how we came to be the way we are, the recapitulation thesis trades on the normative belief that such lives are not to be preferred to the lives of modern, civilized, sophisticated adults. While there is no contradiction here between the world of children as good and as bad and no implication that children's development is not impaired by fear, the belief remains that their nature is human nature in its least attractive state.[26] Insofar as children are seen to be more like our protohuman ancestors than like us, they will tend to be treated according to the moral norms which guide our treatment of non-human animals and not those which guide our treatment of adult humans.[27] This is precisely the state of affairs which gives Gareth Matthews cause for concern when he criticizes the recapitulation thesis:

> Whereas it is certainly good to be warned that a child's ideas may, in a given context, be quite different from yours or mine, to maintain that children live in a pre-scientific and even pre-rational world is arrogant and inappropriately condescending...we must guard against letting [the recapitulation theory] caricature our children and limit the possibilities we are willing to recognize in our dealings with them as fellow human beings.[28]

David Archard concludes his discussion of Ariès's separation thesis by noting that "the way we see the differences between children and adults owes everything to what concerns us about being adults in the world."[29] I will assume that Archard means our anxieties in adulthood influence our reading of childhood as a state of human being which is and ought to be isolated from the real world in one way or another. In the popular imagination, childhood often represents a state of being full of joy and optimism about the future. It is not difficult to see how such a view might incline one to hold that the more protected and protracted that state is, the better off human beings as children will be.

The Way We Were: Age Improves the Past

Adult Canadians, as well as others, always seem extremely angry about youth crime and the intensity of their anger appears to be a function of age.[30] The older we get, the worse the young seem to be. Since everyone gets older, the young just keep getting worse and worse. As I write this, there are, alongside the usual complaints, public demands for stiffer regulations and sanctions in Canada's Young Offenders Act.

The common refrain is that children need more and more forceful discipline, not less. Curiously, the increase in concern is not clearly connected to any actual overall rise in youth crime and may instead be due to an increase in the number of charges laid (which may not correlate with an increase in incidents) and frequency and intensity of youth crime media reporting—especially violent youth crime.[31] The media claim they are just giving the public what it wants.[32] If it is true that whatever the cause, the adult public wants to think of youth primarily in terms of youth crime, then it is fair to suggest that adults want to compare themselves favourably to children. The recapitulation thesis captures this sentiment. Perhaps it would be better for adults if there simply were no children at all.

In her novel, *The Children of Men*, P.D. James creates a world in which children are no longer being born. As she introduces this world to the reader, the novel's narrator writes: "Like a lecherous stud suddenly stricken with impotence, we are humiliated at the very heart of our faith in ourselves. For all our knowledge, our intelligence, our power, we can no longer do what the animals do without thought. No wonder we both worship and resent them."[33] The novel goes on to explore the effects which the end of procreation would have on the world of adults and concludes that the consequences would be disastrous at every level:

> Man [*sic*] is diminished if he lives without knowledge of his past; without hope of a future he becomes a beast. We see in every country in the world the loss of that hope, the end of science and invention, except for discoveries which may extend life or add to its comfort and pleasure, the end of our care for the physical world and our planet....The mass emigrations, the great internal tumults, the religious and tribal wars of the 1990's have given way to a universal anomie which leaves crops unsown and unharvested, animals neglected, starvation, civil war, the grabbing from the weak by the strong.[34]

We do not need a novelist to show us that the results of universal infertility would be very bad for a very long time, finally culminating in the disappearance of human life altogether. This final result would, in itself, have little or no moral interest. Save, perhaps, for the indisposition of pets left to fend for themselves and the extremely remote pos-

sibility that our extinction would destroy the world's ecosystem on a
scale far grander than the Ice Age, there is simply no harm to the world
in our species' demise.

The moral concern comes in long before this eventuality. With no
more children being born alive, the possibility of a future, understood
as we have always understood it, is removed. James's vision of a world
without children is of a world without hope; a world without industry
or creativity; a world exhausted. This world exists a step beyond the
one described by Thomas Hobbes in the seventeenth century — one he
called the "state of nature"[35] — though in a different direction from the
one in which he chose to take it. In Hobbes's precivilized world, rationality is based exclusively in self-interest. But it is in one's self-interest
to produce offspring in order that they may produce for you, preserve
what you have made and care for you in your great age. As such,
Hobbes's story of how human beings move from the state of nature
into a civilized state relies mainly on the felt importance of protecting
one's offspring into their own adulthood. Remove the possibility of offspring and a significant motivation for living under the "rule of law" is
also removed.

The ongoing presence of children is critical in many ways to the
continuing existence of the "modern scientific" world which the recapitulation theory celebrates as, so far, superior to it. If, as Archard suggests, we see the difference between children and ourselves in terms of
our own concerns about being adults in the world, and those concerns
involve maintaining our scientific prowess, political arrangements and
technological wizardry among other things, why don't we want to see
children as scientists, politicians and technologists, not to mention
philosophers, parents and artists *in training*? Why don't we want to see
them as requiring the very same conditions of personal security for their
development as flourishing, self-determining citizens that we demand
for ourselves? What is it about being an aging adult that discourages
this positive view of children? Could it be that the ineliminable features
of childhood which distinguish it from adulthood are simply thought to
pose a threat to our incredibly sophisticated way of life?

It may be that as aging adults, we feel our hold on this sophistication becoming more and more tenuous. We were taught that the disposition necessary to maintain that hold was initially made habitual in us

against our nature. Even once the more hostile view of children had been challenged by the "seed" view, Sutherland notes that in 1894, Canada's New Council of Women handbook advised that "instead of blaming their child, or fate, for any failure, parents were expected to shoulder the responsibility for surrounding their youngster 'with conditions contrary to its nature.'"[36] If the project to denature children failed, we were led to believe that chaos and evil would take over. We manage to maintain the "unnatural" habit of civility for a long period of time but as the worlds of science, politics and technology become more complex or strange to us — once, for example, we are long out of school — the habit is severely strained. We sense that our ability to be civil and sophisticated is under attack by forces which are under the control of the young. (If we are also poor, it is the young and rich who we resent.) If this is what concerns us most about being aging adults in the world, then, since the world of children represents its vanguard, that world is a growing threat to what we have achieved. We achieved the telephone. They will achieve the obsolescence of the telephone. We achieved law and order. They will achieve chaos and evil. Popular media exploits this irrational fear confirming it with regular reporting and depiction of youth violence. Often, such violence is an expression of protest against the destruction of the environment, poverty and the erosion of democracy. But the media rarely gets to the details of such protest nor does it often provide detailed coverage of nonviolent youth protest on such issues.

Resistance to Change

The tendency to see children as out of control, pests, inferior moral beings, as stupid or ridiculous, malevolent, lazy, ill-behaved, unrealistic, selfish, greedy, vicious or all of the above works to develop the deep belief that we, as adults, are somehow justified in defending ourselves against them; are justified in protecting our world — so superior to theirs — from them by exerting control over them. If children, in this case, are not forced to adapt to the world we have made, they will not do so and if children do not grow to fit into that world, it will collapse. P.D. James's world of no children at all may be seen as a metaphor for such a world. Instead, however, of a long vapid decay, what we have in the case of grown-up human beings who have not been civilized is an overwhelming of the civilized world by forces instinctively bent against its preservation.

Our intuitions regarding self-defence and defence of property are well worn. One is justified, in almost all the world's moralities (both customary and philosophical) to use all reasonable and necessary force to preserve oneself from harm and even to protect one's property.[37] As such, resistance to abandoning the view that corporal punishment is morally permissible or required might depend for its tenacity on the fear that civilization and the security it provides will be lost if children are treated with the same consideration which all adults, because they have already been civilized, merit. This fear depends for its reasonableness on a view of children which simply cannot be rationally maintained. Whether or not children lack all the adult sentiments or habits of civilized behaviour, we know that, with few exceptions, they lack neither the rage nor the anxiety response to threats of or harm to their persons that adults have. Because of the rage and anxiety any assault on one's physical security causes, the systematic or legally condoned use of violence against any human being tends either to produce a violent though perhaps more deviously violent character or a broken, selfless character.[38] This is why assault is illegal, why the corporal punishment of adults has been abandoned in our society and also why it ought to condemned in the case of children.

Children are not different from adults in the way they would have to be to justify the claim that they do not need the full protection of their persons. I have allowed, however, that children usually lack the information and skills (both physical and intellectual) which, since it calls for both self-sufficient and cooperative agency, truly independent and successful living requires. Such inexperience, however, calls for education, patience and forbearance from adults and not violent punishment. I assume that most readers, while not necessarily against the use of certain sanctions, would be very averse to being spanked or slapped on a new job, for example, or in a new relationship, for disobeying a rule, making a mistake in judgement or even for causing harm to others as a result of an ill-timed attempt to act independently. Yet it is precisely for these sorts of reasons that children are hit and why such assaults have been justified in our courts of law.[39]

We have acknowledged over time that employers must not beat their employees, nor is beating convicted criminals morally acceptable or legally permitted according to most Western customary and philosophical moralities and law. Learning and improvement, we have discovered, best takes place in environments where the pupil need not fear for his or her bodily security at all. As Mill suggested in the late nineteenth century, as Kant had observed in the eighteenth and as I argued above, children are likely to be more and not less vulnerable to the pain and anxiety of corporal punishment than adults are. As a rule, the unavoidable immaturity of children does indeed distinguish them from adults. However, this difference does not support the view that children deserve less in the way of protection from assault than adults do. Quite the contrary. The only differences between children and adults that can be rationally acknowledged morally require that they be afforded at least as much—or more—and not less security of the person protection than adults enjoy.

6

. . . .

The Paradox of Child
Protection

O f the many moral arguments advanced in favour of corporally punishing children, only one of those considered supports its conclusion. The strict self interest argument is, however, not
really an argument from morality at all since it entirely discounts the
interests of children and does not aim at the greatest good of the greatest number.[1] From the point of view of a philosophically utilitarian
moral position, the case for corporal punishment fails.[2] What this
means is that any customary moral belief which requires or allows its
use — regardless of the cultural, ethnic or religious pedigree of such a
belief — cannot be morally justified in a way which a diverse society
such as ours can recognize as legitimate. I have also argued that
beneath resistance to being persuaded by the moral argument against
corporal punishment is a view of children as different from adults in a
way which does not hold up under critical scrutiny. While poetically
evocative, the view of children as angels, savages or both has no basis
in fact and as such must not be allowed to influence social policy

---

Notes to chapter 6 are on pp. 268–72.

regarding their treatment. Instead, we should regard children as moral persons at a stage in their lives where they are acquiring the skills they need to survive and, more importantly perhaps, to learn what they will need to know to continue to grow as happy and productive persons. While this does mean that as developing beings, they may need to be temporarily denied certain rights of political participation as well as certain liberties (the liberty to drive a car, for example), it does not justify denying or limiting their basic moral entitlement or their legal right to security of the person.

In this chapter, I want to explore the problem raised by the implication which follows from the immorality of corporal punishment that, as a society, we have a responsibility to children which extends to making moral and perhaps even legal judgements about how individual parents fulfill their childcare duties. As we will see later on, a great deal of the criticism against morally condemning corporal punishment or removing legal justification for it is based on fears that doing either will lead to what Barbara Amiel calls "family statism."[3] There is no use denying that the Government of Canada is involved in the families of the nation. Many of its ministries, not to mention the Criminal Code, exercise jurisdiction over the welfare of children in families. A great deal of legislation and policy sets out in writing what the obligations of parents are and imposes limits on what parents may do to their children in fulfilling those duties. However, there has always been — and continues to be — an understanding that parents must have some private room to interpret these requirements and manoeuver within those limits according to their individual views and cultural commitments concerning child welfare.

One jealously guarded area of parental discretion and familial privacy is that of child discipline. If the government is seen to step too far into this area, parental discretion and familial privacy will be seen as threatened. Privacy and the room for parental discretion it affords are important features of our liberal social and political ethos. If we cannot expect privacy in our homes, then one of the foundations of our social and political order will have crumbled. The suggestion that through the agency of our government, we ought, as a society, to morally condemn corporal punishment, strikes many concerned about familial privacy as just such a threat.

The relationship between a government and its children is one that has been explored from time to time in the history of philosophy. The choice has often seemed to be between direct government control of childrearing and so the dissolution of nuclear or extended families as we know them, and a hands-off approach where the heads of families have absolute authority over their members. Little attention was paid in the past to less extreme options. But this is changing. A handful of philosophers, Gareth Matthews and David Archard among them, are now taking the issue seriously.[4] In what follows, I explore both past and current thinking on the problem of state and societal responsibility when it comes to raising children. My aim is to debunk the argument that the state should not end special protection for parents and other childcare givers who use or wish to be able to use corporal punishment as a means of disciplining their children and students.

The State as Parent

In *The Republic*, perhaps the most famous work of ancient Greek philosophy, Plato, Aristotle's teacher, laid down a blueprint for what he thought was the perfect society. It was to be watched over by a philosopher king who, it was presumed by Plato, had special knowledge of the true, the good, the real and the beautiful. One of this society's essential features was its just or harmonious nature. The roles of its citizens were to be designated according to their talents which broadly fell into three categories: ruling, guarding and craftwork or production.[5] Together, these three categories of civil activity mirrored the three aspects of the soul and when all were in good working order, the result was perfect justice.[6] When the role of the guardians (or keepers of the social order) is discussed in the *Republic*, it is decided that both men and women will be considered for duty and that none of those who are selected will raise their own children. Instead, the children of guardians are to be raised in common by the state.

Plato's reasoning on this score is, in part, that if a guardian, particularly a female one, was allowed to have an intimate attachment to her child, she would be less able to perform her civic duties. But there is a deeper consideration. Like all other roles in the perfect society, the role of parent ought to be assigned only to those citizens who have a special talent for it. Since those selected to be guardians have a special talent for enforcing the laws they cannot also have a special talent for crafting or raising children, or so Plato's thesis implies. It must be granted to Plato that he saw that expertise in policing was not a qualification for good parenting. Nevertheless, when it came to the rearing of children, Plato's conception of the perfect society has not faired well. While experiments of the sort Plato envisioned have been tried here and there throughout the world with greater and lesser success, none have dominated in the way Plato apparently thought they should.[7] While Plato concluded that parent-centered childcare schemes are contrary to the interests of the just state, few today share this view.

The Nuclear Family

Preferring a parent-centred approach relies on the intuition that on balance no one is more likely to care about the welfare of a particular child than its biological parents. This intuition does not overlook the possibility that some biological parents do not feel any emotional attachment to their offspring nor does it ignore the possibility that a surrogate parent may feel a great deal of love for the child brought into his or her life. It expresses the view that because of the physical bond between them, a child's biological parents are most likely to be the ones whose emotional interest in seeing the child thrive is strongest. This strong subjective feeling of attachment leads biological parents to identify the child's interests and needs with their own and, as such, provides a much more powerful and reliable motive for protecting children than either duty or a job-related sense of obligation would. As such, where the interests of the state as a continuing entity are bound up in the welfare of its children, those interests are best served by the parent centered approach.

I happen to agree that close, long-term, stable and personal relationships between children and their caregivers (biological or not) are our best bet for raising happy, well adjusted children and that the easiest method of providing these conditions is through the small extended or nuclear family. However, I want to point to a problem raised by blind faith in this model. When, as a society, we allow the reasonable intuition that children are safest in this sort of childrearing situation to lead imperceptibly and without further justification to the belief that they are safe under such circumstances, we risk blinding ourselves to real dangers which threaten children as a result of isolating them in the private realm. Insofar as the blindness is willful, we, as a society, collude in the harms which occur to them there.

Trust No One

The evolution of the conceptually private realm really took off in the seventeenth century. John Locke, a social and political theorist, physician and teacher, devised a theory of government for England in which the powers of the state were severely restricted by the will of the people. It was Locke's view that while the state as it stood at the time could protect the ordinary citizen (customarily male) from his neighbouring enemies, there was no one with sufficient power to protect him from the state.[8] To better protect individuals and their property from state aggression or interference, Locke proposed that a new system of representative constitutional government be instituted in which the government or state could be officially sanctioned for unlawful actions against its citizens. In addition to regular elections, his proposal involved the constitutional separation of various state powers. Bound by constitutional rules, the legislative branch of government made laws but was not to administer them. This was to be left to the executive branch which would thereby have the power to sanction the legislature should it break the rules by which it was bound, or make laws which violated the will of the people as this was expressed in their constitutional documents.

The society which Locke faced and continued to envision was one where women and children lived in the private shadows cast by men who participated in the public enlightened world of politics, commerce, church affairs and national defence. It was believed by most men that the well-being of their women and children needed to be protected from adult males by adult males and was best protected by their husbands, fathers, uncles and so on. Regardless of how bad any particular woman (or child) had it at the hands of her male protectors, it was clear on this view that since no one else had as strong an interest in her welfare, she could not hope for better.

Preference for parent-centred child-rearing is based on the same sentiment which grounded the preference for husband or male relative-centered care of women (and children) in Locke's time. Both depend on the view that physical proprietorship (be it sexual, biological or contractual) is a better foundation for proper care of the weak than an abstract sense of the common good or moral duty and while it was not always workable (Locke financially supported workhouses for the poor and workhouse orphanages), it was to be preferred. We know from experience that even if this is correct, the parent-centred approach to childcare in no way establishes the actual safety of such arrangements. This must be shown independently of the fact that other arrangements are worse. Statistics establish that in our society, human beings are in greatest danger between birth and the time they enter school.[9] As such, children as a group are not as safe under the care of their parents as we might like to think even though their parents may indeed be their best bet for protection.

The world which John Locke was attempting to change was one in which your most powerful protector could be your worst enemy.[10] But while it would be naive to overestimate the extent to which we may rely on the good graces of our government today, it is surely not the case that we have quite as much reason as seventeenth- and eighteenth-century British subjects did to doubt its intention to protect us in our pursuit of "life, liberty and security of the person." As such, we need to see the role of our government as it is: that of protector limited by a set of principles and rules which we have freely embraced and enshrined in our constitutional documents. The question which must be faced in the present context is the extent to which such a state has a moral obligation to ensure the protection of children by their parents.

David Archard's Modest Collectivism

Treating the well-being of children as though it followed automatically or naturally from what their biological (or nuclear) parents believe is in their best interest is to make the mistake of assuming parental infallibility. Clearly, parents are not infallible when it comes to their children's welfare. As such, the well-being of any particular child need not be regarded as the sole province of his or her parents. It is clear from the data and evidence collected on the consequences of corporal punishment that leaving their care entirely to parental discretion poses risks for children as a group.

If the parent-centred approach is best and yet not good enough, if possible, it must be augmented. In simpler societies than ours, the need for augmentation is recognized and satisfied within the tribal or close-knit community model where the welfare of children, even if most closely guarded by their biological parents, is seen to by all or many other members of the group. But ours is not a simple society. In Canada, as in other large states, overseeing the general welfare needs of all children is taken care of by largely impersonal state institutions. In the case of individual children, the state, acting through the courts and various social services, also plays a vital role. In order to maintain a successful parent-centred approach, the government and its agents must carefully balance the values of familial privacy on the one hand and child protection on the other. It may not be possible to define the precise balance implied here. However, David Archard argues that it would involve:

> A significant assumption of collective responsibility for child-care, a 'diffusion of parenting', a collective valuation of children and a significant extension of children's rights...all children merit the best possible upbringing, [modest collectivism] presumes that some ways of bringing up children are better than others and thinks that this necessitates a measure of collectivism.[11]

The mere mention of collectivism in the same breath as childcare may strike some as a harbinger of family statism. But a certain amount of collectivism is already at home in Canadian society. Our national health care policy and child tax credit system, for example, express what are clearly collectivist values or values which express our concern as a people to care for Canada's children. What Archard is suggesting here is that the state go further—that it set up a system of ongoing government supervision for all prospective and actual parents. Such a system, like other national programs, may very well be deployed at the local level through regional or community boards and health clinics. But however sensitive it is to the particular needs and circumstances of this or that parent in this or that community, such a system of supervision would dramatically change the relationship between the state and the family which now exists.

For instance, the amount of privacy parents have in disciplining their children would in principle be sharply curtailed.[12] While the focus of government action in this sphere must be the welfare of children and not the privacy rights of their parents, the value of privacy ensconced within the ethos of liberalism which those rights express cannot simply be ignored. If the rights of parents to privacy are to be curtailed then the payoff in increased child welfare has to be real. Would children be safer under Archard's modest collectivism than they are now?

The Paradox of Child Protection

Let's return to Locke for a moment. He advised adult male citizens to arrange for their security by setting up a representative constitutional government divided into separate and independently authoritative branches. The old fear that your monarch and his or her minions could be your worst enemy was initially assuaged by the prospect that your most powerful governors came from your own community or class and by the knowledge that if they did violate your security of the person, for example, without what was agreed by all to be a just cause, you could sanction them, petition for redress or lobby to remove their democratic authority to protect you. While the old fears were never completely erased, it seemed that this new arrangement went far enough to justify any final leaps of faith. The situation is markedly different when the vulnerable group is children and the potentially dangerous group is adults.

Children cannot politically arrange for their own security. Even if we grant that some older children or youth are capable of doing this; capable of participating in a political process whereby their interests as expressed by them will be heard and taken into serious account, there will be many younger children who would necessarily be excluded from such a process. Since it is these younger children who are at greatest risk from their adult protectors, involving older children in the decision-making process concerning child welfare will not solve the problem of protecting the younger ones. As such, we must focus our attention at the level of young children — say, 12 and under. Would their interests be protected under Archard's collectivist proposal in a way which does not trigger the paradox of child protection?

The paradox of child protection involves the tension between the necessary conditions of protecting young children and the fact that young children are at greatest risk from the adults who protect them. Young children, it may be said, cannot protect themselves or each other from harms, defence against which requires adult or near-adult strength, knowledge or experience. In the present context, all harms to children caused or threatened by adults count as such harms. To protect children from such harms, it is therefore necessary to enlist the help of adults. The tension is immediately clear. Children must rely on adults to protect them from adults. Women were once cultivated to depend upon males to protect them from males. The problem then was as clear as the problem for children is now. When you are successfully taught to place complete trust in one or more adults to protect you from harm, you do not believe that those adults will harm you. Even if you are harmed by one of them, you may find it hard to regard what has happened to you as a harm. If you do come to see this, you may not believe there is anything you can do about it. You may now be as uncertain of the trustworthiness of all those adults you have been taught to rely on for protection as you are of the strangers you have been taught to stay away from.

In principle, adult women, if they were informed or trained, could defend themselves against or leave the men who were supposed to be protecting them. The situation cannot be remedied this way in the case of children. We might try to distinguish between good and bad adults and say that children must rely on good adults to protect them from bad adults. But how will children make this distinction? They must rely on adults who describe themselves as good to instruct them. These are usually their parents. The problem of children's inescapable vulnerability does not go away. We need (and ought) not characterize this vulnerability in terms of inferior cognitive or moral status. The fact that children necessarily lack the sort of strength, information and experience only time will provide suffices to make them a poor match for an adult intent on hurting them. As we saw in chapter 2, parents who use corporal punishment against their children are intent on hurting them as a means of achieving their compliance. From a child's point of view, this means that good adults may intend to hurt them in which case a reliable distinction between good and bad adults is virtually impossible for children to make.

That their vulnerability is unavoidable and that they are at greatest risk from the adults who protect them does not mean that no young child is safe at home. The fact that most children survive these years does not, however, undermine either the claim that they are statistically the most hazardous years for them or that when it comes to those harms to children for which adults are held responsible, these are usually their parents or other caregivers. These facts at least serve to call the belief that our current social arrangement for the protection of young children is adequate into serious question. As we try and explore possible solutions to this dilemma however, the paradox of child protection looms once more.

David Archard recommends that the rearing of young children become much more a matter of community and state interest than it is now. In other words, young children ought not to be left to the discretionary care of their parents only. As many adults as is practicable should become involved in their day-to-day tending and the state must regularly monitor their caregivers. Once children begin school, school authorities could monitor them as well. Unfortunately, statistics also show that young children are at some risk of harm from neighbours, state officials and school teachers. In fact, children are at greatest risk in the hands of those whom society designates as their protectors regardless of who is so designated. The popular belief that parents and all of these other adult groups are especially concerned and expert at protecting the interests of young children creates a false sense that those interests are always well protected. But if not these adults as their protectors, then which ones? The paradox of child protection remains unresolved.

One is tempted to imagine specially programmed robots—androids whose prime directive is to protect and never harm the child in their protection. Ray Bradbury's *I Sing the Body Electric*[13] is a good example of such a vision. In Bradbury's short story, Fantoccini Ltd. promotes one of their most popular items, a robotic grandmother:

> For you who have worried over inattentive sitters, nurses who
> cannot be trusted with marked liquor bottles and well-meaning

> Uncles and Aunts — we have perfected the first humanoid-genre minicircuited, rechargeable AC-DC Mark V Electrical Grandmother. The Toy that is more than a Toy, the Fantocinni Electrical Grandmother is built with loving precision to give the incredible precision of love to your children. The child at ease with the realities of the world and the even greater realities of the imagination, is her aim.[14]

When I was a child, I was told that I had a guardian angel and had to wear a scapular[15] under my clothing. My Italian friends wore amulets which their parents expected would ward off "the evil eye." These are expressions of parental desperation in response to the paradox of child protection. The robot solution is also just an optimistic fantasy the dark side of which was made famous by HAL the homicidal onboard computer system in Stanley Kubrick's film *2001: A Space Odyssey*. In the end, it appears as though the paradox cannot be resolved. Given the fact that, contrary to Thomas Hobbes's fanciful hypothesis that "men as if but now sprung out of the earth, and suddenly (like mushrooms) come to full maturity, without all kinds of engagement to each other,"[16] humans are born in a state of extreme vulnerability and utter dependence, we have no choice but to pass through a period in which our safety is ultimately uncertain. Can anything be done to minimize the risk?

While David Archard's modest collectivism does not solve the paradox of child protection, it can act to minimize the risks to young children which their childhood necessarily imposes. The more adults regularly involved in their day-to-day care, Archard supposes, the greater the chance that the dangerous impulses of some will be kept in check by others. But for such a system to have this effect, many more adults in our society, and especially adults authorized by the state to supervise and assist parents, will have to be rationally persuaded that in addition to being seriously harmed by physical and sexual abuse, children are also at serious risk from corporal punishment and that this risk is morally unacceptable. Merely increasing the number of watchful adults will have no effect if every additional eye is jaundiced by the benign view of corporal punishment.

In addition to this change in moral attitudes towards corporal punishment, the libertarian attitude that your neighbour's children are no concern of yours must be dislodged—not an easy task.[17] But the difficulty of the task hardly speaks against taking it up. The consequence of not doing so is the status quo. Since current arrangements do not ensure the safety of young children and this alternative would go further to achieve that end, philosophical morality requires the modest collectivization of childrearing.[18]

Trusting Government

Tragically, we must grant that no amount of adult surveillance can guarantee the complete safety of children in our or any other society. Will increased state involvement in families nevertheless improve the current situation? When it comes to the role of the state, it is clear that our attitudes towards the good intentions of government officials are going to be skeptical. Ours, like other liberal democracies, is in part an anti-authoritarian society—one in which the actions and claims of government are rarely accepted at face value.[19] Watching government watching parents would go some distance in minimizing the sorts of risks which attach to trusting it—risks which the history of residential and parochial schools show are all too real. It is clear that in any case, ordinary Canadian citizens must individually develop the moral, social and political will to make the safety and security of all children a high priority—higher than and so a limit on parental discretion and familial privacy. Archard acknowledges this in his call for an extension of children's rights. Harm, he argues, is something every child has a moral right to be protected from. While not every physical interference with a child can be considered harmful, corporal punishment, since it hurts children, does not benefit them and poses demonstrated risks for a variety of serious harms to them, is something every child is morally entitled to be protected from.[20]

Increased government involvement can also express itself in parent education. In order to present as comprehensive a strategy as possible for the minimization of risk, the attitudes, training and resources of those on the front lines of childcare in Canada must be developed towards and not away from securing the safety of children.

Parenting in a Vacuum

The problems contributing to bad parenting practice are legion. All new parents begin with no experience and most without any special education or training. Even a second child presents a novel challenge in many ways. And those with lots of experience caring for the children of others have a surprise waiting with one of their own. The effects of this feature of parenting cannot be underestimated. With your own child, the responsibilities multiply exponentially. You not only have the responsibility of this or that child's afternoon amusement or flu or arithmetical competence. You have the responsibility of securing the necessary conditions for this human being's happiness in life; her future; his ability to succeed. And during their early years, the responsibility is never interrupted. The potential for this responsibility to overwhelm parents is great and we generally deal with it by focusing our attention at any one time on its specific details.

Our ability to remain fixed on the long term objectives of parenting is also undermined by pressures which bear in upon us from outside — economic pressures, health worries and tensions in our adult relationships. We may try very hard to keep such pressures at bay; to protect our children from their fallout. But in the process of trying to protect them in this way, we tend to isolate ourselves as parents from ourselves as active adults and citizens and may end up parenting in a vacuum. Parenting in a vacuum is the worst place to parent given the concerns at the bottom of the paradox of child protection. It is clearly dangerous for young children. But given the effects which the responsibility of parenting has on parents themselves, it is also very bad for adults.

Prior to and during World War I, women collectivized their home and childcare efforts as a matter of course. While largely isolated from the world of men (whether the world of men was in the fields, factories or at the Front), they were not isolated from one another.[21] After World War II and its mass movement of women into the industries of war, economic exigency was used to get women out of the job market. A commercial push occurred towards the nuclear family dwelling as well as towards the role of the wife as the sole person responsible for the maintenance of her home and children.[22] Constant borrowing and sharing was replaced by redundant individual ownership of the tools of the trade. The proverbial "borrowed cup of sugar" became a symbol of earlier times.

Since the 1950s, women have therefore borne the brunt of parenting in a vacuum. Men long argued that all and only women are naturally suited as individuals to the rigours of childcare. That such arguments are no longer acceptable is not because men are also individually suited to this job and not because all and only women are collectively though not *individually* suited to it. More importantly, such arguments are no longer acceptable because no one is individually suited to rearing children all on his or her own. To say that no one is individually suited to parenting in a vacuum is not to say that no one is suited to parenting or even naturally so. Rather the effects on parents of any gender of attempting to care for their children cut off either ideologically, materially or emotionally from their wider community are so corrosive of their ability to remain healthy, happy and clear-minded, that their very sense of themselves as dignified human beings is seriously threatened.[23] If we imagine someone individually suited for this job, we would have a human being without any sense of, need for or claim to human dignity. Almost every type of human being has been classified in this way at some time in history. We now reject any suggestion that there naturally are or ought to be such human beings.

Childrearing education, prior to the emergence of the nuclear family, had been conducted informally under the condition of many teachers; many eyes. When the nuclear family became the norm, you generally had one teacher: your parental unit.[24] In both cases, parenting education was largely a matter of what psychologists call "modeling" or the informal acquisition of parenting norms through imitation, custom and habit. While the interests of children may have been better served under the many eyes model than they are under the single eye model, the failures of the former cannot be ignored. Whatever superiority the many eyes model has, it rests on the better conditions for women as primary caregivers which collectivism provided. Without as much pressure on them individually, women may have had an easier time parenting than their individualized children would in the 1950s. Nevertheless, both models of childcare restrict the principles of parenting to the norms of tradition and preserve the determination of parenting practice for those who accept these norms. As such, morally problematic norms such as the acceptance of corporal punishment tend to go unchallenged.

The old views of children as angelic innocents pure of heart or savage miscreants incapable of human reason or judgement have tended to inform most customary or popular parenting education and practice. Unless parenting education becomes formalized according to many of or the same criteria which govern other systems of public education, we have little reason to think that this situation will change.[25] I have argued that it must. And while I am not competent to devise such a system of public parenting education, there are many who are.[26] The factors involved here are numerous and complex. Some are so deeply situated in our feelings, beliefs and practices that unearthing and uprooting them cannot help but have unsettling individual and social consequences. Feminist philosophers have been doing similarly disruptive work for three decades and the seismic effects continue to be felt.[27] But there have been other deep attitudes which have been successfully removed or transformed — belief in the economic necessity or moral justification of slavery for example.

Today's parent is likely to be someone who, while not completely determined by external pressures, is nevertheless under a great deal of pressure from the world of work and finance. Trying to separate oneself as the subject of those pressures from oneself as the subject of the ones at home can only lead to the feeling that one is parenting in a vacuum. This should be avoided since it exacerbates rather than ameliorates the paradox of child protection. Pressures which bear in upon us from the outside must be seen as part of a continuum of pressure parenting society's children involves. As David Archard has argued, many beliefs and intuitions regarding the separation of the private and public arenas must therefore be dislodged when it comes to childrearing. This is not to say that we must either give up our privacy entirely or that everything must be become privatized. As I hope my points against both Plato and the "ultra" nuclear family have shown, both consequences are morally undesirable. But some give is indicated.

We should affirm the moral desirability of opening up all parenting to full public policy concern. Given the fundamental importance of security of the person to their development as happy, successful human beings, one of the foremost moral principles of parenting in a fishtank must be to do no harm to children. Perhaps, among other things, we need a Hypocratic Oath for new mothers and fathers, all teachers and other child caregivers. As neighbours concerned to combine our efforts with those of the state, we ought to be prepared to instantly and actively protect children around us when we observe their parents or caregivers hurting them and as prepared to accept such assistance when we are the ones placing our children at risk. Finally, as citizens, we ought to ensure that our government acts well on our behalf regarding legislation for children's welfare, supervising and educating all parents (not just those already at risk for harming their children) and that it in no way condones or, worse, justifies harming them.[28]

7

· · · · · · · · · · ·

Corporal Punishment:

Its Defenders

Morally speaking, we ought to, individually and collectively, adopt a much more tolerant attitude towards state monitoring of parental childcare, revise our feelings and beliefs about meddling in the childcare behaviours of others and take a much more serious, formal approach to parental childcare education. Doing so promises to give children better protection than they now have and not at the cost of giving up reasonable entitlements to the use of discretion in their disciplining. What follows is a critical analysis of the views of two spokespersons who defend the morality and practice of corporal punishment of children in the arena of public opinion and of the position of one contemporary philosopher who has written on the issue. The first public defender of corporal punishment is an American, Dr. James Dobson. His book *The New Dare to Discipline* is a popular self-help book for parents.[1] The second is Barbara Amiel. Ms. Amiel has been a regular contributor to the country's many *Sun* news-

Notes to chapter 7 are on pp. 272–77.

papers. The philosopher is David Benatar, whose paper "Corporal Punishment" addresses many of the arguments I have presented here and in which it is argued that none of these arguments supports the claim that nonsevere forms of corporal punishment must be prohibited.[2]

Dr. Dobson's *New Dare*

In the opening chapter of the second edition of his popular *Dare to Discipline*, Dr. James Dobson writes that he does not "believe in parental harshness"[3] and allows that "the judicious use of corporal punishment"[4] is consistent with parental love. From remarks he makes later in the book, we may construct first, what he takes to be a definition of "judicious" corporal punishment, second, his normative argument for its use and third, his defence of corporal punishment against its critics.

The Definition

Dobson defines "judicious corporal punishment" as a natural learning process which involves (a) the infliction of a minor but "stinging"[5] physical pain, (b) preferably caused by a switch or paddle,[6] (c) to the buttocks,[7] (d) of a willfully antagonistic child not younger than fifteen months[8] and not older than twelve years of age,[9] (e) by a calm, rational parent or authorized parental agent, (f) who has never abused a child and does not enjoy inflicting such pain.[10] The use of a device for making contact is preferred here since, according to Dobson, "the hand should be seen by the child as 'an object of love.'"[11] It must be noted up front that this preference implies that hitting a child is not an act of love and so is at odds with his view of corporal punishment as consistent with parental love.

Dobson restricts the use of corporal punishment first, to (d) cases where a child has acted in a willfully disobedient manner and secondly, to (e, f) where the punisher is a calm, rational parent or authorized parental agent who has never abused a child and does not enjoy inflicting such pain. With respect to the first restriction, he writes that "heredity does not equip a child with proper attitudes"[12] and that "truly, the toddler is a tiger!"[13] Perhaps without knowing it, Dobson is assuming the recapitulation theory of childhood though in tones more reminiscent of ancient Greece and medieval Italy than contemporary child psychology. His comment about heredity implies that it equips human beings with improper (uncivilized) attitudes which must be denied expression and that on balance, a young human being is more like a nonhuman animal than like an adult human one. I have argued, along with thinkers such as Gareth Matthews, that these assumptions are morally dangerous in that they have no foundation in fact and encourage adults to treat children disrespectfully or to see the harm they cause children as of little account. Further, treating children as proto-humans who can learn from and tolerate corporal punishment in order to turn them into full human beings who would not tolerate it for any purpose is practically contradictory.

With respect to the second restriction, Dobson is right to deny the use of corporal punishment to the agitated or sadistic parent or to one who has abused children in the past. Is he also right to allow it in other cases? What remains after the emotional parent is excluded is the outwardly cool, calm but reluctant punisher. This parent model was exploited in the film *The Yearling*[14] when a father played by Gregory Peck delivered blows to his young son's buttocks as the child was bent over his knee—blows which were represented as causing Peck's character deep emotional and so greater pain than they caused the child. One may also recall a similar portrayal (though the punisher is not represented as very reluctant) from Ingmar Bergman's film *Fanny and Alexander*.[15]

The mythology of the cool but reluctant punisher (usually male) transposes the reality of what is being done to whom by turning the physically violent figure into an object of sympathy. The child victim is portrayed as having forced the parental aggressor into a situation where he must endure the suffering of imposing a violent penalty on a loved one. "This is going to hurt me a lot more than it hurts you" is still a standard preface to the corporal punishment episode. Its absurdity underlines the insidiousness of the ideal corporal punisher Dobson endorses and this effect is not lost on the purveyors of sadistic pornography nor, it seems, on the hosts of countless Internet sites where spanking is now offered as a commercial service. It is also the case, perhaps less problematically, that Dobson's exclusion of the abusive parent begs the question of child abuse by assuming rather than arguing that not all cases of violence towards children are abusive.[16]

Next, Dobson argues for the epistemological merits of corporal punishment on the grounds that the pain of corporal punishment is comparable in its effects to the pain of being burnt by a hot stove or bitten by a dog.[17] But the analogy is counterproductive. The relevant similarity is supposed to be in the consequences of experiencing pain. The child naturally comes to know that he must avoid the stove or dog.[18] If the analogy holds, then the child will naturally learn to avoid the parent or being caught. But avoiding the parent or being caught is not the lesson Dobson wants children to learn. He wants them to avoid willful disobedience. To learn this lesson, children must connect the pain of corporal punishment to the infraction rather than to the parent or to the fact of having been caught. But this association requires the ability to connect distant events to present pain—an ability which is typically not yet well developed in a young child. Long before such complex lessons are learned, the child has adapted to the requirement for improved stealth and in a perfectly natural way. The analogy between hot stoves and "a good smack" is productive here only if the purpose of corporal punishment is to improve the ability of disobedient children to avoid adult detection. Since on Dobson's own terms, the purpose is to train children to avoid disobedient behaviour in the first place, his definitional analogy between natural learning and learning through corporal punishment fails.[19]

With respect to the means of delivery, Dobson's view that switches and paddles are "neutral" in comparison to the hand is bizarre. Their special design and exclusive use as weapons of corporal punishment fit them into a clearly non-neutral category. And while a belt, for example, when it is holding up someone's pants, may be considered neutral in the context of weaponry, as soon as it is out of its loops and coming down on someone's buttocks, it is a weapon. Further, it is not clear why Dobson's reasoning against hand contact would not work as well against a hand-held switch or paddle. In both cases, the child knows that the hand is being used and if he or she cannot actually see what is going on—likely in the case of being beaten on the buttocks—the paddle is experienced as a mere extension of the hand. Finally, as I noted above, Dobson's preference for a punishing instrument other than the hand since the hand "is an object of love" involves him in a contradiction. Either corporal punishment is consistent with parental love or it is not. If it is, then using the "loving" hand should not be excluded by his theory. If it is not, then corporal punishment must not be used. He cannot have it both ways.

Dobson writes that no child under the age of fifteen months should be corporally punished presumably because such children have not yet formed the capacity for willfulness apparent at later ages. Later on in the text, Dobson suggests that such attitudes are usually only present around three years of age and as such, children under three should not be corporally punished. There is a clear tension here which leaves it to individual parents to decide when their 15 month to 3 year old child is capable of "the greatest antagonism."[20] Even infants are capable of causing parents great antagonism though do not intend to cause it. The issue is therefore the age at which a child is capable of intending to cause their parents this sort of grief. Dobson does little to settle this question and in fact obscures it.

In short, Dobson's definition of corporal punishment is a minefield of contradictions and obscurities as well as false empirical assumptions, and as such is in no shape to define the occasions of its judicious use. Like other treatises on the benefits of corporal punishment which attempt to respond to the many criticisms launched against the practice (considered later in the book), Dobson's manipulation of the various definitional elements leaves the reader a considerable amount of latitude when it comes to actually deciding what counts as an appropriate application of this discipline strategy. As we will see when we examine the legal environment on the question of corporal punishment, this vagueness is often exploited to justify serious physical injury to children.

The Normative Argument

Dobson's normative argument in favour of using corporal punishment runs as follows. Children often express a desire for autonomy or to control themselves and their surroundings by testing parental limits (rules and/or patience). Such testing ought to be viewed as an attempt to defy legitimate authority. Defiance of legitimate authority is socially dangerous—Dobson refers to this danger in terms of "dangers in the social world, such as defiance, sassiness, selfishness, temper tantrums, behaviour that puts his life in danger, etc."[21] Since such dangers ought

to be avoided, the child needs to learn to adjust his or her defiant attitude. Dobson then says that "an appropriate spanking is the shortest
and most effective route to an attitude adjustment"[22] and implicitly
concludes that it ought to be used in the course of childcare.

Dobson's normative argument depends on a number of false or
dubious premises. First, the claim that all forms of defiance of legitimate authority are socially dangerous is unargued for. One presumes it
would involve the view that the possibility of society depends upon
the unswerving conformity of the individual to the group which holds
power; that the presence of individuality threatens social order to such
an extent that in the interest of group survival, it must be stamped out.
This is reminiscent of the social order argument which John Stuart Mill
disposed of over one hundred years ago. There may indeed be situations, however, in which the integrity and safety of a group is threatened by individual dissent: if we were describing a military battalion
on patrol in enemy territory for instance. In situations of this sort, the
survival of the group is rightly upheld over the rights and even the
lives of its individual members. Apparently, Dobson thinks that raising
children is a similarly treacherous mission — that children acting on
their own are the family's worst enemy.[23] If this were true, it is not clear
why even more severe measures against them would not be called for.

The sociopolitical underpinning of the claim that all defiance of
legitimate authority is socially dangerous is representative of "bunker
mentality." This may have been reasonable on the doorstep of the
American War of Independence and may still be popular in some seg-
ments of the U.S. population today, but it is in sharp conflict with the
liberal ideology of individual rights which sees the welfare interests of
individuals (including though not restricted to the interests of the
groups of which they are members) as fundamental. As such, Dobson's
argument makes a false assumption describing the normal task of childrearing in terms of, say, surviving in a war zone.

Dobson also claims that "an appropriate spanking is the shortest
and most effective route to an attitude adjustment." This claim trades
on a confusion between behaviour and attitude. As we will see later,
spanking has been shown to correlate with immediate behavioural
compliance in a limited case. But the changes Dobson is after in attitude require time and reflection and, as John Stuart Mill argued in the

nineteenth century, avoiding the use of corporal (as well as verbally humiliating) punishment. Dobson is therefore mistaken about corporal punishment being "the shortest and most effective route" to attitude adjustment if by that term is meant a positive change to what the child internalizes concerning the moral worth of good behaviour. If, on the other hand, Dobson intends this term as a mere euphemism for their outward behaviour then he must acknowledge that his behaviouristic program of child discipline is indistinguishable from those we use for nonhuman animals. Even in the case of training nonhuman animals, however, many people have rejected the view that harsh physical punishment is justified on the basis of its results finding instead that non-violent humane approaches work as well if not better. As such, Dobson's normative conclusion that such punishment must be used when an attitude adjustment is called for is at best unsupported by the evidence and at worst, false.

Dobson Defends His Position

Dobson responds to several criticisms of his position: 1) that corporal punishment has a demonstrated tendency to escalate into abuse, 2) that the use of corporal punishment in the disciplining of children has a tendency to make them more aggressive and violent than children who are not punished in this way and 3) that children who are corporally punished will suffer lifelong problems with self-esteem. These criticisms as well as Dobson's responses to them should be familiar by now. Dobson counters first that "just because a technique is used wrongly…is no reason to reject it altogether,"[24] second that the attitude adjustment which follows the pain caused by corporal punishment does "not create aggression in a boy or girl, it helps them control their impulses and live in harmony with various forms of benevolent authority throughout life…because it is in harmony with nature"[25] and third that "a boy or girl who knows love abounds at home will not resent a well-deserved spanking."[26]

At first glance Dobson's first *reductio ad absurdum* counterargument is fair. If any instance of misusing a technique counted as a reason for abandoning it, we would have to abandon all techniques. But Dobson equivocates on the term "used wrongly" here. He has to show that there are flaws in the statistical arguments inductively establishing the tendency for use of corporal punishment (either alone or in combination with other factors) to pose a risk for escalation to abuse ("used wrongly") of children. Instead, he makes a logical point about the conceptual distinction between the merit of a technique and the competence or incompetence of its users ("used wrongly"). As such, he does not address the abuse objection at all.

Once again, the empirical issue is not whether most parents who use corporal punishment go on to inflict what we currently acknowledge as serious physical damage to a child. Most do not. But when other factors even less strongly associated with child abuse combine with the use of corporal punishment, the risk of abuse is significantly greater. In addition, nearly all parents who are convicted of abusing their children began with a commitment to using corporal punishment against them and continued to believe that their abusive acts were just more of the same. Dobson may have in mind the concern that if only parents who were convicted of abusing their children are sampled for the purposes of these studies, then the studies are biased towards users of corporal punishment who have other serious problems — problems which lead them to misuse the correct corporal punishment technique. But such a concern would once again beg the question of what counts as misapplication of the technique assuming rather than arguing that all parents who abuse children must be misusing it.

Belief in the effectiveness and justifiability of corporal punishment is known to be a strong predictor for its use (regardless that this belief has no demonstrated basis in fact) and its use, especially in combination with various stresses on parents, is a risk factor, even if small, for child abuse. But it must also be noted that its being a risk factor for abuse is not the only reason for morally condemning corporal punishment. As I have argued, there is overwhelming evidence that it is a significant risk factor for many other child and social harms even where most people would agree it has not escalated to an abusive level and virtually no evidence at all for its being strongly correlated with the positive outcomes its users aim at. The debate over the connection between corporal punishment and child abuse will be revisited in the concluding chapter.

With respect to his second defensive move, I have already argued that Dobson's epistemological analogy between the natural and parental delivery of pain is unintelligible. His view then, that corporal punishment is a "natural" form of teaching children how to behave, is virtually meaningless. This leaves him without any argument to support the conclusion that corporal punishment is a natural method of child control.[27] One might also point out that "harmony with nature" is a logically poor foundation for curbing natural impulses and that empirically speaking, being hit is hardly conducive to developing the ability to "live in harmony with various forms of benevolent authority throughout life." Dobson is presuming a view of nature which is both contradictory given his heredity theory of "proper attitudes" and at odds with the facts.

Finally, to the objection that children who are corporally punished will suffer lifelong problems with self-esteem, Dobson writes that "a boy or girl who knows love abounds at home will not resent a well-deserved spanking."[28] The objection raises the problem of how a child who is subjected to corporal punishment can be confident in the first place that love abounds at home, suggesting in turn that corporal punishment causes children to feel hated or resented by their parents, damaging their self-esteem. In response, Dobson invokes a contextualist argument appealing to the principle that no episode of physical violence can be judged harmful to self-esteem on its own. This principle seems reasonable. The voluntary barroom brawl or boxing match are typical examples of subjection to violence which need not result in a moral or legal harm to one or the other party. Dobson must show that the so-called judicious corporal punishment episode is this sort of situation: specifically that children know they are respected before they are ever physically punished, see the consequent harm as an expression of that respect rather than a withdrawal of it and their role as victim of corporal punishment in terms of their voluntary and co-equal participation in the corporal punishment act.

There are at least two problems for Dobson here. First, those situations in which violence clearly does not damage self-esteem are not punishment situations at all. Rather they are combat situations where each participant consents to being hurt and sees him or herself having some real chance to hurt the other. Given the inequalities as well as lack of consent in the punishment situation, the child's dignity must be assured prior to and not by the first physical punishment episode—

perhaps by having been affectionately disciplined for its first fifteen months. A normal fifteen-month-old who has never been violently punished and never even been threatened in that direction will then, supposedly, take the first beating in stride. If this is Dobson's expectation, it is ludicrous. Children feel loved and respected in the first place because they have been treated with kindness and patience and not assaulted or threatened with assault. As I suggested in chapter 6, a violent change in parental response to their misdemeanors is likely to deeply undermine their family feeling, not reinforce it. Once again, Dobson begs the question of how children will interpret corporal punishment. He assumes they will see it as parental love instead of arguing for this claim.

In conclusion, Dobson's complex definition of "judicious corporal punishment," his normative argument for its use and his defence against his critics are all guilty of begging the question, vagueness, category errors, contradictions, equivocations and other fallacies, as well as false empirical assumptions. As such, his argument for corporal punishment is not rationally persuasive. At the bottom of that argument is the implicit assumption of a world view opposed to Dobson's own explicit insistence that he is against parental harshness as well as to his view of children as especially vulnerable. The implicit world view is informed by the recapitulation theory and sees proper parenting as the forced implantation of the firm disposition to obey and conform to existing authority by means of threats to and actual violation of the bodily security of children. It presumes, against common sense and all experience, that when all children turn twelve, provided they have been corporally punished as well as loved, their desire for autonomy will no longer express itself as defiance against parental limits and that the scope of their self-control will automatically extend to all other sources of legitimate authority. Dobson concludes his remarks with a comment on what "will be a sad day for families"[29] referring to the possibility that governments may outlaw corporal punishment against children. "Child abuse," Dobson asserts, "will increase not decrease, as frustrated parents explode after having no appropriate response to defiant behaviour."[30] Let us examine Barbara Amiel's worries in the same vein.

Barbara Amiel's Neoconservative Protest

Unlike Dr. Dobson, Barbara Amiel is no self-proclaimed expert in child psychology. She is also not an expert in the area of corporal punishment. Amiel, arguably, is not an expert in anything. She is a journalist and as such, is a commentator on the expert claims of others. Her writings are not subject to scholarly review nor much, I assume, editorial scrutiny. As such, treating her writings with the same scholarly seriousness and interest with which the views of scholars and experts (self-proclaimed or not) are treated here may strike some readers as odd. But Amiel's views, however unscholarly, have the potential to influence a wide Canadian readership and, it might be argued, reflect commonly held beliefs among that readership. Also, it seems to me that being a public commentator on, rather than an expert in, corporal punishment research should not protect Amiel from serious critical attention. It is for these reasons, among others, that she is included here.

Barbara Amiel wrote in an *Edmonton Sun* piece entitled "Beware the Sinister Arm of Family Statism" that:

> All the philosophical arguments against statism have been made. Now we are simply left with the practical concerns: what parent can exercise any authority over their family after being hauled into court simply for trying to discipline it? Such actions irreparably destroy the consensual basis of the family which is why the state ought to take the greatest possible care whenever interfering with the family unit. Having seen off Nazism and communism, we seem utterly unable to resist the poorer relative — statism. The fix is in. Soon the state will outlaw the slipper, belt and slap.[31]

It is clear from this remark and the general tenor of the rest of the piece, that Amiel believes the freedom to slap or otherwise strike children for the purpose of correction is necessary for the maintenance of parental authority which is in turn necessary for the protection of the nuclear family. Since the nuclear family is the cornerstone of democratic society as we wish to preserve it, this freedom must not be interfered with. Amiel insists that if the state attempts to block this freedom, it will illegitimately usurp natural parental authority in the family — established in the minds of the children, if one follows Amiel's reasoning, via the parent's sovereign administration of corporal punishment.

And from there, it is a very slippery slope to replacing the nuclear family with the state as family — that is, Plato's *Republic*.

Amiel argues that a lack of proportionality characterizes public opinion on this issue. Either, she says, we turn a blind eye to even the most horrendous and arbitrary tortures of children or we call in the state to act as parent in even the most innocuous of physical punishment and correction situations. False dilemmas aside, Amiel's solution, to interfere in family punishment practices only when they cross some line, is of no theoretical or practical value. But her point about the unity of families and its connection to the practice of corporal punishment, following Dobson, needs serious consideration. Allowing that no one is actually suggesting that the state become the *de facto* punishing authority in each and every family, it remains for us to examine the view that in prohibiting corporal punishment or removing its legal defence, the state would in effect be destroying the basis of family unity. This is strong stuff. How well does the conclusion hold up?

The conclusion rides on the importance of children's recognition of a proximate and unified authority in the family and the manner in which such authority is established. There is little to argue against on the first score. As I have suggested, young children in particular require close supervision and quick, consistent responses to their dangerous behaviour so that they are protected from harming themselves and others, and so a useful conjunction is eventually set up in their minds between action, responsibility and consequence. As to the means of establishing the necessary authority, however, it is clear that corporal punishment is not the way to go.

Those who support corporal punishment as a means of maintaining family unity implicitly assume the recapitulation theory arguing that children of all ages are incapable of regularly responding positively to mere restrictions on their liberty where behavioural problems have arisen. According to this view, children do not always take such parental attempts at discipline seriously or seriously enough, and as a result lose respect for their parental figures. Here, children's respect is understood in terms of fear and awe inspired by the prospect of pain. As such, the authority of the parent and so the maintenance of the unity of the family appears to require that parents administer physical pain in the course of educating their children.[32]

Given the serious problems with the recapitulation theory, Amiel's implicit reliance upon it undermines the connection she sees between the prohibition of corporal punishment and the dissolution of the family which, it is granted, could follow from the breakdown of even healthy parental authority. Children are not the "mindless beasts" the recapitulation theory assumes they are. And in any case, we know from the experience of trained animal handlers that corporal punishment is not required to establish authority.[33] Unless one is prepared to grant (as the strict libertarian or deontologist might be) that the freedom to corporally punish is justified by something other than its consequences, since it is, on balance, harmful to children, morality demands that other means be used to maintain family unity.

Even under state monitoring, parents remain free to choose other means of maintaining their authority based on what fits with the family's cultural or other normative commitments. As such, admitting the guardianship of state when it comes to adult-child relations does not mean forfeiting either the privacy to which adults, in their voluntary associations with one another, are usually entitled or the liberty to raise their children according to the dictates of their customary morality.[34] Amiel's opinion that it does implies the view that parents have a natural right—a right above and beyond those granted by the state—to hit their children for the purpose of improving their behaviour or attitudes. As we saw above, Dobson also prevails upon nature to support his position and with the same weak result. We have already seen John Stuart Mill reject such arguments. Natural rights arguments tend to proceed from a claim about how things have always been or how God says they ought to be, directly to a conclusion about how in fact, they ought to be. This type of argument can be used to justify or promote anything from breast feeding to cannibalism and has been used to justify religious toleration as well as slavery and the disenfranchisement of women. There are numerous problems, as we have seen, with arguments based on natural law even when their conclusions seem acceptable. But even if one accepts them in this case, unless there are circumstances in which nature affords no other or no better means to parents for maintaining family unity than hitting their children, the argument from nature for this practice fails.[35] As we will see below, Amiel has also attempted just such a demonstration.

Violations of an individual's entitlement to security of the person may only be morally justified under the reasonable expectation that they will prevent immanent and more serious harms to the individual or to others endangered by the individual. From the point of view of all involved, threats to a family's integrity could count as such a harm and under certain circumstances, one may use physical violence against those who pose such threats. But this is a far cry from saying that a family's integrity requires or even justifies the use of physical violence against its children — as if the children of the family were somehow on par with the thief, vandal or murderer crawling in through the bathroom window.

Amiel's argument takes the form of a natural law argument that is based on the recapitulation theory and, as such, it does not work. No family dissolves as a result of the failure of the parents to use corporal punishment against their children. Families might dissolve as a result of a failure of parental authority but parental authority does not fail because of a failure to corporally punish. Rather, authority fails as a result of not using other means to establish it. Like Dobson, Amiel problematically assumes rather than argues that other means are not or are not always available. We know from experience that the use of physical violence is neither necessary nor optimal to maintaining group cohesiveness in the long term. Unless families differ categorically from other groups in this respect, it is reasonable to conclude that maintaining longterm family unity does not require the use of physical violence either. Amiel must show and not assume that families are importantly different in this respect. Since she does not, her family statism argument against prohibiting corporal punishment fails. The family statism argument will be revisited in the concluding chapter.

Barbara Amiel's Louder Neoconservative Protest

In a much later *Montreal Gazette* piece entitled "The Case for Corporal Punishment,"[36] Amiel concludes that "without arbitrary authority, many parents and teachers simply will stop raising kids." Here, it seems, is a much more desperate attempt at justifying corporal punishment — one which echoes Dobson's despair when he writes that, "Child abuse will increase not decrease, as frustrated parents explode after having no appropriate response to defiant behaviour."[37] There are in fact two arguments in Amiel's piece which need to be distinguished. The first concludes that corporal punishment is necessary for the all important "classical education" of children. The second speaks specifically to the conclusion about parenting above.

Amiel begins the first argument by upholding the value of a "classical education." She claims such an education equips the individual with an ability to "speak and write with a fluency that is truly enviable." As she puts it, her "informal research" shows that whatever is necessary for a successful classical education must be socially endorsed and that according to famous people like George Orwell,[38] corporal punishment is one such necessity. Orwell arrived at this conclusion after reflecting upon his own "wretched" school experience — he had been beaten twice at St. Cyprian's for bedwetting, for example. Referring to the beating as a "barbarous remedy," he notes that it nevertheless worked.

In Orwell's recollection, his bedwetting stopped not after being beaten once (it continued after the first beating) but later after a second beating. Bedwetting is a developmental phenomenon not a moral or behavioural problem and as such, it is likely that his bedwetting would have stopped in any case. Orwell (or Amiel's version of Orwell) concludes that because his bedwetting stopped after the second beating that being beating per se caused the bedwetting to stop. This reasoning is fallacious. As critics of those studies which show strong correlations between corporal punishment and harms to children are always quick to point out, mere regular correlation much less a single instance of correlation is not enough to show a causal relation. Amiel, in addition to illegitimately extending Orwell's expertise as a novelist to education and child development, goes on to repeat his mistaken inference.

Based on the recollection of another product of the British school system — M.W. Gibson, Assistant Chief Constable of the Bedfordshire Police — Amiel concludes from the fact that he is an articulate and thoughtful individual who was beaten at school for getting a B- in History that his "enviable" fluency is the result of having been corporally punished. Arguments of this sort also commit the *post hoc ergo propter hoc* fallacy[39] and are often used to justify the infliction of pain and suffering. For example, using this bad argument form, we could also claim that had Orwell or ACC Gibson been sexually abused, poor, chronically ill or orphaned just before they stopped wetting their beds or improved on their history exams, that these circumstances cause one to get As or stay dry through the night. Alternatively, I might reasonably claim that being beaten as a child played a key role in my developing a special commitment to the welfare of children. But if I inferred from this that being beaten as a child is a necessary condition of devoting oneself as an adult to child welfare, you would rightly think me unreasonable. The mere fact of sequence (first "A" happens then "B" happens) is not sufficient to show causal correlation ("B" happens as a result of "A" happening). Amiel's first argument for the necessity of corporal punishment makes the mistake of assuming it is. She commits a classic reasoning fallacy and as such, gives us no reason whatsoever to accept her "corporal punishment/classical education" conclusion.

Amiel's second argument in the piece aims at offering support for her conclusion that "without arbitrary authority, many parents and teachers simply will stop raising kids." It is connected to the first argument when Amiel writes that she agrees with Orwell that corporal punishment is "a barbarous remedy." "If a parent or teacher has better methods than corporal punishment at their disposal they are infinitely preferable." She goes on to list such methods in terms of character traits: "personality, wit, an ability to psychologically influence children or be an effective role model and so on." Next, on the supposed empirical grounds that few parents and teachers have any of these traits or "methods," she concludes that most parents and teachers must resort to corporal punishment to "raise children somehow." "If they cannot employ a certain amount of arbitrary [sic] authority, including corporal punishment, they turn to the only other solution which is to stop raising their children." Correctly assuming that a widespread failure in this regard would be morally unacceptable, Amiel concludes that state interference with the sovereignty of parents and teachers to corporally punish children must be avoided.

There are several serious flaws with Amiel's reasoning here. First, her use of the term "arbitrary" is problematic. Assuming she means to use the term in its usual sense (without rational justification), the parental exercise of "arbitrary" authority would mean that parents are allowed to treat their children according to impulse rather than reason. Clearly, Amiel is not supporting open season on children. Rather, she supports a certain amount of legal space within which parents may use their discretion when it comes to disciplining their children — a space otherwise circumscribed by restrictions imposed by the state. I have argued that such a space is consistent with the demands of philosophical morality provided that it does not include permission to assault children. Amiel argues that it should include this permission on the moral grounds that not including it will be worse for children and society. Her argument for this moral claim is based on an empirical one that few parents possess alternative resources for raising children. Such resources, she contends, are only to be found in character traits which impress the reader as "native" to an individual rather than acquired.

Amiel fails on two points here. First, she actually ignores the possibility of alternative methods of raising children altogether, electing instead to focus on parent or teacher personality. While intelligence may be an issue, regardless of a parent's or teacher's personality, he or she can learn successful nonviolent methods of dealing with children.[40] Secondly, even when it comes to character traits, there is a certain amount of learning which obviously takes place. If this were not the case, it is hard to see why we should try to teach children to be good people or admonish adults to be good role models. Wit, for instance, is a product of quick mindedness, knowledge and a sense of humour. All three can be developed, distorted or destroyed. So, even if we assume that Amiel's claim that few parents or teachers have the necessary qualities for peaceful childcare is true, this hardly shows that such deficits are irremediable.

If Amiel agrees that corporal punishment is a "barbarous remedy" and is not to be preferred to nonviolent methods of childcare, then given the possibility of realizing the conditions for the use of such methods, she should be arguing for their realization. Instead, she argues that most parents and teachers lack personality, wit and the ability to be a role model for children and instead must resort to assault as an alternative to abandoning them. She then argues that many parents in the West have in fact abandoned their childcare duties, the result of which is "ghastly children who grow up to be even worse adults: undisciplined, unfit for life."

Amiel fails to see just how deeply this last claim undermines her thesis. Neither Britain[41] nor Canada nor the United States — places where one assumes the "ghastliest" children live—has either morally or legally moved to interfere with the authority of parents to corporally punish their children. Quite the reverse. Therefore, the putative fact that parents in the West have abandoned their childcare duties and produced a generation of n'ere-do-wells cannot be attributed to such interference. Amiel may, at this point, argue that it was the popularity of children's rights and permissiveness in the 1970s that encouraged a whole generation of parents to keep their hands off their children. This is a complicated issue and one which I will not go into in great detail here. Suffice it to say that such an appeal would fail. The movement to which Amiel might refer in support of her position never enjoyed popular appeal. Its problems, both according to the media and in practice, were due to confusing respectful parenting with no parenting at all.

The assumption, of course, that children are much more ghastly today than in the past is underdetermined by the evidence offered in its support. Adults compare children today to the way they recall children were in the past. Such recollection is usually based on generalizations from heavily edited, puffed up memories of their own childhood behaviour. It is a powerful psychological tendency of growing older to see the past as somehow better than the present—to see the past's children (ourselves) as somehow better than today's. My teenaged son suggested to me that his sense that the world of his childhood was better than the world he now knows is due to the subjective quality of his recollection. "I didn't know about all the bad stuff when I was young so of course the world I remember seems much better to me than the world I know now does." This is not to say that there are no things that are worse about the world now compared to the world of seventeen or even fifty years ago, but it clearly demonstrates that personal recollections cannot be relied upon to establish such claims. It is sadly a short but fallacious step from this revisionist tendency of personal historicizing to conclude that perceived differences between older and newer ways of treating children can explain the alleged generational change for the worse in their demeanor. Put this shaky reasoning all together and you get the normative view that children ought to be corporally punished so that they will be more like we imagine children were when we were young. Note that the same type of argument can be used by men to deny women equal rights, to justify infanticide and gericide, to support slavery or any number of social arrangements which we have come to see are immoral.

In the end, it is more likely that factors such as sheer exhaustion following from poverty, ignorance of effective and respectful childcare practices and lack of serious public support for remedying both are the ones that cause parents and teachers to give up. Amiel argues that the preferred options for disciplining children are not available to most parents. Does she mean that most parents are not aware of them? If so, the remedy seems self-evident. Does she mean that most parents, while aware of them, are so intellectually and emotionally backward that they are incapable of using them? If this is what she has in mind then her readers should know this.

In conclusion, both of Amiel's arguments in her second attack on those who would like to see corporal punishment abandoned as a childcare practice fail to persuade. Amiel depends on the emotional appeal of a couple of hot button issues—state interference in our daily lives, "ghastly children"—to convince her readers. But if we allow mere emotive response to guide policy, there is nothing standing in the way of the persuasive power of arguments similarly designed to justify the most obvious of immoral practices. In the end, Amiel's position rests upon the claim that most parents and teachers are incompetent to deal with children except as their unenlightened jailers or animal trainers. Such a claim involves, as we have seen, extremely dubious assumptions about both adults and children (not to mention prisoners and nonhuman animals)—assumptions which, it seems, are difficult to dislodge.

David Benatar and Robert Larzelere: The Philosopher and the Social Scientist

In his 1998 paper "Corporal Punishment,"[42] philosopher David Benatar argues that critics of corporal punishment are wrong to insist, on moral grounds, that "corporal punishment should *never* be inflicted."[43] Benatar lists seven points made against corporal punishment by its opponents. The list accurately surveys the strongest arguments put forward here so far: "corporal punishment leads to abuse...is degrading...is psychologically damaging...stems from and causes sexual deviance [I look at this argument in chapter 10]...teaches the wrong lesson...leads to unquestioning obedience...does not deter."[44] One by one, Benatar claims to dissolve the objections by showing that since none of them demonstrate that the infliction of "infrequent pain without injury"[45] has the morally problematic results which would be necessary to justify its moral condemnation, this form of corporal punishment escapes the net of those objections. Since at least one form of corporal punishment survives the strongest arguments against the practice, one cannot validly claim that corporal punishment is never morally justified.

While Benatar himself uses the term "physical punishment" to include actions such as beating, hitting, spanking, paddling, swatting and caning,[46] it is fairly clear that he means to isolate spanking in what escapes the objections he reviews. "I am not suggesting that [the infliction of pain without injury] is the most problematic form of corporal punishment, but I shall focus on it because it seems to be the mildest level of corporal punishment at which the disagreement enters."[47] In what follows, I concentrate on weaknesses in Benatar's argument.

The first is Benatar's failure to provide a clear definition of what would amount to "mild and infrequent corporal punishment."[48] The second is Benatar's reliance on the research of Robert Larzelere for a critique of the findings and studies which suggest that no form of corporal punishment is free of risk for a number of highly undesirable outcomes for children and society.

Just how we understand "mild and infrequent" physical punishment is crucial to the merit of Benatar's overall argument. If it is difficult or impossible for him to settle on a definition, allowing corporal punishment which is mild and infrequent while disallowing all other types will fail to be action guiding and as such, fail one important test of a moral norm. Also, if he has not clearly shown what types of corporal punishment survive criticism, then he has failed to show that any actually do. With respect to the term 'mild,' there is no explicit definition offered beyond "pain without injury." This, however, is extremely vague. Benatar may have in mind the use, for example, of "no more than two open-handed slaps on the thigh"[49] or buttocks but he does not say so explicitly. When it comes to ensuring that no morally objectionable forms of corporal punishment occur and so imposing restrictions on its use, Benatar suggests that only certain offences be punishable in this way, that only certain implements be used for it, that the "number of blows" be regulated and that we only hit places on the child's body which are the least apt to be injured when struck.[50]

In order to be action-guiding, Benatar's rule must give parents and teachers a fairly clear idea of what sort of assault is permitted by the term "mild." The term "reasonable," as it often appears in criminal statutes for example, may be said to suffer from the same vagueness. But the term "reasonable" has a certain objective content: it refers us back to what our social community is seen to most commonly and publicly endorse. The term "mild" has no such referent. While a large range of noninjurious assaults may fall more or less within its ambit, there will be many types of hitting contested at the margins. It is also a comparative term—one that may be used to rank two types of assault even though both may be severe. Parents (and judges) have a tendency to favourably compare the punishments received by today's children to ones they received as children from their parents and teachers finding the former mild in comparison to the latter. Benatar may believe that he has provided the necessary content here by referring to "pain without injury." But caning was adapted from earlier forms of beating children which had resulted in serious injuries and even death and was considered a humane form of physical punishment. The notion that we should not injure children in the course of physically punishing them is hardly new. Nevertheless, when it comes to defining "injury" Benatar is silent. I believe it is safe to assume that he means "harm" yet as I argued earlier, harm must at least include all forms of damage to the child's body which interfere with its normal functioning. If a caning results in the inability of the child to sit or walk comfortably for any period of time, then a harm or injury has occurred. Benatar himself cites a case of paddling in which the victim suffered a hematoma. All this points in the direction of excluding the use of implements for the purpose of corporal punishment, yet Benatar clearly allows them when he allows that some restrictions on the use of implements are recommended by his position. Yet in this case, perhaps it is not the use of such implements that is morally problematic, according to Benatar, but rather the number of blows allowable for any one episode. While he seems to object to the "twenty" that caused the victim of paddling his serious injury, he does not say how many would have been permissible. As I argued earlier in the case of Dobson, Benatar has given parents and teachers no unequivocal guidance here.

As for the matter of "infrequency," Benatar cautions that using corporal punishment in anger is ill-advised since "children are likely to be punished more often and more severely if it is done in anger."[51] Instead, he recommends that the punishment be delayed so that it may be administered in a "cool and methodical and not passionate"[52] frame of mind. During this cooling off period, he states that parents and teachers will be in "a better situation to conduct a fair inquiry and determine an appropriate punishment."[53] Benatar thus introduces the possibility that conducting an informal trial of sorts is a necessary precondition of meting out corporal punishment but he does not elaborate. He sets aside worries that in the event of a delay between bad behaviour and punishment, children will not make the right connection between their bad behaviour and its consequence on the grounds that "children at school already have the capacity to understand that a punishment inflicted now can be for a wrong committed at some significantly earlier time."[54] But he is "inclined to agree" that such delays will be lost on "very young children." Nowhere does Benatar say that preschool-age children ought not to be hit and as such we are entitled to infer that according to his position, they should be hit, if hitting seems appropriate, without due process and as soon as or very shortly after they have behaved badly. This in turn implies that very young children will be hit more often and more severely than school aged ones. Will the term "infrequent" therefore allow more and worse assaults for preschoolers than school-aged children? Benatar does not appear to have thought this through. In the end, no clear indication is given regarding how often counts as the infrequent use of corporal punishment. Once again, Benatar employs a very subjective criterion at an extremely crucial point in his overall argument—one that can hardly be described as action-guiding.

Finally, Benatar admits that while enforcing such rules in schools "could be monitored in a variety of ways...punishment within families is less easily monitored."[55] He concludes that "because it is even more difficult to monitor parental compliance with an unqualified ban on corporal punishment than it is to monitor parental compliance with a ban on only severe physical punishment, this monitoring problem provides no support for the elimination of all corporal punishment in homes. What is called for is a sensitization of those (such as doctors and teachers as well as children themselves) who are well placed to detect abusive punishment."[56]

Benatar's view here is incoherent. He seems to intuit that without adequate monitoring, parents will be unable or unwilling to comply with the spanking rule he proposes and correctly sees that this monitoring problem could easily derail his practical position. As we saw earlier, Barbara Amiel seems to think that due to the same monitoring problem, we must leave parents to make their own decisions about hitting their children. Benatar is not as open-minded about this as Amiel. He seems to realize that the vague mild and infrequent rule would be difficult if not impossible to follow without direct and constant guidance from or monitoring by experts. He also knows that it is not realistic to expect the state to engage in this sort of regulation. But he does not want to draw the conclusion Amiel does. Instead, Benatar argues that while it would be difficult to monitor parents in the home for compliance with his rule, it would be much more difficult to monitor compliance with a rule which says "never."

Does this reasoning make sense? If monitoring is difficult in either case, it is because unless a family has already come to the attention of the state, there are no easy means for legal, objective observation of what goes on inside the home. There are some ways of doing this. Sound travels. Children reveal or display the effects of physical punishment at school, or to neighbours and relatives. And as Benatar himself notes, doctors are also in a position to detect problems. Occasionally, parents hit their children in public view. Occasionally, you are a witness in the home of someone who strikes his or her child. Benatar claims that in the absence of official monitoring, it would be easier for you or a neighbour, teacher, doctor or passerby to judge that a parent has complied with the mild and infrequent rule than it would be for any of you to judge whether or not a parent has struck a child at all. Surely, one must reason the other way. Whether or not a child has been struck is a fairly simple either/or distinction — an objective fact. But whether or not a child has been struck mildly or not mildly is, as I have argued, a matter of interpretation — a subjective evaluation. There is likely to be a great deal less disagreement over the former than the latter and so if it is difficult to ascertain *whether* a child has been hit, it will be even more difficult, in most cases, to tell whether a child has been hit "mildly" or "not mildly." Also, while in public an observer may not even be able to tell with any confidence that the adult striking a child is the child's parent or teacher or a stranger. And without a broader context for interpretation, there is no way of knowing how frequently the child has been hit. Benatar does not raise the issue of strangers (nonparents and nonteachers) hitting children and I assume this is because he would reject the idea that this was in any way permitted by his position. Under the guidance of a complete ban on corporal punishment, one would not require any information beyond what one could observe to condemn the act. He might have been trying to argue that it is easier for the state to tell when a child has been seriously abused than it is to tell when a child has been spanked. The abused child might show up in a hospital emergency ward, for instance. Whereas a child who has merely been spanked would not. But his argument here is in support of the claim that because it is easier to tell when a child has been corporally punished in violation of his mild and infrequent rule than it is to tell when they've been hit at all, banning all hitting is unrealistic. Clearly, most instances of violating that rule will not end up in hospital emergency wards. And so, his reasoning would still be flawed.

The second and equally important weakness in Benatar's argument stems from his reliance on Robert Larzelere for refutations of empirical evidence which purports to show strong correlations between nonsevere forms of corporal punishment such as spanking and highly undesirable outcomes for children and society. Larzelere has been very influential on the procorporal punishment side of the debate alleging that studies which claim to show these correlations are inconclusive at best. This is, for the most part, Benatar's response to the empirical arguments which suggest otherwise. One undesirable outcome for children which gets attention in the social science literature is aggression. In response to the concern that "being subject to the willful infliction of pain causes rage and this gets vented through acts of violence on others" Benatar says that "there is insufficient evidence that the properly restricted use of corporal punishment causes increased violence."[57] We can infer that by "properly restricted use of corporal punishment," Benatar means something like "no more than two open-handed slaps on the thigh" used "infrequently." As I argued above, however, it is unclear from other things he has to say about restrictions on its use, that this is the only type of corporal punishment that satisfies his criterion. However, even if we charitably assume that this is all he has in mind, problems arise for his objection.

That objection is supported by reference to concerns raised against Murray Straus's studies which purport to show "that even infrequent, noninjurious corporal punishment can increase one's chances of being depressed."[58] Straus's studies and others also purport to show that similarly "restricted use of corporal punishment" increases the incidence of child aggression. Benatar objects that "the main methodological problem is that the studies are not experiments but post facto investigations based on self-reports."[59] While nonexperimental, self-reported data definitely has its limitations, in order for Benatar's objection to stick, it would have to be true that no data collected in this way is useful to researchers. Yet, we know that with the proper controls and caution in drawing conclusions — both of which Straus and others have been careful to observe[60] — such data can be valid and reliable. Two further problems with this complaint need attention. The first is that randomized experimentation on levels of aggression following the corporal punishment of children would require a group of children be subjected to the infliction of punitive physical pain for the purpose of data collection. Ironically, the ethical problems with this sort of human experimentation are well known.[61] The second is that, ethical questions aside, there actually have been non-randomized experiments in which children have been spanked and observed for their compliance levels. Joan Durrant writes that in 1986, Larzelere himself,

> Examined the relationships among the child's age (three to seventeen), frequency of spanking, and frequency of discussion. He found that discussion had no moderating effect on the relationship between corporal punishment and aggression towards siblings in any age group....It is important to note that corporal punishment was never inversely related to child aggression — even for those children whose parents frequently used discussion.[62]

Benatar does not make reference to this early work of Larzelere's.

Aside from the matter of its costs, Larzelere has more recently argued that experimental evidence shows that contrary to the conclusions of studies such as Straus's, the moderate use of corporal punishment has certain benefits. In support of this claim, Larzelere cites Lovaas whose experiments on autistic children purported to show that accompanying a loud "No" with the occasional slap on the thigh improved these children's ability to control themselves.[63] Further, he cites Forehand and McMahon who argued that experimental evidence showed that "a carefully prescribed spanking" was "effective in enforcing compliance to time-out."[64] If one stops reading Larzelere there, it would appear that Benatar has some initial grounds for objecting to the view that all corporal punishment should be prohibited. However, Larzelere goes on to note that the "barrier method" which involves no corporal punishment as well as the combination of non-corporal punishment and reasoning produce the same rates of compliance and behaviour moderation in normal children. It must be noted first that with regard to the benefits referred to in procorporal punishment studies for normal children, these always are in the domain of immediate compliance only. Second, in the works to which Benatar refers, Larzelere fails to include the conclusions of the very researchers he relies on which state that where the results are inconclusive, noncorporal punishment strategies ought to be preferred.[65] In short, whatever benefits the moderate use of corporal punishment might appear to have in certain very narrow circumstances, there is substantial evidence of long-term risk for antisocial behaviour as well as for many other undesirable outcomes from its use. In addition, even according to Larzelere (and despite the conclusions he comes to) there is no evidence that corporal punishment with or without reasoning tends to be more effective than nonviolent methods of child discipline.

Benatar claims he has shown that arguments against all forms of corporal punishment fail—that such arguments trade illicitly on the rightful condemnation of dangerous hitting and child abuse. He insists that the evidence to which such arguments appeal does not show that mild and infrequent hitting has any undesirable outcomes for children or society. Indeed, Benatar argues, this "moral" form of corporal punishment has some benefits. I have shown that Benatar fails to support his conclusion. As such, the argument against all forms of corporal punishment survives his challenge.

A recurring problem for all those who defend the practice of corporal punishment is most assuredly one of definition. Even if we set aside disagreements within their ranks over whether "paddling" or "caning," etc., should be permitted and focus on those who would only ever allow "two open handed slaps on the thigh," serious problems remain concerning how much force may be used and how frequently this technique should be used. Everyone—even on the pro-corporal punishment side—is agreed that we should never injure children, that too frequent spankings are counterproductive and that it is unrealistic to expect that parents can be forced to comply with vague moral or legal rules designed to prevent so-called noninjurious and infrequent uses of corporal punishment from escalating into more problematic forms. And even if evidence of the risk factors for using corporal punishment is inconclusive, it is nevertheless strongly suggestive. As such, it is reasonable to conclude we should err, if we are to err, on the side of caution and that all forms of the practice ought to be prohibited. A moral (and legal) prohibition is clear and unambiguous—no hitting allowed—and there is no danger of incurring any of the risks found to correlate with the practically infinite number of ways in which a child may be assaulted. The defenders of corporal punishment of children in Canada and elsewhere have therefore failed to provide any moral or rational justification for the practice.

8

• • • • • • • • • • •

Corporal Punishment and Special

Defences in the Law

I t is time to consider the moral issues surrounding corporal punishment in terms of their legal realities and implications for
Canadians. Moral and legal philosophers have spilled a lot of ink
exploring the relationship between the shoulds and should nots of
morality and the musts and must nots of law. For the sake of my discussion of the legal issues surrounding corporal punishment, I assume
there is some relationship between the two but that it does not clearly
privilege one over the other. Historically, the question of this relationship has evolved within a debate which opposes those who think that
morality is the final authority when it comes to rules of conduct and
those who think that codified law is. More recently, the terms of this
debate have shifted to admit the position that a need for an absolute
ranking of the two is unnecessarily divisive. In what follows, I presume
this more recent view. While the recommendations of morality may
indeed determine the creation of law, once law is created, it assumes an

Notes to chapter 8 are on pp. 277–81.

authority which morality—even philosophical morality—must acknowledge. In practice this means we all should obey the law even if we come to believe that a particular one violates our moral principles.

Now, having said this, it is important to note that there is nothing stopping the creators of law from building safeguards and mechanisms into it which leave room for changing or repealing laws as legislators or the will of the people see fit. Such devices are, however, normally installed in a way which requires considerable consensus and the observation of onerous procedures so that their use does not compromise either the rule of law or the democratic process. In Canadian society, there are two well-known ways in which the law may be decisively altered: through new legislation and through Supreme Court rulings. Citizens have important roles to play in either case. We may lobby our representatives to enact new laws or alter or repeal existing ones or we may decide to elect a political party which has promised to make the changes we desire. If they do not, we may vote it out of office next time round, sending a clear message to the one that takes its place. On the other hand, we may, either individually or collectively, launch or participate in a court case challenging a particular existing law, leaving it to Canada's highest legal authorities to decide whether it is, indeed, valid. In the case of Section 43 of the Canadian Criminal Code, such a challenge was made in 1999 by an Ontario group called the Canadian Foundation for Children, Youth and the Law to the Ontario Superior Court. That challenge was unsuccessful and a case was prepared appealing the Ontario court's decision to uphold Section 43 to the Ontario Court of Appeal. More will be said on the prospects for a Supreme Court case in light of the Ontario decision in chapter 9.

Whether we lobby our political representatives or take more formal legal action, our motivation may be strictly moral. We think a particular law demands something of some or all Canadians which violates what we may regard as our moral rights. But while political representatives may be directly influenced by such appeals, our judges must take great care in how they are admitted for legal consideration. In order to influence the Supreme Court, a moral entreaty against an existing law must find a black letter partner in The Canadian Charter of Rights and Freedoms. For it is only those moral values which have been enshrined in the Charter which properly guide the Court's decisions. Whether efforts to change a law are better directed at Parliament or the courts, when people organize themselves around such causes, they often target both.

As we will see in what follows, while morality takes a back seat to the rule of law when the courts are involved, pursuing a legal challenge to the Supreme Court of Canada does not quite mean leaving morality out of the picture. This is because the Charter of Rights and Freedoms contains a special device which permits the Court to consider moral questions when deciding on the constitutionality of individual laws. That device is found in Section 1 of the Charter and leaves open the possibility that some laws, even though their application violates the rights and freedoms of some individuals, may nevertheless be constitutionally acceptable.

In the present context, the discussion need not concern itself with the enactment of new law — something that only elected governments are duly authorized by the people to do. Rather, I am concerned with an existing provision in the Criminal Code of Canada, namely Section 43, and so one which either our political representatives or the courts may assess. The government could repeal the law if it saw fit to do so; if the Supreme Court found the law offended the Charter, it would be declared null and void. One way or the other, I argue the law in question should go.

While the state is obliged to enact positive law and policy in a way which enables Canadian citizens to understand and comply with such changes, the state must also take a leadership role in areas of common interest where existing law is concerned.[1] Changes to Canadian law and policy on matters such as capital punishment, gun control and tobacco advertising have been implemented on the basis of expert evidence and advice and a sense of impending rather than existing attitudinal change. Expert evidence and advice has long called upon the government to repeal Section 43 of the Criminal Code which provides a special "justificatory" defence against the charge of assault for defendants who stand in relation to their child victim or victims as parents, teachers or persons standing in the place of parents. These calls have been attacked in turn by individuals and groups representing a variety of "family values." So far, the government has declined to act, implicitly aligning itself with the pro-corporal punishment side of the

debate.[2] Apparently, it senses no attitudinal change on the horizon. Nor
does it seem to appreciate the deep legal tensions which the presence
of Section 43 gives rise to in the context of Canadian law as a whole.

Perhaps there is no impending attitudinal change. However, if one
takes the long view of changes which have already taken place in
Canadian law, this view seems untenable. What those changes point to
is a tendency to find fewer and fewer groups of people appropriately
subject to corporal punishment. They also point to a lower threshold of
tolerance when it comes to the severity of the corporal punishment of
children. One might then try to argue that the deep legal tensions produced by the presence of Section 43 are simply the price we have to pay
for the fact that human beings are not born well-behaved. I have
argued that while certain developmental differences between adults
and children make certain differences in how we treat them necessary,
this fact does not justify corporal punishment. As such, the matter of
whether the corporal punishment of children should be legally justified is one which ought to be fully examined in the light of public and
political discussion and judicial evaluation if necessary.

In this chapter, I present and comment on the legal substance of
Section 43 of the Canadian Criminal Code. This discussion is broken
down into three sections: the first is on the general question of rights
and privileges as it pertains to the legal effect of Section 43, the second
is on the context and nature of common-law and special defences in the
law, in particular special defences for "persons in authority" and the
third offers a philosophical critique of Section 43. In the next chapter, I
discuss, failing such a legislative repeal, what might happen in the face
of a Supreme Court challenge to it. I conclude that there are sufficient
grounds for a Supreme Court of Canada declaration that Section 43 is
unconstitutional.

The Legal Substance of Section 43

Rights and Privileges

Section 43 states that any parent, teacher or person standing in the
place of a parent is justified in using physical force as a means of correction of a child or student as long as the force used is reasonable
under the circumstances. As such, it only justifies the use of physical

force by parents and teachers against children when the purpose of using it is improving children's behaviour or character. According to the equality guarantee in Section 15 of the Charter and the rights guarantee in Section 7, all Canadians have a right to security of the person — a right which can only be limited when the fundamental principles of justice require it. All criminal law must be consistent with Charter provisions since the latter is a more authoritative legal document. Nevertheless, arguments proceed too quickly when they conclude that Section 43 is invalid because it violates Sections 7 and 15 of the Charter.

It may be argued that when charged with assault, the successful use by a parent or teacher of a Section 43 defence has harmful effects on children and further that its use is immoral since its net effect on society is to endorse violence against those who cannot defend themselves. A successful use of Section 43 legitimizes the assault in question and so increases the likelihood that assaults on the victims will continue and perhaps intensify. And as a public exoneration and prescription, the presence and successful use of Section 43 helps perpetuate a moral, social and political environment of sanctioned violence in which the corporal punishment of children, regarded as the best way of or last resort for disciplining them, is merely one aspect of an alarmingly dangerous world. But it does not follow from the fact of being implicated in such harms nor even from the fact it violates children's rights that Section 43 is unconstitutional, since these are consequences which are sometimes accepted as the cost of fundamental justice.

To see the tension caused by the coincident presence of Section 43 and various provisions of the Charter more clearly, the philosophical distinction between a right and a privilege needs to be introduced. Parents, it may be said, possess a common-law right to claim and raise their children as their own. This right is, however, conditional. For the state may take your children away from you if it satisfies a court of law that you are an unfit parent. It is generally assumed, however, that this right implies parents are entitled to use considerable discretion in the upbringing of their children. Without such discretion, the value of multiculturalism, for example, would be unrealizable. Included within this notion of parental discretion is the leeway to discipline children in ways which comport with individual parental values and attitudes. In this way, it might be argued, though at a stretch, where parental values and attitudes are pro-corporal punishment, parents are legally entitled to use this form of discipline in raising their children.

In stating the tension as such, we appear to have a conflict of legal rights: the legal right of parents to discipline their children as they see fit versus the legal right of children to security of the person. It is presumed that the state must protect all of its citizens in the possession of their legal rights. Yet here, the state cannot do this consistently. So far and in this case, the state has chosen to protect what it considers the rights of parents over those of children. But the view that the tension between parental and children's rights must be resolved in favour of parents is seriously undermined by the fact that parental legal rights are not actually involved in this conflict. The logical stretch described above from a limited common-law right to raise their own children to a legal right to use violence against them as a means of correction is an extreme and ultimately unwarranted one.

We live in a society which considers the basic good of security of the person a "super" value and which repudiates the expression of all values which call for or ignore its violation. We express this repudiation through countless interdictions in law against acting either publicly or privately on values which require or involve harming others or interfering with their interest in personal security. Someone may, for example, value the warrior virtues and feel it a matter of honour to violently avenge even verbal attacks. While anyone is free to hold this value, assault law prohibits its practical expression. Citizens who are parents and teachers, however, are treated differently from other Canadians when it comes to the manner in which their assaults on their children or students are judged. Assaults are permitted provided the harm is reasonable and occurs to one's child or pupil as a means of correction. So while the general rule is that no value provides a legitimate reason for assault, the value of correction in the limited case of parents and teachers stands as an exception to that rule. What Section 43 does for parents and teachers therefore, is release the general "harm" limit on the expression of values which restricts the behaviour of all other persons not connected in either of these ways to children. Having released the general limit, Section 43 puts in its place a special limit whereby only those harms which result from reasonable parental or teacher discipline are permitted. This exception to the general harm limit clearly rests on the presumed instrumental importance of physical pain in the education of children. Section 43 therefore confers a legal privilege on Canadian parents and teachers which the general population does not have. Wesley Newcomb Hohfeld has argued that a privilege "is one's freedom from the right or claim of another."[3] As a privilege, the permission for parents and teachers to hit children for the purpose of their education logically implies that children indeed have a legal right which is limited in this special case not to be hit even for this purpose.

The distinction here between a right and a privilege is crucial for the argument that Section 43 ought to be declared legally invalid. Section 43 does not create a conflict between the legal rights of parents and the legal rights of children. As such, this is not a contest between two equally strong prior legal entitlements to be decided upon the consequences of failing to protect one or the other. Instead, Section 43 creates a conflict between a privilege and a right. Privileges are legally weaker than rights and are normally granted on utilitarian grounds. The state finds that the common good will be better served in particular cases if the protection of the right in question is traded off for the privilege of violating it. So long as that finding is empirically justified, the privilege may stand. But should such justification be lacking, the right must prevail. In the absence of empirical evidence supporting the maintenance of the privilege and given empirical evidence that the use of corporal punishment is counterproductive, the right of children to security of the person ought to prevail in law.

It may be objected, however, that the legal privilege to hit their children is not weak at all since it is derived from parents' "natural right" to do with their children as they see fit, and as such enjoys the weight of a legal right. We have seen a little bit of the historical basis for such claims in chapter 2 as well as in much of what Dr. James Dobson offers in defence of corporal punishment. But we have also seen John Stuart Mill's response to such claims. In short, Mill rejects appeals to so-called natural rights as grounds for political or legal rights. His rejection of natural rights as such grounds is based on the claim that political and legal rights must be acknowledged as binding on all who fall under them while "natural rights," due to reasonable controversy surrounding their authority, cannot be. In spite of the legal history of the privilege to corporally punish children, it cannot be argued today that it derives its authority from a natural right. As such, it may not be legally fortified by the strength natural rights enjoy in the minds of those who uphold them.

If one disagrees with the separation of natural and conventional law implied by this response, then one would have no easy grounds for objecting to a weighty legal privilege for husbands to hit their wives or even whites to enslave blacks. One could counterargue that there is in fact no natural right of husbands to hit their wives, for example, but then this claim would have to be justified to those who disagree and it is far from clear how this debate would be settled without appealing to something which is not a natural right. It is for these reasons, among others, that the separation between natural and conventional law is now generally upheld in the legal systems of multicultural states.

In what follows, I analyse the meaning of Section 43 in detail. Having argued that there is no moral warrant for the corporal punishment of children, I now argue that there is no legal one for the privilege of using it.

Legal Defences in Context

Once again, Section 43 of the Canadian Criminal Code states that:

> Every schoolteacher, parent or person standing in the place of a parent is justified in using force by way of correction toward a pupil or a child, as the case may be, who is under his [*sic*] care, if the force does not exceed what is reasonable under the circumstances.

Two aspects of the law as it is stated require our attention. First, the phrase "force by way of correction" needs some explanation. Traditionally, the term "correction" used in legal theorizing simply meant physical chastisement or hitting as punishment. In the eighteenth and nineteenth century, *Blackstone's Commentaries on the Laws of England* stated that a father "may also delegate part of his paternal authority, during his life, to the tutor or schoolmaster of his child; who is then *in loco parentis*, and has such a portion of the power of the parent committed to his charge, viz. that of restraint *and* correction, as may be necessary to answer the purpose for which he is employed."[4] Clearly, two types of discipline are distinguished here. The first is restraint, which I have argued is the only sort which can be morally justified though it is not always justified. The second is correction. In lawyer James Boswell's 1791 biography of Samuel Johnson, the author reports that on being questioned concerning the matter of cruelty towards children, Johnson responded that "No instrument of correction is more proper than any other, but as it is adapted to produce present pain without lasting mischief."[5] Clearly, the term correction was a euphemism for hitting as punishment.

The phrase "force by way of correction" meant "force by way of hitting as punishment" and was clearly intended to address this particular form of chastisement and distinguish it from all other forms as standing in need of explicit justification under the law. It also distinguishes what we have come to call "corporal punishment" (this is our euphemism for hitting as punishment) from all other uses of force, be they specially protected elsewhere in the law or not. While general usage of the term "correction" has lost this exclusive emphasis, that emphasis is key to understanding what continues to be the practical purpose of Section 43. In order to stay focused on that practical purpose, I assume, in what follows, the traditional connotation of correction according to which merely restraining actions are excluded.

The second matter which calls for attention is also raised by *Blackstone's Commentaries*. Traditionally, the authority of teachers and other nonparental caregivers to correct pupils derived from the natural right of parents to chastise their children in this way. That is, if a teacher had permission to correct children, this was only because it was tacitly or explicitly given them by a parent. This delegating relationship left it open to any parent to refuse to give the permission in which case, a teacher would not be legally protected if he or she corrected that parent's child. Section 43, while in most senses very much in line with legal tradition, subverts the legal ability of the parent to refuse such permission to teachers and other nonparental caregivers by giving the authority to corporally punish children directly to caregiving nonparents. Even if a parent does not want his or her child to be corporally punished by teachers, teachers are legally protected in doing so. Section 43 therefore leaves it open to courts to interpret the teacher's privilege to correct as intrinsic to the teacher-pupil relationship rather than as derived from the parent-child relationship. However suspect the natural parent privilege to correct or corporally punish children is, surely a natural teacher privilege to do so is even more suspect. If the authority of Section 43 is indeed based in legal tradition on the privilege of parents to discipline their children, then its subversion of one of the mainstays of legal thought on this matter—the derived nature of the teacher's privilege to correct students—casts a shadow on that authority. As we will see later, the Law Reform Commission of Canada has noted this feature of Section 43 and found it problematic.

When considering the legal effect of Section 43, it is important to see that it is not a "Thou shalt not" criminal provision but rather a *defense* against the "Thou shalt not" charge of assault or assault with a weapon. In spite of its implications, its specific purpose is protective rather than prescriptive. Whenever someone is charged with an offence, it must be possible to mount a defence on his or her behalf. Otherwise, the charge itself would constitute a conviction and for very good reasons, our system of justice does not run this way. You may of course defend yourself by claiming that "it wasn't me." But often, that option is not open. Defences in the law acknowledge the force of extenuating circumstances surrounding the commission of otherwise unlawful acts. For the most part, they speak directly to the mental element of criminal liability by granting that certain states of mind make complying with the law as it stands too much too ask or impossible. In some situations, the law allows that complying with a particular rule can even be wrong. There are three groups of common-law defences which persons who "did it" can use at trial to try to avoid conviction. These are the defences of necessity, excuse and justification. I will discuss each of these below. These defences are discussed in the General Part as well as under specific sections in subsequent parts of the Canadian Criminal Code.[6] Common law, which includes the reasoning of the judiciary on each defence, lays out their meaning in greater detail.

There are some defences, however, which are specified in the main body of the Criminal Code. These are known as "special defences." While a special defence may be categorized as one or another common-law defence, it is distinguished from common-law defences in that its availability is much more restricted. The "specialness" of a special defence refers to the fact that not just anyone who finds themselves accused of a particular crime can avail themselves of the shield against criminal liability the special defence affords. Most special defences in the law assume that when certain relationships hold between a victim and a defendant, otherwise clearly unlawful acts may not, in fact, be unlawful. Special defences may therefore be said to confer legal privileges on persons in certain roles or relationships.

Section 43 appears in that part of the Criminal Code which deals with the special circumstances of persons in authority. Three groups of such persons are referred to under three separate provisions: "Every schoolteacher, parent or person standing in the place of a parent" (Section 43), "the master or officer in command of a vessel on a voyage" (Section 44) and "everyone…performing a surgical operation upon any person for the benefit of that person" (Section 45). It is therefore granted in law that certain acts which may cause serious harm to individuals and which, because of this, must be made illegal, should be allowed when the actors are individuals with a grave responsibility to protect the greater good of all those for whom they are responsible. The presence of these three special defences for persons in authority is a clear sign of a utilitarian moral theory at work where what is morally called for is that act or policy which will promote the greatest good for the greatest number. For here, we have the implication that while there is no doubt the acts in question may result in serious harm to individuals, that harm is outweighed by the greater good.

In the background of this brief discussion of the Criminal Code context in which Section 43 appears are the three general categories of defence alluded to earlier: necessity, excuse and justification. The law is not entirely blind or insensitive to the vicissitudes of life. Occasionally, these vicissitudes may become exigencies which, however rarely, may compel reasonable persons to act in ways which violate this or that criminal law. The most familiar example of the circumstances of necessity is the pilot attempting to crash-land a malfunctioning aircraft in an area where she must, for example, either crash the plane in a crowded schoolyard or in a used car lot. Either way, serious damage is likely but she must do one or the other. That is, she has no choice but to risk breaking the law: on the one hand the law against killing innocent persons or on the other, the law against damage to private property.[7]

While it is unlikely that a pilot who crashed in the car lot and survived would be charged with anything in this dramatic example of a necessary but destructive act, there are cases in which charges would likely be laid. It may be less than clear from an objective point of view that the agent had no other choice but to break the law (what about the empty field?) or less than clear that the agent chose the right the law to break (she decides to crash land in the schoolyard). In such cases, a defendant might still try to prove his or her innocence on the grounds of necessity. The defence of necessity is also available to anyone who has chosen, in an emergency situation, to save his or her own life at the cost of another's so long as he or she reasonably saw these as the only options.[8]

The doctrine of necessity points to our utilitarian moral sensibilities regarding emergency situations in which one must choose between the greater and the lesser harm.[9] In cases where the defence of necessity is invoked, certain circumstances must be shown to have held at the time of the act in question. If they can be shown and cannot be placed into doubt by the Crown, then the defence will be successful. The definition of such circumstances found in case law is formal and a wide variety of particular circumstances may satisfy it. Also, the defence is available to anyone who thinks they can satisfy its conditions — that is regardless of their relationship to the victim or victims of the consequent harm.

In addition to circumstances of necessity, the law recognizes that due to something about the physical or mental state of a person who acts in an otherwise criminally harmful way, it would be useless if not of greater harm to convict that person of a crime. In this case, the law allows for a variety of "excuse" defences.[10] The defence of excuse is normally used to defeat the court's presumption that the defendant was mentally fit at the time of the offence. To be found guilty of most crimes, the Crown must show that when he or she acted, the defendant satisfied the requisite mental element of the charge in question. For example, to be convicted of "personation"[11] the Crown must demonstrate that the accused intentionally impersonated someone else for the purpose of fraud. If the defence can show instead that the defendant could not have formed the requisite intent due to some form of mental defect (for example, due to mental imbalance at the time, the defendant believed he or she was the person), he or she may be found not guilty of this crime. If such a defence is successful, the defendant is excused from criminal liability for the act. What is crucial about the defence of excuse is that even if successful, the law still regards the act in question as wrong. Suppose that by the numbers, more and people come to be let off on excusatory grounds for manslaughter. While this might be reason to study the water supply or human genome, it would in no way be seen as grounds for rethinking the immorality or criminality of the offence of manslaughter.

Finally, the defence of "justification" proposes to the Court that while the offence in question was committed by the defendant and with the requisite mental element, the defendant acted rightly under the circumstances. Since the action was a right action, it logically follows that the defendant was justified in doing what he or she did. The Law Reform Commission states, for example, that "whatever is authorized by law must also be justified and any force needed to do it must be justified as well—otherwise the law speaks with two voices."[12] Self-defence is treated as a defence of justification as is "defense of property" and "advancement of justice."[13] The Commission argues that the need to defend our property "comes close to the right of self-defense."[14] Here we have the familiar cat burglar scenario where I am justified in using force against an intruder in my home even if I am sure that he does not mean to harm me. The "advancement of justice" is a justification for the use of force which is typically used by peace officers acting in the line of duty—where "the accused may have actually been promoting a value recognized by law."[15] Presumably that value would rightly have greater weight in the court's eyes than any value accorded to the victim's security of person in the circumstances. So, for example, a police officer who pushes a suspect to the ground to prevent him or her from escaping lawful arrest would be justified in doing so on the grounds that the harm to the community should the suspect escape is greater than that to the suspect from injury in the fall.

Section 43: Criticism

In concert with these common-law defences as they are laid out in The General Part and developed in case law are, as I noted above, special defences laid out in the body of the Criminal Code itself. In particular, the Criminal Code provides special defences against criminal charges

when the defendant is "a person in authority" though not a peace officer. Sections 43, 44, and 45 of the Code afford special protection from
criminal liability to parents, teachers, persons standing in the place of
parents (S.43), captains of vessels (S.44) and surgeons (S.45) when their
actions interfere with individuals in ways which would otherwise constitute criminal assault. In the case of Sections 43 and 44, the defence is
clearly one of justification. Section 45 does not make the ground of the
defence clear stating only that as long as a number of conditions are met,
the surgeon is to be considered "free from liability."[16] Their language
strongly suggests that each provision does in fact confer a privilege on
persons who stand in the designated relationship to the victim. As such,
not just anyone who strikes a misbehaving child with an electrical cord,
a mutinous sailor with a yardarm or cuts open a woman in labour distress may claim in their defence that they were justified in doing so.

As a special justificatory defence, we may presume that the presence of Section 43 follows from the fundamental principle of justice
that "whatever is authorized by law must also be justified and any
force needed to do it must be justified as well."[17] In the background of
Section 43 is the educational relationship of the caregiving adult-child
situation — a relationship which is authorized by law and which explicitly allows that where correction or hitting as punishment is reasonable
and needed to maintain that relationship, the person doing the hitting
is to be protected against conviction.

I grant that the educative purpose, among others, of the caregiving
adult-child relationship is rightly acknowledged by the law. And were
the use of correction or hitting as punishment in fact required for that
purpose, hitting in this case would also be legally justified. Section 43
assumes that hitting as punishment is often or at least sometimes necessary to educate children. And behind this assumption is the identification of caregiving adults with police officers and ship captains as
well as children with adult criminals and sailors. This assumption is
simply false and elides the important distinction between the educational training role of parents and teachers, and the law and order
enforcement role of police and naval officers — a distinction which even
Plato implied was necessary in his ideal society. For it must be noted
that in 1972, the Canadian Criminal Code was amended to remove this
protection for Correctional Officers (the designation is now anachro-

nistic) the effect of which was the cessation of all officially sanctioned corporal punishment of inmates in Canadian penal institutions. This change in the law expressed the belief that hitting, while it might occasionally be required to enforce law and order, was not an acceptable means of improving behaviour or character.

It may be argued that Section 43 is meant to function when and only when child care circumstances become just like the circumstances a police officer faces when arresting a dangerous suspect or a ship captain faces in case of a mutinous crew or life-threatening storm at sea.[18] As such, even if it could be shown that Section 43 logically entails the violation of the security of person rights of children and grants that ultimately, the use of hitting is never educative, this would not show that it was not legally justified.

The parent or teacher as peace officer or ship's captain may, in this case, argue that he or she is justified in the use force in the advancement of justice. But in this case, the parent or teacher would nevertheless be subject to the same restrictions in the use of such force as actual peace officers and ship's captains are. I will not rehearse those restrictions here.[19] Suffice it to say that the general rule is that no more force than is necessary to prevent escape or injury to others may be used. In any case, the rationale behind Section 43 as a special defence for parents and other childcare givers who assault children in the course of educating them collapses. At best, this response indicates that parents and teachers ought to be explicitly included in the category of persons who are protected by the advancement of justice defence against assault.

In this case, we would have to ask ourselves, as a society, whether we want the legal authority of individual childcare givers over children to convert to authority on par with that of recognized police or military authorities. The permission given to police officers, especially, is a moral compromise which we make reluctantly and execute very carefully. Police officers, since they have this privilege, are painstakingly selected and highly trained and supervised. If one really wants to defend the parental use of corporal punishment on the same sorts of grounds the use of violent interference by the police is justified, then it is time to start handpicking parents and subjecting them to routine investigation, report writing, and ongoing training.[20] Until such time these measures are in place, the advancement of justice justification for retaining the legal corporal punishment of children is simply not available.

The government has not been altogether uninterested in the legal tensions surrounding Section 43. In its 1982 report on defences, the Law Reform Commission concluded that due to a lack of consensus on the matter of corporal punishment, the Section 43 special defence should not be repealed.[21] Two years later in 1984, however, another group of commissioners was somewhat more circumspect in its conclusions. The 1985 working paper "Assault" began by assuming, for the sake of argument, that an analogy between the state and families supported the retention of Section 43. Since the "state must have the right to use force as the ultimate sanction to enforce its laws…parents must be legally entitled to similar power to buttress their authority and must be entitled, in addition, to authorize teachers and others [sic] to use force for lawful correction."[22]

From this analogical premise, the Law Reform Commission proceeded to critically analyze the case of corporal punishment. It determined that on the basis of the analogy with state power to use force, parents were entitled to use it in emergency situations only. However, the Commission concluded that since the use of force in emergency situations is already legally protected under the general defence of necessity, no special defence was needed to protect it.

As it stands, however, Section 43 protects something else — namely the use of force in the case of "chastisement" which the Commission admitted was a "controversial issue."[23] In any case, the Commission noted that the analogy between state and parental authority breaks down here and so cannot be used to justify Section 43 as it stands. As such, some other justification must be sought. The Commission then considered the cases for and against the legal sanctioning of corporal punishment of children. On the "against" side, the Commission noted these, by now familiar, arguments: "wrongly institutionalizing violence," "archaic reflection of parental right," "contributing to the serious problem of child abuse" and "blurring the basic message of the law that violence is off limits."[24] On the "for" side, the Commission also listed familiar arguments: "spanking is widely accepted," "removing this right would constitute unwar-

ranted interference with family privacy" and "[corporal punishment]
is a necessary disciplinary measure of last resort…[it] is a traditional
and practical system."[25]

The Commission then noted that the "ultimate question is whether
corporal punishment is even necessary"[26] and provisionally concluded
that since the use of force outside of emergency situations is "less easy
to justify"[27] that "the rule in Criminal Code Section 43 should be abol-
ished."[28] However, when considering the practicality of its abolition,
the Commission hesitated. As far as teachers were concerned, it was of
one mind. "In our opinion, therefore, section 43 should be repealed as
a defense of teachers."[29] But when it came to parents, a majority concluded that a special privilege for parents to use corporal punishment
against their children ought to be retained in law. The Commission
considered the matter in terms of worse outcomes. The majority was
not persuaded that "prosecutorial discretion" would avoid "wheeling
the engines of law enforcement into the privacy of the home for every
trivial slap or spanking."[30] The Commission took such "wheeling" to
be a worse outcome for children than being slapped or spanked or, of
course, worse when we take what case law under Section 43 allows. To
its credit, the report included the views of a minority of commissioners
that such a weighting preference is anathemic to the principles of justice observed everywhere else in Canadian law. For this minority,
"experience suggests that there is probably too much, not too little,
institutional tolerance towards domestic situations, and it is doubtful
that a special exception in the Criminal Code is required to protect families against over-zealous enforcement."[31]

In the end, the Law Reform Commission appeared philosophical
about the implications of retaining Section 43 protection for parents.

> The singling out of children, whether on the basis of age or a
> relationship of dependency, raises concerns about how far the
> State may go to deprive individuals of their "security of the
> person," and whether those embraced by the exception would
> enjoy the "equal protection" of the Canadian criminal law. The
> language and spirit of the CCRF [Charter] is not without rele-
> vance to this issue, forcing each of us to examine our own view
> of what can be "demonstrably justified in a free and democratic
> society." In the end, this has a great deal to with moral choices
> about how children should be treated in our society.[32]

In short, while the Commission saw in 1984 that there were no *legal* grounds for the retention of any part of Section 43, it decided that there were moral ones for retaining some part of it. Since removing Section 43 allowed for the remote possibility of a parent being approached or charged by police for a administering a "trivial slap or spanking" and the even more remote possibility of being convicted for assault under such circumstances, the protection it afforded parents must be retained. The possible harm to an adult caused by overzealous police interference in the home was believed to be so much worse than the actual harm to children from being hit that the latter harm was regarded as the price to be paid to avoid the former. I have argued that such beliefs, since they are based on a number of false or incoherent theories about children and adults and do not take into account empirical evidence concerning the harms to children which corporal punishment invites, are without rational merit.

The explicit consideration at work in the Commission's reluctance to recommend wholesale repeal is the worry over what Barbara Amiel called "family statism." Such worries are also without rational basis. Amiel and others use the standard and completely fallacious "icy slope" form of argument where one step on the way down the hill of state reach into families will precipitate an unbreakable skid into Plato's Republic, Big Brother and the destruction of democracy. What such arguments typically ignore are the many factors operating within society and law to "grade and sand" the road. If we focus on the issue at hand instead of imagining what could logically happen, we see very clearly that prohibiting the inclusion of corporal punishment in their child discipline repertoire need not come into conflict with the entitlement of parents to a great deal of privacy and discretion in this regard.[33]

It is also worth noting that many of those who use the family statism argument in support of Section 43 also appeal to the analogy between the state and the family cited by the Law Reform Commission. As we saw in the latter case, for the analogy to work, we must hold parents to the same standards of professional conduct to which we hold officers of the state and do so in the same way. The training, certification and surveillance of all parents as well as the requirement for detailed reporting of all incidents would be comprehensive and ongoing and therefore far more intrusive than what is implied by the repeal of Section 43. Even David Archard's modest collectivism does not go this far, relying instead on incorporating parent education into the regular school system and for monitoring, on already existing local community health clinics. Also, as I noted earlier, according to Section 43, the state directly authorizes teachers and other nonparental care-givers to corporally punish children. It therefore sidesteps parental authority and ought to cause great concern to those who worry about family statism.

The Commission's argument for retention of the parental privilege to assault rests upon the view that the probability of harm to parents arising from being called to account for hitting their children is greater than the probability of harm to children arising from their being hit and that, in case either sort of harm actually occurs, the harm to parents is worse than the harm to children. This view will be revisited in the concluding chapter. As the Commission states however, balancing these probabilities and harms naturally leads us to a consideration of how a constitutional analysis of Section 43 might go. While this section of the Criminal Code is in clear violation of certain Charter protections, it may be "saved" by the limit also found in the Charter on the extent to which the rights of individuals may be protected when such protection threatens our free and democratic society.[34] In the next chapter, the constitutionality of Section 43 will be examined in detail.

9

• • • • • • • • • • •

The Legal Challenge

for Section 43

The fact that Section 43 confers a legal privilege upon parents and teachers and neither establishes nor expresses a legal right for them to corporally punish their children ought to persuade the government that repealing Section 43 would not imply the Big Brother scenario which opponents of repeal are so fond of rehearsing. It would simply imply that empirical facts do not support the view that the common good is best served by extending that privilege. Repealing Section 43 in this case is simply a matter of adjusting law to fit the facts as they are currently seen by those experts charged with the responsibility of finding and interpreting them — something governments do all the time. As I noted earlier, however, the Government may not be so easily persuaded of these facts or of their obligation to make the indicated legislative changes. In the face of its continued resistance to act, we may have to conclude that the Government would prefer that the courts handle the matter. If this is what the Liberal and

Notes to chapter 9 are on pp. 281–82.

Conservative Governments have been up to, then they have wrongly put their political fortunes ahead of the welfare of Canadian children.

But again, perhaps the weight of this privilege is not so easily dismissed. It is true that its history is deeply rooted in natural law and the idea that parents have a natural right to "chastise" children in this manner. Samuel Johnson's view of the matter in 1772 was that "No severity is cruel which obstinacy makes necessary for the greatest cruelty would be, to desist, and leave the scholar too careless for instruction, and too much hardened for reproof...punishments, however severe, that produce no lasting evil, may be just and reasonable, because they may be necessary."[1] Johnson's reasoning was very much in keeping with the jurisprudence of the day—jurisprudence we have inherited. Blackstone, for example, notes that "The duties of children to their parents arise from a principle of natural justice and retribution. For to those who gave us existence, we naturally owe subjection and obedience during our minority, and honor and reverence ever after...."[2] It followed from this principle that the parent's "power" over the child was "sufficient to keep the child in order and obedience... [that] he may lawfully correct his child, being underage, in a reasonable manner."[3] But even here, the roots of the legal privilege in natural law were not regarded as sufficient for its justification, for the commentary continues, "for this is for the benefit of his education."[4]

While it is true that its questionable roots do not invalidate the legal privilege or power to corporally punish children, it is also true that they do not justify it. The history simply explains how the present law came to be. When it comes to such justifications *we* look at consequences to the common good and coherence with our fundamental legal principles as these are expressed in the Charter and elaborated in case law. The legal privilege to corporally punish children is therefore not allowed to derive legal strength from natural law and as I have attempted to show is contradicted by the facts and our fundamental principles of justice.

Given the tendency to reject the use of corporal punishment for other groups, why the lingering reluctance to reject its legal defensibility in the case of children? Perhaps other changes in the law have all along been enacted on the assumption that adults are not like children and so may not be treated in the way children must be in efforts to control their behaviour. I have argued at length that this assumption does not support the practice of corporal punishment. One may instead argue that the tide of change has not quite come in—that what I have suggested is a reluctance to extend the full right of security of the person to children is really just the last fraying thread of a soon-to-be dead and buried view. In this case, we must not overstate the maritime analogy—the tide of change will not come in on its own. In spite of his belief that he was expressing a principle of natural law, when Samuel Johnson said that "To impress this fear is…the duty of a parent; and has never been thought inconsistent with parental tenderness,"[5] he was at best reporting an unfortunate cultural norm. This same norm lurks behind the justificatory façade of Section 43 and appears to be informing the Government's resistance to legislative change.

Did the 1984 Law Reform Commission report "Assault" steer the Government away from such change when it gestured towards a constitutional analysis? Possibly. In what follows, we will examine some speculations on how such an analysis might go. I conclude there are grounds for a constitutional disqualification of Section 43.

A Constitutional Challenge

Sharon Greene has argued in "The Unconstitutionality of Section 43"[6] that it could not survive a constitutional challenge. Greene does an excellent job of running us through the questions which a Supreme Court would ask to make such a determination. These questions combine to form what is referred to in Canadian jurisprudence as the Oakes Test.[7] The Oakes Test is applied if and only if the court agrees that the law in question does violate a Charter right or freedom. As we have seen, such a violation is not enough to show that the law should be invalidated. Canada's Charter of Rights and Freedoms contains a provision in Section 1 for the constitutional validity of laws which violate certain individuals' rights or freedoms but which are also deemed "demonstrably justified in a free and democratic society." Whenever a law or policy or regulation is brought before the court because someone thinks it is unconstitutional, provided the court agrees it violates a Charter right or freedom, it must decide whether or not it is saved by Section 1. If the court finds in favour of the complainant or applicant, the law in question is thereby invalidated or declared "no law." How is the court to tell whether an offending law is saved by Section 1 of the Charter? The Oakes Test has been formulated in response to this question.

The Oakes Test is an analytical tool which the Supreme Court of Canada uses whenever it agrees that a certain law or rule violates an individual right or freedom. The test determines whether or not an offending law or "limit" on an individual right or freedom is a reasonable and acceptable one given the high value and particular scope we place as a society on the ability of all to act as free citizens in a democracy. As such, the imposition of this test implies that while individual rights and freedoms are of ultimate importance, since these can come into conflict, there may be circumstances in which the harms to some of having their rights or freedoms violated by a law is necessary to prevent the greater or more serious harm which would result to others in the absence of such a law. We must be careful not to read too much into this concession to circumstances, however. As we will see, the Oakes Test imposes a very tough standard of demonstration in this regard. Nevertheless, the mere presence of Section 1 of the Charter makes it clear that the law is partly informed by the utilitarian moral point of view. The Oakes Test is therefore concerned mainly though not exclusively with weighing the respective harms to persons caused by limits on their rights or freedoms against those of others and to cause as little harm overall as possible given the aim of preserving individual freedom in a democratic society and the assumption such freedom is necessary for human flourishing.

The test itself has two main parts, both of which must be passed in their entirety for the offending law to survive a challenge: the Valid Objective part and the Proportionality part. The Valid Objective part asks whether the purpose of the law in question is legitimate. A law whose purpose is to deny women access to public institutions, for example, would not pass the Valid Objective part of the test since, as a society, we no longer consider this aim consistent with those of freedom and democracy. However, it is possible for a law to have a legitimate purpose even if, as it is stated, the law is a bad one. For instance, it might be argued that Canada's old abortion law was struck down not because it had an illegitimate purpose (though, it might also be argued it did), but because the manner in which it sought to achieve that purpose—say, to protect women and unborn children from the dangers of incompetent or unscrupulous abortionists—violated the rights of women. Clearly, just how its purpose is identified is crucial to how a law will perform on this part of the test.

If an offending law passes the Valid Objective portion of the test, it is then subjected to the second part. The question then is whether the manner in which the law seeks to achieve that objective is also valid. The Proportionality part of the Oakes Test helps answer this question and has three stages in turn. First, given its objective, is the "limit" on individual rights or freedoms fair, rational and not arbitrary? Second, is the limit as minimal as can be given the law's purpose? And third, supposing that the law in question passes both this first and second stage of the Proportionality part, is the harm caused by the limiting law significantly less serious than the harm which would be caused without it?

As noted, the outcome of the second part depends very much on what is initially identified as the aim or purpose of the law in question. Greene identifies the aim of Section 43 as follows, "to keep children 'in order and obedience' and to correct children for the benefit of their education."[8] While I believe her conclusion that Section 43 should fail the Oakes Test is right, I am not convinced that this is the actual aim of Section 43. Greene notes that this aim is often quoted in Section 43 judgements and rightly argues that it stands in the background according to the tradition of British common law which informs it. But as I have demonstrated, Section 43 is first and foremost a defence. As such, while its ultimate purpose may be to ensure the civilization of children, its specific aim is to protect those whose prima facie criminal behaviour falls under its purview.

More to the point then, it may be argued that the aim of Section 43 is to provide a sphere safe from criminal penalty for parents, teachers and persons standing in the place of parents who correct children in the course of fulfilling their legal duty to provide for children's "necessaries" and education. We ought to understand the meaning of "correct" here in the traditional "hitting as punishment" sense I noted earlier. As such, Section 43 justifies caregiver assault against children in special circumstances. It therefore provides a privileged sphere for parents, teachers or persons standing in the place of parents where they may use assault under circumstances which would not ordinarily defeat criminal responsibility.

As stated, Section 43 gives certain persons extra protection from legal sanction. Is this objective constitutional? This is an extremely complicated issue. First, the purpose of Section 43 draws a suspect distinction between adults as childcare givers and these same adults relative to children for whom they are not directly responsible. Adults have the same duty of non-interference towards children not in their care — regardless of how "badly" they are behaving — that they have towards other adults. Relative to children in their care, however, these same adults may breach this duty regardless of how minor the misbehaviour. Second, the purpose of Section 43 distinguishes all adult citizens from all child citizens. The courts have clearly stated that adults caring for other adults (the mentally handicapped, for example) may not violate their bodily security in the course of providing for or educating them and, as such, may not use a Section 43 defence if they do. We must conclude that it is not their size, age, experience, independence or greater knowledge which qualifies caregiving adults for this defence. And so its purpose has no obvious connection to ensuring the welfare of those in society who need adult care. I suspect that it has to do with something like the anachronistic status of adult childcare givers as "property owners" (children, along with wives, were once considered legal chattel). But I confess that beyond this, I am unable to make more sense of Section 43's purpose. Perhaps the Government in defending its law could come up with a better explanation but I am skeptical that it could offer anything which would not offend the court. In short, the specific defensive purpose of Section 43 is either incoherent or in serious violation of the principles of freedom and democracy which inform our Charter.

Let us assume, however, that the Supreme Court takes a different view of this purpose and decides that it is legitimate. Will Section 43 pass the Proportionality part of the Oakes Test? There are three stages to this and all must be passed in their entirety.

First, given its purpose, is Section 43 a fair, rational and nonarbitrary limit on the rights or freedoms of children? This question asks if Section 43 makes sense to us as an effective way of achieving its objective. It is here where the difference between the aim of Section 43 as stated by Greene and its aim as I see it becomes crucial. Greene concludes that given the aim of teaching children discipline, Section 43 fails this stage of the Proportionality part of the Oakes Test. She argues, as I have throughout this book, that there is no evidence that permitting parents to corporally punish their children for bad behaviour is an effective way of improving it. In fact, there is continuous and consistent evidence to the contrary. But given the defensive purpose of Section 43, the law is clearly and not arbitrarily connected to its aim. If, generally speaking, the aim is to preserve parents, etc., from legal sanction for using disciplinary violence against their children, then allowing that the use of such violence is "justified" makes sense as a way of achieving that aim. I expect that if Section 43 passed the Valid Objective part of the Oakes Test as discussed above, it would pass this stage of the Proportionality part of the test as well.

Next, our attention turns from the interests of parents, etc., to those of the persons whose rights are violated by the presence of this law, namely children. In turning our attention to the interests of children, the Oakes Test now takes account of the overall consequences of Section 43's application.

Does Section 43 minimally impair the rights or freedoms of children? Here Greene is on target. Two considerations among others serve to show that it does not. The first is that given its wording, Section 43 is "impermissibly vague, resulting in an exceedingly low, variable, and arbitrary judicial threshold as to what is deemed acceptable force."[9] Its purpose and actual use imply and so allow the protection of parents, etc., who inflict a wide variety of injuries on their children or students for anything from not doing homework to talking back to hitting siblings. With this much room for interpretation, the law, Greene argues, fails to be adequately action-guiding. In addition to the problem of identifying when corporal punishment is legally defensible, is the problem with attempts to limit the sorts of corporal punishments permitted. Section 43 limits these to "reasonable" forms and as such refers to community standards on this question. The absence of any clear standards is problematic here as the discussion of David Benatar's efforts in chapter 7 illustrated.

Nevertheless, in the face of complaints as to its vagueness, in his 2001 decision, Justice McCombs of the Ontario Superior Court found that Section 43 did not fail in this regard. On the grounds that it specifically excluded all uses of force which were primarily motivated by anger, were aimed at instilling values which run contrary to what the community endorses and which could not reasonably be expected to succeed in teaching the victim a lesson (the child was too young or mentally handicapped), McCombs argued that Section 43 was not vague because "it is not so lacking in precision that it fails to provide sufficient guidance for legal debate or to provide an intelligible standard."[10] On the question of when corporal punishment is legally defensible, McCombs may be right. But on the more important question of what sorts are defensible, his reasoning is inadequate.

A second reason for arguing that Section 43 is not minimally impairing has to do with the fact that many other countries have successfully eliminated similar provisions from their Criminal Codes.[11] The experience of such countries surely counts as strong evidence that defences such as Section 43 are not required to cut parents a bit of legal slack in discharging their childcare duties.

Contrary to McCombs, I believe that Section 43's vagueness cannot be denied or, for that matter, eliminated with more precise wording. Its problematic vagueness centres on the notion of "reasonable force." This notion points to a relationship between the type of misbehaviour which calls for correction and the degree of force used to do the job. Excluding the cases which McCombs excludes, is the latter proportionate to the former? McCombs insists that the community must be consulted when answering this question. But in practice, the courts have often assessed reasonableness by asking whether the defendant believed that the force used was proportionate to the child's misbehaviour. Even if the belief was questionable in the view of such courts, they have, on occasion, decided that as long as an accused has a "completely honest and genuine belief that circumstances existed justifying the use of force in the context of the Code, s. 43 removes all or much of the culpability in the offense of assault."[12] Such decisions imply that as "impermissibly vague," the wording of Section 43 leaves it open to all courts to assess the force used for its sincerity and not for its reasonableness at all. We may be clear as a society about certain examples of what will count at one end, as reasonable or at the other end, as unreasonable discipline on a continuum between the two. But the gap between clearly reasonable and clearly unreasonable punishment on such a continuum is wide—too wide to give meaningful content to this law. Without an objective test for reasonable force (and it is doubtful one can be determined), the door is left open to over-reliance on the subjective point of view, leaving the children of unreasonable caregivers the most vulnerable to state-sanctioned violence.

In addition to being inadequately action-guiding for the courts, Section 43 is arguably vague in terms of its ability to inform Canadian parents about what it allows. Based on actual interpretations of the courts, Section 43's wording is not precise enough when it comes to what sorts of corporal punishment are allowed. In some cases where the term "reasonable" is used, more precision than an implicit reference to "community standards" is not required. But in this case, there are no clear standards beyond the worst cases of child abuse to refer to and, as I argued in chapter 7, proposals for such standards — for example, "two sharp slaps to the thigh" — are unlikely to succeed.

As long as the wording of Section 43 leaves it open to the courts to exculpate any parent, etc., who did not "abuse" his or her child, and who it accepts really believed his or her child deserved whatever they got, and as long as many other countries have found it possible to protect parents, etc., in the discharge of their disciplinary duties without this sort of special defence, Section 43 surely cannot be said to "minimally impair" the rights of children. Indeed, in practice, it holds those rights hostage to parental incompetence and the absence of community standards on so-called non-abusive physical punishment. Having arguably failed to satisfy a necessary condition of the Oakes Test, Section 43 is an invalid limit on the rights of children. But let us assume that somehow, once again, the court sees things differently and proceed to the final stage of the Proportionality part of the test.

Granting that, in any case, the rights violations to children are significant, are they significantly less serious than the harm which would be caused to parents etc., should Section 43 be removed from the Criminal Code? Here, things get pretty thorny. Should Section 43 pass the second stage of the Proportionality part of the Oakes Test, I assume it would be on the grounds that as it is stated, it does not sanction unreasonable violence against children — that what is "reasonable" are only those corrective punishments which involve things like spanking, slapping or rapping and pinching. The court may in fact take this view. In *R. v. Ogg-Moss*, and as quoted in Greene, the Supreme Court stated that "any section which authorizes otherwise illegal physical violence should be strictly construed against the actor" suggesting that "otherwise illegal violence" may be legal.[13] Further, in *R. v. Dupperon*, the Saskatchewan Court of Appeal stated that if a child's injuries were "life, limb or health" endangering or resulted in disfigurement, that Section 43 could not be applied.[14] The Supreme Court might therefore adopt a narrow reading of Section 43 where no violence resulting in any degree of physical injury would come under its protection. It may, on these grounds, conclude that Section 43 is indeed minimally impairing of children's rights, given the need to achieve its legitimate objective. It may dismiss the experiences of other countries as irrelevant to ours at the present time. If it proceeded with this view, the third "balance of harms" question would be whether harms caused by these purported narrowed limits on children's rights are less significant morally- and constitutionally-speaking than the harms to parents, etc., in the form of sanctions which might result from their conviction for assault if there were no Section 43. Put in this light, it is certainly less than clear that a court which has already determined that Section 43's objective is valid and that it minimally impairs the rights of children would conclude that children are worse off with the law than both they and their parents would be without it.

There are thus two places in the Oakes Test where Section 43 might fail. It might fail the Valid Objective part. I think it fails this part. But even if it passed the Valid Objective part, it might fail the test for "minimal impairment" under the Proportionality part. I think the case for failing this part is as strong as, if not stronger than, the case against passing the Valid Objective test. However, if it passed on both of these questions, I think it is highly unlikely that it would fail the Oakes Test. If Section 43 survives a constitutional challenge, then it seems to me this must be on the grounds that like the lower courts, the Supreme Court accepts the possibility of reasonable violence against children and finds that Section 43 is not vague when it comes to specifying what constitutes such reasonable violence. The deep legal entrenchment of this possibility would, I imagine, have large and harmful consequences to Canadian justice. But such an outcome would not preclude the possibility of Governmental legislative change. The ball, having been passed to the courts, would be tossed back, in this case, to Parliament.

The case presented here for Section 43's unconstitutionality rests primarily on the illegitimacy of its objective and its failure to be adequately action-guiding for both those that care for children directly and those who do so indirectly, namely the courts. For those who see the law as simply immoral, this legalistic argument for its rejection may sound somewhat hollow. Be that as it may, it is precisely this sort of argument by which the courts are persuaded in such cases. You will not find the courts striking down laws for the simple reason that many or even most people find them immoral. Nevertheless, when it comes to fine-grained interpretation of hazy areas in the law, the Supreme Court of Canada has in the past and can be expected to continue to appeal to sources outside the "four corners of the document"[15]–sources, for example, which represent authoritative empirical findings in the society which that law governs. It will find, in this case, that justifying the use of correction risks such serious harms to children and the society in which we all live that they cannot be outweighed by the benefit to their parents, etc., of being shielded from criminal sanction for using it.

Technically speaking, the legislative repeal or constitutional striking down of Section 43 would not bring any parental action to the interest of law enforcement which is not of interest to it now. Recall that Section 43 is a defence. Its existence assumes that a certain punitive act has already invited a criminal charge of assault which in turn implies the act has met a certain threshold test.[16] What Section 43 does is provide a handy shield against conviction in many such cases. That shield consists in the intention to improve behaviour or character. Removing Section 43 will therefore have the effect of making this intention no defence for assault. But as we have seen, there are other defences available to any person charged with assault. In this sense, the removal of Section 43 must be seen as a small step but only a step on the way to full prohibition of the corporal punishment of children. Only under full criminalization would convictions for light spanking be conceivable. Yet, as a step only, this approach to eliminating the corporal punishment of children need not end in its full criminalization. Other countries have used different legislative means for warning against its use. In the next chapter, we look at the worries of those who complain that repealing Section 43 would lead to an all-out attack on parents who are, after all, just trying to do their job.

10

· · · · · · · · · · ·

What About Spanking?

Corporal punishment is immoral. The tendency of its use to undermine rather than strengthen children's sense of personal security which is in turn required for leading happy, healthy lives not only fails to promote the greatest happiness for the greatest number, it contributes to promoting the reverse. The same empirical and moral reasoning I have used to reach this conclusion is at the bottom of the Charter right to security of the person. The extremely high value Canadians place on this right must be considered when the authority of existing law is at issue. Though Section 43 of the Criminal Code of Canada does not initially presume to comment on the morality of corporal punishment, it implies that it is a legally justified strategy for improving children's behaviour or character. If this is true, then corporal punishment must be the only way of protecting something we value even more than the security of the person of individual children—some value fundamental to a free and democratic society

Notes to chapter 10 are on pp. 282–88.

implicitly included under Section 1 of the Charter. Careful review of Section 43's history as law and of knowledge about the history of corporal punishment as a practice reveals that none of the possible candidates — social order or the security rights of most others for example — survives critical scrutiny as such a value.

Consequently, Section 43 is in sharp conflict with the Charter. Given that the Charter is the final arbiter of those values which we have agreed as a people may be expressed in our laws, Section 43 ought to be repealed. The grounds upon which such uses of violence have been morally justified in the past no longer have any rational or empirical warrant (if they ever did) and any existing legal justifications for the use of corporal punishment that might be proposed (for example, "the advancement of justice") do not in fact justify it as a means of discipline at all.

In the course of examining and criticizing arguments for the moral and legal acceptability of corporal punishment, I have glossed over a few worries which many parents express concerning the disciplining of their children. Does spanking count as the sort of punishment which would fall under what is morally condemned or legally prohibited here? If so, might parents who spank their children for the purpose of improving behaviour or character be breaking the law if Section 43 were removed from the Criminal Code? Will Canadians endorse criminal sanctions for offenders as the Italians have or will they, as the Swedes have done, adopt a more nurturing and educative approach to dealing with those who insist on hitting their children?

I have also claimed that Section 43 as it now stands does indeed imply that the use of corporal punishment is a justified means of improving children's behaviour or character. The wording of Section 43 is not explicit on this matter stating only that force is justified as long as it "does not exceed what is reasonable under the circumstances." There are other forms of force which parents and teachers typically use to discipline children: time-outs for instance. In what follows, I take up this second question first. While the law as it is stated does not specify that corporal punishment is justified as a means of "lawful correction," case law illustrates that the wording of Section 43 has been interpreted by the courts not only as covering it but also as designed with it in mind.

Once this has been shown, I move to the question of spanking. There are three aspects to this question which need attention. The first is the moral status of spanking in the context of harm. The second is the legal status of spanking in the context of assault. The third is the "policy" status of spanking in the context of our social and political commitment to the welfare of Canada's children and the importance of parental authority and discretion which may be said to follow from the liberal democratic value of personal autonomy. I conclude with a separate discussion of the special circumstances faced by teachers.

Section 43 and "Corporal Punishment"

As Section 43 is worded, there is no specific reference to "corporal punishment" as the sort of force protected from criminal sanction. Wording is important here, given the tendency of our courts to give legal priority to the written law. Were Section 43 challenged on the grounds that corporal punishment is not a constitutional means of improving children's behaviour or character, the court might note that while this may be true, the law as stated does not include corporal punishment and as such need not be declared invalid on these grounds.[1] As I noted earlier, there are other forceful means of improving children's behaviour which do not involve causing them pain. I have argued, for instance, that whenever you are close enough to hit a child, you are close enough to physically remove him or her from the scene of danger or hostility together with a "No" and ought to do so on moral grounds even if the child resists. I assume, but will not argue here, that throwing objects at children would not be protected under Section 43. Surely this sort of physical intervention is also a use of force and one which would rarely be permitted by law when the parties are both competent adults and the circumstances what they usually are when such action is reasonable in the case of children.

Perhaps, one might argue, it is only those types of force which do not involve hitting children that are protected by Section 43. While it may indeed be the case that these are the only sorts of forceful interventions that ought to be protected by Section 43 (and are already well protected under the general defences reviewed earlier), they are not, in fact, the ones which the law has been designed or used to justify. A few examples from Canadian case law between the years 1899 and 1992 should suffice to demonstrate that Section 43 is specifically intended to shield parents and teachers from criminal prosecution for hitting children with or without the use of a weapon.[2]

Canadian Case Law on Successful Use of Section 43

As it happens, between the years 1899 and 1992, the majority of cases where Section 43 was successfully used as a defence involved teachers and not parents. This is as expected. While no one may be around to protest or report a parental use of excessive corporal punishment whose concerns would be taken seriously by authorities, if a son or daughter comes home from school suffering from any obvious effects of being struck by a teacher or school official, a parent might just want to press charges.[3] Teachers, as I discuss below, are therefore more vulnerable than parents are to criminal investigation in these circumstances.[4] What does case law tell us about the meaning of Section 43? In what follows, I rely on lawyer Corinne Robertshaw's research for the Repeal 43 Committee.

In 1899, the Crown brought a charge of common assault against a school principal for strapping a fourteen-year-old boy on the hands with a leather strap for breaking the school steps. The principal was acquitted on appeal on the grounds that "any correction, however severe, which produces temporary pain and no permanent ill" is justified by law.[5] In 1910, a schoolteacher was charged with common assault for strapping a fourteen-year-old boy (who "refused to get his lessons up") across the shoulder when he refused to hold out his hands.[6] Also acquitted on appeal, the court found that this teacher did "what she was legally and morally bound to do." A school principal was acquitted on appeal for common assault in 1927 for a "strapping 'on that part of her anatomy...specifically designed for corporal punishment'" which "left bruises and welts."[7] In *R v. Corkum* ten years later,[8] a schoolteacher charged with common assault for strapping a ten-year-old boy "on both hands causing bruising and swelling" was also acquitted on appeal. These cases illustrate that while lower local courts were prepared to exclude these forms of corporal punishment from legal protection, higher courts with the "big picture" in view, held fast to what they perceived was the intent of the law on this matter.[9]

In addition to cases where Section 43 was used successfully (Robertshaw lists eighteen) were cases where its failure was nevertheless informative with respect to the intent of the law. Of the twelve cases in this category cited, four defendants were nevertheless absolutely discharged, two were conditionally discharged, one was given a suspended sentence, one fined $10 and another $400 with eighteen months probation[10] and three were given prison sentences (thirty days for a father; one year for a foster mother; one sentence of unknown length). In the $10 fine 1951 case, a school teacher, Mr. Campeau, was charged with common assault for knocking the hands of two boys—ages six and eight—against the back of a desk "dislocating the finger of the six-year-old and causing bruises and swelling to the eight-year-old" as well as repeatedly striking a nine-year-old boy on the "upper arm with a stick."[11] On the defence's appeal to Quebec Superior Court, the teacher was found guilty again and given a $10 fine. Judge Bissonette dissented from his appeal court colleagues' guilty decision, arguing, among other things, that: "The right of correction or corporal punishment is one of the attributes of paternal power and, like it, flows from natural law…[it "would be imposing extreme hardship upon the father or the schoolmaster" and "granting the Attourney General a right of constant watchfulness and control over what are called 'these little rules of domestic discipline'] if [we were to say] that if the effect of the corporal punishment surpasses by a slight degree what was prudently intended, there is assault and consequently a criminal offense."[12]

Other cases throughout the twentieth century confirm the claim that while Section 43 does not explicitly state that corporal punishment is protected by it, this form of punishment is what it is meant to and does protect. Slaps on the face, blows to the head, buttocks, back and legs with leather and plastic belts, sticks, extension cords, rulers and bare hands causing bruises, abrasions, contusions, swelling and bleeding have been judged "reasonable," "allowed by 43," "not excessive," and "well within the range of accepted punishment."[13] As late as 1992, when a mother was given an absolute discharge (having pled guilty) for repeatedly striking her eleven-year-old daughter with a belt for "lying about why her room was untidy," the trial judge stated that "Parents are entitled to use a belt, given the circumstances. There are welts, but I guess you expect to find welts when you use a belt."[14]

Even in cases where Section 43 was not a successful defence, the question of the reasonableness of corporal punishment per se is set aside. In *R. v. Ogg-Moss* (1981), for example, a counsellor at a facility for the mentally challenged was accused at trial of common assault for hitting a resident (with the mental age of five) several times on the head with a metal spoon for spilling his milk. The trial judge dismissed the charge accepting the accused's Section 43 defence that the force used was reasonable. On appeal by the Crown to the Ontario Court of Appeal, the court set aside the Lower Court's acquittal on the grounds that the accused did not stand in the sort of relationship to the victim that Section 43 required and as such, the defence it offered was not applicable. Nevertheless, the accused received an absolute discharge. In its reasoning, the appeal court held that Section 43 had to be strictly interpreted "since it deprives an individual or group, of the protection normally offered by the criminal law, namely the right to be free from unconsented invasions of physical security or dignity."[15] But as noted, its decision to disallow a Section 43 defence in this case was not based on the question of reasonable force. "Section 43 authorizes the use of force only where this is for the benefit of the education of the child. The person applying the force must intend it for correction, and the person being corrected must be capable of learning from the correction."[16] Clearly, while the accused was convicted of common assault in this case, the grounds for his conviction lay in the incapacity of the victim and not in the harmful nature of his act.

In addition to the statistics on Section 43 cases from their brief, the Repeal 43 Committee provides a list of the twenty-two Canadian children between the ages of three months and five years who died as a result of injuries sustained under the corporal punishment of their parents in 1977 alone. These injuries include skull fractures (three months, four months, five months, two years, three years), rupture of the liver and pancreas (ten months), virus infection during hospitalization for lacerations and broken ribs and legs (twenty-two months), peritonitis (seventeen months), asphyxia (five years), bowel and leg trauma (eighteen months), ruptured intestines (twenty-two months), perforation of the bowel (seventeen months), concussion (four years), shock (seventeen months), hemorrhage of the heart (due to punching) (two and one-half years) and abdominal trauma (two and one-half years).[17]

While these statistics do not speak to the question of whether Section 43 allows corporal punishment, they are a sad reminder of the dangers to very young children implied by the paradox of child protection and raise the issue of the connection between corporal punishment and child abuse. Let us now turn to the first question noted earlier: Does spanking count as the sort of corporal punishment which my position on its immorality finds unacceptable?

Spanking: Where It All Starts

To answer this question, three separate but related issues must be identified. The first has to do with the morality of spanking. The second involves the legal matter of whether a spanking constitutes assault according to its legal definition. And third, the question of spanking needs to be looked at in the context of the overall issue of child discipline as an obligation imposed upon individual parents in a free and democratic society which honours the nuclear family model of childcare.

Many parents and teachers defend the use of corporal punishment because they understand such punishment as never going beyond spanking in the first place or what is necessary for self-defence or restraint in the second. In the latter instance, the connection between defense and correction is problematic. Indeed, according to *R. v. Ogg-Moss*, the law does not permit the use of Section 43 defenses when the assault in question was intended to protect self or others from danger. This is because it is far from clear that using physical violence in such cases is intended to improve behaviour or character. In addition, the defense of necessity is presumably available in such circumstances. In any case, this defence of corporal punishment implies that while physical punishment beyond spanking might or might not be harmful to children, punishment which stays within these limits is definitely not harmful. Physical punishment of children which is not harmful ought not to be considered morally or more importantly, legally wrong. The courts, it might be concluded on this view, may simply have to get up to speed on this issue by altering their interpretation of reasonable force so that it does not include the sorts of punishments listed above as acceptable according to existing case law. As we will see, the problem with this argument is in the claim that certain instances of hitting children do not involve harming them. I will address the problems and worries of teachers separately. Spanking is, perhaps, what most people think of when they think of a child being hit. It is widely considered a nonsevere form of corporal punishment. As was noted in chapter 7, David Benatar sees it as that form of corporal punishment which invites the most controversy when the morality of the practice is at issue. Since it is regarded as nonsevere, many, if not most, parents do not think there is anything wrong with spanking their children as a means of improving their behaviour or character. So, before we explore the concerns of parents raised when it is suggested even spanking is morally problematic, we need a definition of spanking.

The Morality of Spanking

On a continuum between severe and non-severe forms of corporal punishment, I grant that spanking is closer to the nonsevere end than the severe one. Nevertheless, it must be said that one can also distinguish between severe and nonsevere spankings and so the classification of spanking as simply nonsevere is misleading. Instead, I would like to begin by distinguishing between punitive and nonpunitive spanking. For my purpose here, the delivery of a punitive spanking involves the bringing down of the hand or an object once or more than once on the clothed or bare buttocks of another with a degree of force sufficient to convey the spanker's real disapproval or anger with some aspect of the other's behaviour or character.[18] Typically, in order to be an effective punishment, the degree of force used must cause the other pain.

There is another sort of spanking—nonpunitive spanking. Nonpunitive spanking also involves the bringing down of a hand or an object on the buttocks of another. But there is little or no force used and the intention is to convey familiarity or affection. The no-force nonpunitive spanking is often referred to as the "love pat." This form of spanking follows women into their adulthood and except among familiars, is generally considered unwelcome physical contact. Among parents and children, the love pat may be used to hurry a child along or express affection. While I would argue that this type of nonpunitive spanking is not entirely unproblematic, I grant here that it is not condemned by my moral argument against corporal punishment.

The use of force in nonpunitive spanking is more complex. What I have in mind here is the sado-masochistic practice of sexual spanking. Here, the intention is to convey feigned disapproval or anger. Do a search on the Internet for the term "spanking" or "corporal punishment" and site after site of "erotic spanking and corporal punishment" scroll by. Irwin A. Hyman notes that many teachers seem to believe that the "the best route to a student's mind is through his behind."[19] But the truth is more disturbing. In a fanciful exercise intended to highlight what Hyman thinks is the strangeness of spanking, he writes that "the nerves of the behind, the place on children's bodies that gets spanked the most, are also hooked with the nerves that go to the sexual organs. Parents give kids a pain in the behind by spanking them and then say that they love them at the same time."[20] Philip Greven has written extensively on this subject in his book *Spare the Child: The Religious Roots of Punishment and the Psychological Effects of Physical Abuse.*[21] Sexual arousal is often experienced in the context of a confusion of pain and pleasure. Many adults go one step further requiring pain before they can feel any sexual pleasure at all. This need is catered to by the booming sado-masochism industry. Spanking with the hand as well as with paddles and other implements is, judging from the Internet, one of the most popular means of satisfying it. Greven concludes that:

> The roots of sadomasochism can often be traced back to the experiences of childhood, to actual encounters with punishment and pain, to the imposition of power and control by adults over the bodies and wills of children....So long as children are beaten by adults, the obsessions with domination and submission, with power and authority, with shame and humiliation, with painful pleasure—all hallmarks of sadomasochism—will remain an enduring consequence of the ordinary violence and coercion done in the name of discipline.[22]

Tremeear's Criminal Annotations supply a summary of an interesting case given the above. In *R. v. Taylor* (1985), the accused was charged with among other crimes, sexual assault of a sixteen-year-old female complainant. Mr. Taylor and his wife were the girl's guardians (her mother could not handle her and sent her to live with them).[23] To get the girl to stop using marijuana and smoking cigarettes, he tried several means of disciplining her. These attempts culminated in removing all of her clothing and binding her to a post in his basement where he "delivered several blows to her buttocks with a wooden paddle."[24] Mr. Taylor "was acquitted at trial on the ground that the acts complained of had no sexual connotation." In the absence of such a connotation, the acts in question reverted to ones of common assault and the trial judge held that as such, the accused was justified according to Section 43 of the Criminal Code. While the Alberta Court of Appeal rejected the trial judge's decision, this was on the grounds that he had erred in his view that the acts were nonsexual. The case was retried and the defendant found guilty of sexual assault. It is likely, given the courts' directions in this case, that if the complainant had been six instead of sixteen years old, the accused would have been absolutely discharged.

Forceful nonpunitive spankings which take place between consenting adults are arguably a far cry from the circumstances of *R. v. Taylor* and are not included here in what I think ought to be morally condemned even though again, I am not morally defending them. Also, any spanking for a sexual purpose which an adult administers to a child (regardless of the age of the child or degree of force used) ought to constitute sexual assault and is not, despite the open-mindedness of some trial judges, the sort of spanking which is ever defended by supporters of corporal punishment. Also, I will assume for the sake of argument that popular defences of corporal punishment would not be reasonably extended to cover the other sorts of actions currently defended in the courts—that striking other more vulnerable parts of children's bodies (their heads or hands, for instance) can never be morally justified. The American Academy of Pediatrics definition of spanking includes blows to the body's extremities but I will proceed on the grounds that when we are talking about blows to body parts other than the buttocks, we never use the term "spanking" and that, as such, the term is indeed reserved for striking the buttocks (or in some cases, the thighs). The issue at stake here is the use of the punitive spanking of children—the sort that delivers pain to the buttocks solely for the purpose of improving the child's behaviour or character. Is the bringing down of your hand or an object on the buttocks of your child with a painful degree of force morally wrong, even though its purpose and sole purpose is to convey your disapproval or anger with some aspect of your child's behaviour or character and even though it does not cause any lasting physical trauma?

In short, my answer to this question is yes, it is morally wrong. The issue here is whether this particular corporal punishment strategy is harmful and if so whether the harm outweighs any benefit. In the case of other more severe forms of corporal punishment, the answers to these questions may be clearer. The harm of a punitive spanking, its defenders argue, is minimal. Can it really be enough to outweigh the good it does? It must be noted that the benefits of punitive spanking are no more obvious than the benefits of worse forms of corporal punishment. Longitudinal controlled studies on spanking show that it is not an effective form of discipline insofar as it does not put a stop to unacceptable behaviour without causing it to erupt with greater intensity down the road.[25] Spanking like other forms of coercive discipline, teaches both male and female children of all ages that their behaviour is ultimately a matter of external physical rather than internal rational control. The main lesson is always "don't get caught."

Not all forms of external control are problematic here. The use of certain forms of external rational control may indeed be necessary when it comes to teaching children the norms of behaviour in our society. John Stuart Mill considered, for example, verbal expressions of disapproval from our peers and those we look up to as the most powerful external control on our behaviour. But complete reliance on even this nonviolent sanction ultimately interferes with a child's ability to develop a moral conscience. This internal control on behaviour is instead disciplined through moral guidance by appeal to the child's reason and sympathetic feelings for the well-being of others. Only once these feelings are "laid hold of," does the child begin to develop the self-discipline his or her moral autonomy requires. If they are not, no amount of external control will ever succeed in training a child to be moral—to be a person who may be generally relied upon to observe those norms of a democratic and free society which require concern for others. At most, a child will behave according to those norms so long as the threat of punishment their violation triggers is severe and imminent. If they are, then it is no longer clear that the society in which this is the case is a democratic and free one. And even in the sort of authoritarian or fascistic society which these conditions imply, human beings can generally be relied upon to try to avoid detection or to circumvent punishment. The use of spanking as a regular penalty or penalty of last resort tends, therefore, to make getting caught or punished rather than "bad" behaviour, regardless of how this is understood, the thing to avoid. And to this result must be added the increase in rage levels when one is dealing with assaults to one's person. As the levels rise, the consequences of not developing internal controls become worse; the prospect of internal anger management dimmer. There is therefore no self-disciplinary benefit to spanking children.[26]

Benefits to the punisher alone do not address the issue at the heart of the corporal punishment debate and even if they were to be taken into account, they could not possibly outweigh the harms and risks of harm to children and society in the long run. This last point, however, is in tension with the claim that the harm of punitive spanking is very minimal. This claim denies that spanking has the same effects as worse beatings and that as such cannot be considered harmful to any or the same extent. If one wants to argue, on the one hand, that spanking has no harmful effects, then it is unclear why it would be used at all for punitive purposes. It may be argued that no harm is done since the pain of the spanking is so short-lived but that the pain itself neverthe-less has an improving effect on behaviour or attitude. This argument reveals a lack of understanding where behaviourist techniques of improving behaviour and character are concerned. If the pain is minor and short-lived, it will quickly be forgotten (even though the humilia-tion—something the child may be too young to make sense of at the time—may linger in a sublimated form). To have the desired improv-ing effect, the pain must be severe enough to last for some time in which case harm is arguably done. The defenders of spanking cannot have it both ways.

While it may be true that punitive spanking by a parent need not involve physical trauma, it necessarily involves the infliction of pain by someone the victim loves and depends upon for his or her physical safety and security of the person. As such, punitive spanking risks emotional insecurity and if particularly frequent, may result in more serious psychological problems. There is also the matter of stimulating the sexual organs. Even if this is not the intention, it may be an effect of punitive spanking (especially episodes accompanied by words of love) leading to the sorts of harms associated with deep confusion over the connection between love and pain. Due to the failure to prove any crucial net benefits, punitive spanking cannot be placed in the same category of unwelcome physical interventions as vaccination needles. Consequently, it cannot escape definition as violence and its acceptance and use is therefore unavoidably at odds with the general feeling that violence against children is to be especially condemned. Finally, those, like Barbara Amiel, who insist nevertheless that spanking is not always harmful or violent, cannot deny that its use is a demonstrated risk factor or predictor for a variety of serious harms.[27]

Another issue comes up here. It is a widely accepted norm of moral judgement that the punishment fit the crime. This indeed is one of principles at the heart of the notion of reasonable punishment. The norm is clearly at home within a retributivist theory of punishment where the more radical maxim "an eye for an eye" is also arguably at home. But it may also form part of a consequentialist theory of punishment or one which sees punishment in terms of deterrence. If being judged guilty of a particular offence brings with it a penalty which the members of a jury, for example, find too severe, they might find someone not guilty who they actually believe committed a crime. Over time, the deterrent effect of the punishment in question might be rendered inoperative; the offence in question more common. On either theory of punishment, the norm that the punishment ought to fit the crime seems legally well-justified. Is it also morally justified? That is, is this norm one which we ought to observe in our everyday dealings with one another? From the point of view of a consequentialist theory of punishment, punishments that do not fit moral offences are ones which fail to bring about the desired result. A punishment could fail here by being either under- or overzealous. As long as the desired result is consistent with promoting the greatest happiness for the greatest number (or the least unhappiness for the least number), punishments which fail to do this may be considered immoral. On either theory of punishment, the punishment should therefore fit the offence — be it legal or moral.

Tempers being what they are, it is sometimes a difficult norm to observe but we always ought to aim at doing so even in our everyday dealings with one another. Supporters of corporal punishment and

many others seem to think that children must be excluded from the
scope of this norm and punished more severely than adults punish
one another for the same and even worse offences. If we find out that
an adult friend has lied to us about her income, for example, we
might not say or do anything at all by way of punishing her or trying
to improve her behaviour. But as a society, as evidenced in several
court cases, we seem to think it is fitting to corporally punish children
for lying regardless of the content or consequences of the lie in question. I assume this is because we suppose that the adult already
knows that lying is wrong and knows this because somewhere along
the line, he or she was "corrected" for lying. Children, it might be
argued, must or may be physically punished for certain behaviours
adults are not punished for at all because they need to learn that (as
opposed to why) the behaviour in question is wrong. It is nevertheless a mystery why we seem more forgiving of someone who knows
and understands lying is wrong, and does it anyway than we are of
someone who lies and may not know or understand it is wrong. I will
not pursue this difficult issue any further here except to say that the
norms by which we judge and punish children's behaviour should be
brought closer into line with what we will expect of them as adults.

While some children who lie, steal and damage persons and property may rank right up there with serious adult offenders, those cases
of corporal punishment which come to public light are often notable
for the inanity of the offence for which the child victim was punished.
The Repeal 43 Committee lists, among others, "may have called teacher
'short ribs,'" "impolite and insubordinate," "replied 'saucily'" to
teacher's order to "get to work," "bed wetters," "didn't finish her lessons," "spilled his milk," "gossiping" and being "mean."[28] Since corporal punishment has been shown to be an ineffective method of
improving behaviour and since there are effective nonviolent alternatives for teaching children to behave, to learn self-discipline and to
treat others with respect and kindness, these ought to be morally preferred to spanking or any other form of corporal punishment.

The Legality of Spanking

Would a parent who spanked a child for the purpose of improving that
child's behaviour be considered a criminal if Section 43 were removed

from the Criminal Code? If we regard spanking as "assault" under the law, then, even with Section 43, there is at least a prima facie case for saying that all parents who spank their children are acting criminally. The retention or removal of Section 43 would not have any effect on the prima facie claim. But the legal status of spanking (with or without Section 43) is complicated by the *de minimis* rule recognized by our courts as an important principle of jurisprudence. The courts acknowledge that there are instances of what, by the law's definition, count as assault but which, due to the context or trivial nature of the contact in question, ought not to attract legal attention.

Considering context, imagine, for example, that you are standing in the aisle of a very crowded public bus. Several new passengers have just boarded and are trying to make their way to the back. One of them pushes past, intentionally elbowing you and knocking you off balance into someone who is seated. You apologize to the seated patron and feel like punishing the person who pushed you. There are certainly contexts in which this same shoving behaviour would attract the attention of the law. But in this sort of case and regardless of the desire to retaliate in a more dramatic way, we generally think that a word to the driver will have the desired effect if indeed we think that any action ought to be taken at all. While psychologists may rightly argue that all feelings are legitimate, it does not follow that it is right to express — even in words — or act on every feeling we have.

The issue of triviality is trickier. Let's say that you are in an art class in which the students, seated on high stools at their benches, are busy at work. The teacher is walking up and down the aisles checking on how everyone is doing. Suddenly you feel the teacher stroking your bare shin. He asks you how you are getting along. You say you are doing fine. He smiles and moves on. You feel as if something wrong has occurred and think that the teacher's behaviour should be reported. This sort of behaviour has come to be regarded as inappropriate and institutions such as universities have policies in place which forbid it. But while the teacher may have violated university policy, it is highly unlikely that a court would find the matter serious enough to warrant criminal prosecution.[29] Such matters, the courts say, are best dealt with at the level of individual resolution or institutional policy. While the Americans are very litigious where such behaviour is concerned, Canadians continue to favor nonlegal remedies. Even in the American case, however, the legal remedies tend to be noncriminal.

In other circumstances, the act described in the bus example might be sufficient to initiate a criminal investigation. In the classroom example, if the teacher had scratched the student's shin breaking the skin or if he had stroked a thigh rather than a shin, the law would take greater interest in his behaviour. But given the facts as they stand, both acts are considered minimal by the law. If a report is taken by police, it must be selected from a larger group by the Crown for prosecution. Crown prosecutors must select cases based upon what they think will succeed. There is tremendous top-down pressure at this point. How have the courts decided in the past about such cases? Case law on the *de minimis* principle might encourage the Crown to drop the case. But the Crown just might take a chance. It is then left to a judge — sometimes a jury — to decide the case's merits. Judges are extremely busy people; our courts are clogged. Few people enjoy the costs of jury duty. The suggestion all along is "this better be serious" — so serious that the very costly and heavy hand of the Canadian judicial system is required to sort it out.

Just what police, lawyers, judges and society represented by juries think, at any given time, is serious or trivial is largely a matter of culture and other historically situated factors. "Rule of thumb" is alleged to refer to a rule which was once used to designate the difference between a wife-beating which could be criminally sanctioned and one which could not. As long as the husband who struck his wife with a stick or other implement did not use one which was wider than the breadth of his thumb, the story goes, his assault on his wife could be protected by the *de minimis* rule. Today, the law, mirroring the concerns of society, no longer regards spousal assault as ever beyond its concern. The legal question about spanking may be placed in this overall context. Despite its immorality, does spanking children involve the sort of harm which the law ought to consider minimal and so not proper to its jurisdiction? Or should the law take the route implied by the changes which have taken place in its attitude towards violence against women adopting a principle of zero tolerance when it comes to hitting children?

The Repeal 43 Committee has taken up the worries of parents in this regard and argued that due to several factors including but not limited to the effect of the *de minimis* rule, the removal of Section 43 from the Criminal Code will not result in open season on parents. As I have already argued, there would be no immediate change in the attitude of the law towards spanking. Even in the presence of Section 43, there have been a few cases where parents have been charged with common assault for spanking their children when the spanking occurred in public and was particularly severe. But apart from such cases, spanking has not been of much interest to law enforcement officials. Nevertheless, it may certainly be argued that the main reason spanking has attracted such little attention is that Section 43 states that such punishment is socially sanctioned and legally justified and that case law clearly shows that much worse punishments of children are also allowed by law.

Should the state of the law change so that it no longer defended this practice, this would send a message throughout society that spanking was no longer such a trivial matter. The aura of triviality which currently surrounds the practice of spanking and which influences the police as well as those who witness it would start to fade and eventually, disappear altogether. At that time, parents might be more vulnerable to criminal investigation and sanction for administering disciplinary spankings to their children than they are now, or would be for a period of time following the repeal or invalidation of Section 43. In the end, all reassurances about the moderating effect of the *de minimis* rule would rightly fail to calm the worries of parents who fear the intrusion of the state into their disciplinary regime as well as the loss of their ability to control their children in dangerous situations.

I do not dispute the reasoning or the conclusion of this argument. I believe that if Section 43 is repealed or invalidated, this would begin a long process of changing social attitudes towards spanking children—a process which would necessarily include education in nonviolent methods of protecting and disciplining children. I am optimistic that this process would eventually terminate in the complete social rejection of corporal punishment including spanking in much the same way adopting a zero tolerance rule for wife-beating played an important part in the unreserved condemnation of this once widely accepted "correctional" practice. The effect of a sea change in social attitudes towards spanking would likely mean that parents who continued to spank their children would be regarded by both society and the law as in the wrong. Just how such sanctions would be applied is necessarily a matter which requires discussion and social consensus. As I have noted, though Sweden has a specific law against spanking children, it does not attach criminal penalties to violations. Italy, on the other hand, administers its rules against assaulting or harming children within its criminal law.[30]

The prospect of any sort of punishment targeting parents who spank may strike some of you as excessive. But bear in mind that over the long process of education which would follow this change in the law, your own feelings about spanking could very well change. By the time we get to a stage where a simple spanking invites serious social or legal censure, there would necessarily be widespread social agreement on this matter. We are a very long way from widespread agreement at the moment. Consensus or perfect agreement is, in any case, not required. If it were, I doubt that any significant changes in national social or legal policy could ever occur.

The Repeal 43 Committee raises the question of penalties for corporal punishment in the context of parental fears that light spanking will become a criminal act. I have drawn a distinction between punitive and nonpunitive spanking which makes the latter, for the purpose of my argument here, morally neutral. On these grounds, if by "light spanking" those who fear the repeal of Section 43 mean the nonpunitive "love pat," their worries are overblown and incendiary. I would remind them, however, that if they intend by light spanking some form of punishment, unless a spanking carries with it a significant degree of pain, its use as punishment is unintelligible. They may instead have in mind a spanking which delivers the minimum amount of pain required to effect its punitive purpose — a nonsevere spanking. As long as any lasting pain is involved, regardless of how minimal, my argument against spanking applies.

Furthermore, children ought not to be the subjects of parental experimentation when it comes to discovering minimum yet sufficient levels of disciplinary pain. The problem here is one which Irwin Hyman argues is irresolvable and involves the discernment of the individual parent's judgement when it comes to gauging pain. Just what is the minimum amount necessary to effect a punitive purpose?

Should we be experimenting on our children in order to come to a conclusion? Hyman argues that the answer to this second question must be no. Since there is no way to tell just what minimal is, we must err on the side of caution and stop hitting our children.

The Social and Political Options

Punitive spanking is a form of corporal punishment which must be included in the moral condemnation of all violent disciplinary practices involving children. Like the so-called "mild" forms of the physical punishment of wives and convicts, it deserves to be abandoned along with more severe beatings. I doubt, however, that my argument to this conclusion will have much immediate effect on the attitudes of those Canadians who view things differently. Rational persuasion takes time — arguments need to be thoughtfully considered, critically evaluated. Even if the reasoning and claims involved are accepted, they may need time to sink in; time to work themselves into one's feelings. But I believe that the principle at the bottom of my argument is of such tremendous force that it will eventually prevail in the minds of most Canadians: any use of physical violence against human beings for the purpose of improving their behaviour must be forbidden, regardless of the age of the human being in question and their relationship to their assailants.

It is true that we currently allow police officers to use reasonable physical force against an offender who poses an obvious, immediate and dire threat to the safety of the community, but if and only if the offender clearly resists arrest. We also allow individuals to use reasonable physical force to defend themselves against personal attack. However, neither concession to the use of violence can be intelligently referred to as corrective or aimed at improvement and so neither can be used via analogy to justify the use of corporal punishment against children. Furthermore, the law is very strict about the sorts of circumstances which must obtain before either concession is made. The circumstances leading up to the administration of a spanking or other form of corporal punishment to a child are rarely of the right sort. For one thing, the child would have to possess strength adequate to pose a real threat to an adult. As we have seen, defenders of corporal punishment tend not to endorse its use for the older child. What if a younger child is brandishing a dangerous weapon—a gun, for instance? The moral and legal issues surrounding the question of corporal punishment seem irrelevant, to say the least, in such a circumstance. The law, as has been noted, is explicit on this matter as well. Section 43, since it covers punitive assaults only, may not be used as a defence in cases where the assault in question was allegedly in defence of self or another against some danger or threat of danger.

When the threat of danger or harm posed by an aggressor is morally and legally sufficient to trigger exceptions to our general rule against the use of violence, we may infer that the aggressor is as or more powerful (on his own or because he is armed) than the target of his hostilities. This is what is assumed, for instance, by our notion of justified self-defence. Yet, our attitudes towards corporal punishment show that whenever this use of violence against another has been thought morally or legally acceptable, this has always been in situations where the "corrector/defender" is considered more powerful, for one reason or another, than the so-called "correctee/aggressor." State officials were allowed to strike their subjects, masters were permitted to hit their slaves, men were permitted to beat their wives, teachers are permitted to hit their students, parents are justified when they spank their children.

The culture of corporal punishment is one which sees human beings in terms of drastic contrasts in worth—one where the "superiors" grant one another the right to harm the "inferior" in the latter's "best interest" and without the latter's consent. I have suggested that this culture is guilty of promoting an illusion; that at best, it supports the falsehood that whoever is in power is entitled to express their displeasure on the bodies of those without power. I realize that few if any parents believe that this is what they are doing when they spank their children for misbehaviour. But like it or not, spanking is part of the corporal punishment culture. This culture has a bloody and shameful history and has a much broader influence than that exerted in the typical family discipline episode. Removing Section 43 from the Canadian Criminal Code will not be able, on its own, to bring this culture to an end. And yet, like all cultures which value the oppression of the physically weak and/or politically disenfranchised and realize this value through violent coercion and the maintenance of underclasses, it must not be tolerated in any of its aspects in a liberal, free and democratic society.[31]

Irwin Hyman has argued that the culture of corporal punishment is fueled by the practice of spanking children and Philip Greven has argued that this culture in turn fuels the more widespread culture of violence which is constantly threatening to overwhelm the best achievements of the human race.[32] While their views may seem extreme to some, both authors rely on vast amounts of research to recommend them. In any case, these views must at least be understood and seriously considered. Until the skeptical reader is able to support his or her conclusion that "spanking is okay" in the face of the many arguments and evidence for the claim that it has no improving value and is a statistically significant risk factor for so many undesirable outcomes for children and the adults they will eventually become, erring on the side of caution when it comes to the dangers of child abuse and violent totalitarianism recommend that the practice of spanking ought to be morally condemned and in no way justified in law.

Even in the face of a current lack of voluntary compliance, the government ought to repeal Section 43. But compliance will become necessary if the use of spanking and other forms of corporal punishment is to be brought to a halt. What should be done to further this end? Would, for example, criminal sanctions against parents who are convicted of assaulting their children when the assault was intended in the child's best interest be conducive to achieving it? Or would noncriminal sanctions be more in keeping with the spirit of the principle against corporal punishment? Is the threat of legal sanctions — be they criminal or non-criminal — sufficient to turn the tide towards compliance? Or will public education also be required? Should adults preparing for parenthood be required to apply for licenses? Should, as David Archard suggests, the Government monitor all parents of young children? Will the media have to take the whole matter on board and report on it as attentively as it reports on the national economy or our national health care system? Will any or all of this have any positive effect if the nation's churches choose to speak out against these reforms? Other countries in the world have already addressed many of these questions. Whether their answers will be the right answers for Canadians remains to be seen. But their experiences should be consulted in our efforts to respond.

The Italians

The Italians have elected to pursue the eradication of all forms of corporal punishment in their society through the use of criminal sanctions.[33] As Susan H. Bitensky notes in her article on corporal punishment for the *University of Michigan Journal of Law Reform*, "On May 16, 1996, Italy's highest court, the Supreme Court of Cassation, issued a decision prohibiting all parental use of corporal punishment on children as a childrearing technique. In that decision the court announced as a new juridical principle that 'the use of violence for educational purposes can no longer be considered lawful.'"[34] This decision was preceded by what Judge Ippolito argued was "ongoing legal reforms and political and cultural changes since the end of Benito Mussolini's fascist dictatorship over Italy in 1945."[35] These changes were seen by the Italian court as part of a strong and continuing trend away from the tacit approval of violence which characterized Italy's identity under Mussolini and as one which is expressed in Italy's current constitutional values.

Bitensky also reports that Italy's attitude towards its obligations under international treaties makes its commitments as a signatory to the UN Convention on the Rights of the Child a powerful force for social change. Under that Convention, every child is granted the right, among many others, to be free from all corporal punishments.[36] While in this case, the Italian court took the upper hand introducing a reform into the interpretation of assault law, it is clear from Judge Ippolito's reasoning that it did not regard itself as "making" law. For while it did impose a new interpretation of child abuse such that all corporal punishment of children was now considered abusive and criminal, it did so on what it argued were grounds already well established in existing law and binding under international treaty obligations. This sort of judicial remedy, while possible in Canada, should not be counted upon and ought not to be preferred to a legislative remedy. We may want to take a somewhat gentler approach than the Italians given our very different historical circumstances.

The Swedes

The Swedes (and all other Scandinavian countries) have proceeded along a different path. I will not rehearse all the details of their legislative moves to prohibit all forms of corporal punishment. These are available elsewhere.[37] But it is important to note that prior to prohibiting all corporal punishment of children in 1979, the Swedes had begun their legal journey by prohibiting the use of corporal punishment in schools in 1928. Swedish law continued to provide a defence similar to Section 43, however. In 1957, "this defense was completely removed from the Penal Code in order to provide children with the same protection from assault that adults receive and to clarify the grounds for criminal prosecution of parents who abused their children."[38] What the Swedes found was that this repeal was not adequate for garnering universal compliance and so in 1977 and after several serious child abuse cases, "the Minister of Justice appointed a Children's Rights Committee to review the Parent's Code."[39] In 1979, the Committee's proposal to "include a paragraph in the Parent's Code that explicitly banned the use of corporal punishment by parents" was passed by the Swedish parliament.[40]

The passing of what has come to be known as the "no-spanking law" was accompanied by a concerted government campaign to educate all Swedish parents in nonviolent child discipline. The history of the reform of child discipline practices for the Swedes is much longer than ours. Canadian child clinical psychologist Joan Durrant has written extensively on their experiences as well as on the current state of opinion among Canadians. Durrant concludes that while the differences in histories might imply that Canada needs to catch up before it can consider similar legislation, this may not necessarily be the case. The force of precedent which Sweden has given the world may give countries such as ours an additional reason for acting quickly to repeal Section 43, even though we may fall short of a very high degree of social agreement against corporal punishment.

Dr. Durrant has also argued that "a three-pronged approach is necessary to achieve the goal of reducing rates of corporal punishment and child abuse."[41] One of these prongs is "legislative change [which] would provide a 'symbolic statement' that society does not condone the use of physical discipline."[42] I have argued that the introduction of radical new legal requirements and prohibitions must take into account the readiness of Canadian citizens to comply with such changes and that as such, a new law specifically prohibiting corporal punishment might not yet be timely. I have also argued, however, that governments should take a leadership role in preparing citizens for such radical changes when they are warranted by the facts and values which otherwise guide society. Section 43 ought to be repealed immediately on these grounds.

The Swedish experience suggests that repealing Section 43 will not, on its own, have a dramatic effect on attitudes towards corporal punishment. I suspect that this is because the change is, to some extent, a subtle and legalistic one. However, it would bring the issue of the corporal punishment of children to public debate and prepare the ground for more significant legal reform. It might also prevent courts from dismissing charges against parents and teachers who seriously harm the children they corporally punish. While this would only be a beginning, I believe it is one which a majority of Canadians would be able to support upon serious reflection. This sense of wide public support for protecting children from the harms of corporal punishment is something which is lacking at the moment and which may hinder constitutional challenges to Section 43. In the end, however, I agree with Durrant that a very strong legal position against the corporal punishment of children — including spanking — is going to be a necessary component of an overall successful strategy.

I have not answered all of the questions I posed at the beginning of this section. To do so would mean another book. Many of those questions require empirical information which we do not have at this time. And so at the very least, more money for the necessary research must be allocated. The Government of Canada recently funded a study which examines the incidence of and attitudes towards child abuse and corporal punishment of Canadian children, though in a somewhat limited context.[43] Much more in this vein is needed. In addition, the media must do a better job of bringing the information which we already have to the public. The other side of this debate is well funded and promoted by a number of active right-wing thinktanks under the aegis of "family values" institutes.[44] All those who seek to challenge their position must act with as much if not greater gusto.

I believe that such efforts should include aiming at legislative change and not be restricted to or focused exclusively on judicial intervention. A legislative remedy will always be one which can be affected with much greater flexibility and sensitivity than the courts are in a position to afford. So while I sympathize with the Italian course given their historical circumstances, I suspect that worries about onerous parental childcare responsibilities and discretion over child discipline would be better addressed in the Canadian Parliament than they would be in the Supreme Court. The fact, for example, that so many of those accused and found guilty of commonly assaulting children have been given absolute discharges, implies that our courts are not prepared to impose criminal penalties on them, even though they have been convicted of a criminal offence.

Teachers: A Special Case

The history of Section 43 defence use, as I noted earlier, is dominated by cases involving teachers. This continues to be true. Teachers voice serious concern that if Section 43 is repealed, they will be unable to defend themselves against students and unable to maintain discipline in their classrooms without fear of criminal charges or worse, convictions. As I explained in chapter 8, special defences in the law such as Section 43 acknowledge there are occasions when harm to the one is necessary in order to prevent harm to the many and without the special protections which laws such as Section 43 provide, persons with the responsibility of the many would hesitate to fulfill their obligations and for obvious reasons. This, I agreed, would be bad. The hypothetical situation envisaged by teachers is not unlike the one imagined by Barbara Amiel when she warned that were Section 43 removed from the Criminal Code, parents would "stop raising" their children. I very much doubt that the scenario is a more realistic one when we are talking about teachers and students. However, there is room for a reasonable concern and this needs to be addressed.

One of the reasons which I and many others have offered in support of repeal is that nonviolent methods of improving behaviour or character are available and that they work, given time. Much of what has been said in this regard depends upon there being a loving relationship between the child and the disciplining adult—typically a parent-child relationship. However, many of the features of parent-child relationships which ground the availability and efficiency of nonviolent methods of discipline do not apply in the teacher-pupil relationship. The affection that may exist between a teacher and a student, while often intense, is never the same as that which exists between most parents and their children. If it is, then we tend to think that the teacher has overstepped his or her professional bounds. And clearly as children get a bit older and begin to differentiate between the teacher's and the parent's role, the "love" between the child and the teacher weakens and usually disappears altogether. This does not mean that most children come to dislike or hate their teachers—though some do—but rather that their feelings become more detached. Teachers, therefore, often face people who do not experience themselves as having a great stake in what the teacher feels about them—a very different situation from the one in which parents figure out how to get children to behave. And it is no response to this situation to recommend that teachers just get their students to love them.

Without this powerful reason for listening to and going along with adults, children might be more difficult to handle. Strategies are required which compensate for its absence. Might this lead us to be more generous in the case of teachers when it comes to the use of corporal punishment than we are in the case of parents? While I am very sensitive to the special difficulties which teachers face, I cannot conclude that they warrant any privileges when it comes to hitting children. To do so would force me back to the conclusion that wherever this condition obtains— the condition of detachment let's say—the use of corporal punishment is a viable method of behaviour modification. Yet clearly, this conclusion is unacceptable. The law itself does not admit it. Strangers are not entitled to hit your children for the purposes of their improvement and I doubt that any defenders of corporal punishment would oppose this position. And so we are sent back to the view that teachers, like parents, must develop the skill of nonviolent behaviour management. Unlike parents, teachers are now specifically educated and trained in such methods and so I find their anxiety over the repeal of Section 43 somewhat baffling. But perhaps I have overlooked something.

Teachers face another pressure which parents do not. As I mentioned earlier, the actions of teachers against students are under constant scrutiny by the parents of those children. While the actions of parents may be similarly monitored by teachers, such monitoring cannot be nearly as efficient as it is in the other direction. A parent may have two or three teachers to monitor, a teacher may have thirty or forty parents. A parent can drop in on a teacher just about whenever he or she likes. Teachers may not drop in on parents. A teacher may find that he or she has to use physical restraint in order to prevent a more serious harm. I have argued that the reasonable use of physical restraint in a dangerous situation is not condemned by either my moral or legal argument against corporal punishment and that indeed, its availability is part of what makes corporal punishment immoral. However, if a son or daughter comes home reporting that he or she has been forcefully held or pushed aside or shoved against a wall, etc., by a teacher or school official, a parent might be inclined to pursue the incident. Teachers may have good reason to fear that such a pursuit will escalate into a criminal investigation. Some parents who hit their own children are apt to regard the teacher's behaviour as a hostile intrusion into their natural domain. As such, teachers may feel that they require a "big stick" to warn the parents back and that Section 43 provides just such a warning tool. In its absence, even if open season on parents does not follow, open season on teachers might. This is a reasonable fear.

Historically, the use of corporal punishment in schools was always prohibited long before the question of parental corporal punishment came up. Many more countries have excluded teacher-inflicted corporal punishment than both it and parental corporal punishment, and no country that has prohibited parental corporal punishment has not done the same with teacher corporal punishment. The prospect, therefore, of a moral atmosphere or legal culture which allows teachers to hit students but does not allow parents to hit their children is historically anomalous. I suspect that the move to prohibit school uses of corporal punishment has, at least in the past, been primarily accepted if not motivated by the idea that parents own their children. And it is this view on the part of parents which makes the teacher's situation as an agent of their children's improvement so precarious. It is this view, therefore, that must be dislodged from the minds of all—parents do not own their children. Whatever rights they have in the course of caring for them do not arise from the principles of ownership. When parents send their children off to school, they implicitly agree to share many of those rights with the teachers who must carry on the task of preparing those children for adult life.

The law clearly understands this, if case histories are any guide. And so in this way, we come to see that teachers, while they may have many of the same rights or privileges parents have, cannot possibly have more than parents have. As such, whatever special difficulties teachers face when it comes to managing or improving the behaviour of the children they teach, these must be dealt with in ways which are compatible with the ones available to parents. These special difficulties include greater vulnerability to criminal investigation. But I would argue that not unlike many other professions, this is just part of what makes the profession of teaching young children so difficult.

Finally, it must be noted again that when it comes to what teachers seem most concerned about — the legal use of physical intervention in the course of restraint or self-defence — nothing I have said precludes its use in such cases. Section 43 is redundant and much too "big" a stick for warning off parents who feel their children may have been criminally assaulted. Assault law independently of Section 43 and together with common law defenses such as necessity are clearly sufficient for such purposes. It is worth mentioning here that many provincial education ministries have instituted policies which prohibit the use of corporal punishment in their schools. It is time for the federal government to back them up.

In conclusion, everything I have argued throughout the previous ten chapters should be taken to include spanking. Parents who worry that they will be socially or legally sanctioned for spanking if Section 43 is repealed should be worried about this. Spanking, like all other forms of corporal punishment, is immoral according to my argument and that means that we ought to feel bad about doing it and we ought to criticize others who do it. I have argued that corporal punishment is so bad that we should consider using the law as a means of discouraging its use. For the time being however, it is sufficient that we do not use the law to justify it. I have also argued, along with Joan Durrant, for example, that the law is only one part of a comprehensive strategy for eliminating corporal punishment from our society. Applied and interpreted in our courts, it is a blunt instrument of social reform and as such must be used with caution. The issue of spanking in particular gives us plenty of reason to prefer a potentially more sensitive and comprehensive legislative remedy.

11

• • • • • • • • • • •

Child Abuse and Family
Statism Revisited

C anadian children currently stand as a group of human beings whose members are, as the Ontario Court of Appeal once stated, deprived "of the protection normally offered by the criminal law, namely, the right to be free from unconsented invasions of physical security or dignity."[1] While there may be many good reasons to deprive children of certain rights — the right to vote for example — such reasons do not support depriving them of their right to security of the person or limiting this right in the way Section 43 limits it. This is because the full right to security of the person is practically fundamental to enjoyment of all other rights. The actual value of the right to vote would be questionable if, on your way to the polling station, you could be physically threatened or interfered with by authorities. The right to free expression might not come to much for you if, throughout your childhood, the adults who cared for you spanked you every time you said something they found inappropriate ("Children should be seen and not heard"). As

---

Notes to chapter 11 are on pp. 288–290.

Mill argued, a sense of personal security is one which "no human being can do without; on it we depend for all our immunity from evil and for the whole value of all and every good, beyond the passing moment, since nothing but the gratification of the instant could be of any worth to us, if we could be deprived of anything the next instant by whoever was momentarily stronger than ourselves."[2]

As the law and our current moral attitudes stand, this is the moral and legal situation in which children find themselves. It may be argued that in using corporal punishment, we compel children to remain in the very state of pursuing instant gratification for which they are typically punished. The tenacity of belief in the value of corporal punishment is due at least in part to the conflicted mythology of childhood which has been handed down through cultural and religious belief and practice, especially in the Western tradition.

To break free of that conflicted mythology and the grip which the value of corporal punishment seems to have on our society, it is important to look at the results of empirical studies on this form of child discipline. When we consult these studies, we see for ourselves that this disciplinary strategy tends to produce or risks producing the very same undesirable results we seek to prevent in using it. From this, we must infer that the belief that corporal punishment will be effective is based on something other than the actual improvement of behaviour and character. But on what? In light of the argument presented in the recent Ontario Superior Court case in which Section 43 was upheld, this question and others concerning the nature of how people reason about the connections between corporal punishment and various harms need to be explored a bit further.

The Connection between Corporal Punishment and Child Abuse

The most reasonable advocates of corporal punishment begin by acknowledging that there are risks in using the practice, that too many parents use it excessively, that it should not be used on very young children or teenagers, that it should not involve the head or any other vulnerable area of a child's body, that only the hand should be used and that it should, in any case, only be used as a last resort. In other words, these advocates admit that there are harms and risks of harm associated with the use of corporal punishment. However, they argue, these harms are outweighed by the benefits of using corporal punishment. Therefore, the practice should be permitted and Section 43 should not be repealed.

As stated, this argument fails due to the erroneous assumption on which it relies. There is only one documented benefit of using corporal punishment: immediate, short-term compliance. But many studies show this benefit can also be achieved by using removal, restraint or barriers instead of corporal punishment and so the harms associated with corporal punishment must be regarded as net harms. Other advocates do not deny that the benefits of using corporal punishment might be negligible or achieved just as well with other methods of child discipline. Instead, they argue there is little evidence to support the claims which point to its harms. Since it is a traditional right of parents to hit their children, the practice, which is morally neutral, should continue to be permitted.

Contrary to what this argument assumes, the evidence in support of the claim that corporal punishment is a significant risk for many serious harms is mountainous, well-researched and documented. If it were the case that there was no significant benefit or harm from using corporal punishment, there would, of course, be no reason for the law to be involved one way or the other with the practice. But, even in that case, the question of the practice's purpose would remain unanswered.

There is little evidence of the benefits of corporal punishment and considerable evidence demonstrating the risk of various harms it poses. The risks demonstrated are statistically significant; in many cases strong. But there is one reputed risk which is regarded with especially intense skepticism. One of the most common concerns expressed by opponents of repealing Section 43 has to do with the suggestion made by its critics that the use of corporal punishment by a parent poses a significant risk of child abuse. According to some, existing studies do not support this claim. Is skepticism reasonable in this particular case?

Assume, for the sake of argument, that "abuse" here only refers to what happens in substantiated cases of child abuse — the worst cases of harming children. Research results clearly support the claim that a vast majority of identified abusive parents believed they were administering an acceptable level of corporal punishment when they hurt their children. Studies also show most abusive parents typically began with noncorporal punishments, then moved to moderate and finally more and more severe forms of corporal punishment over time.[3] The implication here is that most child abuse is clearly connected to corporal punishment. With some but very few reservations, all researchers seem quite happy to say that child abuse is an excellent predictor of the use of corporal punishment. Unfortunately, the strength of this connection does not warrant the conclusion that corporal punishment is as significant a predictor for child abuse. Very roughly speaking, to support the second conclusion, the number of parents who use corporal punishment would have to be compared to the smaller number of parents who physically abuse their children. A figure would then be generated which represented a statistical tendency of corporal punishment, considered society wide, to lead to child abuse.

There are no firm national numbers available at the present time on how many parents approve of and use corporal punishment. However, the *Canadian Incidence Study of Child Abuse and Neglect* (2001) provides data on how many Canadian parents were involved in reported cases of child abuse in 1998 and which, of those, involved the use of corporal punishment.[4] Without knowing how many Canadian parents approve of and use corporal punishment, no firm numbers on how many of them go on to abuse their children can be inferred from the findings of the study. However, suppose for the sake of argument, that one parent in every thousand who believed that corporal punishment was an acceptable form of discipline and who corporally punished (say, a mild to severe spanking) his or her children at least once a week would go on to abuse at least one of them. My guess is that such a figure is somewhat conservative. In any case, would such a figure justify the conclusion that corporal punishment is not a significant risk factor for child abuse? If it could be shown that in all or most cases of abuse but in none or few of the cases of non-abusive corporal punishment, other contributing factors were present, such a conclusion might be justified. The parental factors involved here include unemployment, spousal violence, parental history of child abuse, youth of parent, lack of support network, stress and authoritarianism. The child factors include high activity level and handicaps. It is highly unlikely that only those families in which children are abused are ones in which these factors are present. They are factors which affect many if not most families at one time or another. While these considerations do not necessarily justify the claim that corporal punishment is a strong risk factor for child abuse, they just as clearly fail to justify the claim it is not.

One needs, however, to keep in mind the potential consequences of taking the chance that corporal punishment is not, despite the strong evidence it is implicated in almost all cases of child abuse, a risk factor for abuse. A supporter of corporal punishment may not see her parental situation as characterized by any of the other factors associated with abuse. She may conclude there is no danger in corporally punishing her child. But stress from various sources can strike without warning. In this case, the chances of abusing her child increase.

Experts such as Straus defend the claim that corporal punishment is a risk factor for child abuse by showing that when corporal punishment is coupled with other factors which have also been identified as risks for child abuse, the tendency for child abuse to occur is statistically significant.[5] Straus argues there is no one factor which can be clearly identified as the main cause of child abuse. This is because there is no such single factor. "A hard-nosed evaluation would point out that there has not been a definitive experimental study showing that corporal punishment causes physical abuse. On the other hand, that can also be said about every other presumed cause."[6] Cite any factor considered by most people to be more obvious than corporal punishment as a risk for child abuse. It will simply fail to be true that most parents affected by that factor will abuse their children. The majority will not. Taken each on their own, one would have to conclude that there are no significant risk factors for child abuse.

I suspect that those who conclude that corporal punishment is not a strong enough risk factor for child abuse to warrant prohibiting it on those grounds would deny there is nothing we can do to prevent or reduce the incidence of child abuse. Clearly, the majority of Canadians (including those who support Section 43) abhor child abuse and are quick to criticize the Government for not doing enough to prevent its causes when cases of child abuse come to light. This reaction implies Canadians believe there are real risk factors for child abuse and that these must be identified and controlled for in the most vigorous manner possible.

Our expectations, however, when it comes to justifying action on any particular factor, seem to run right alongside our favourite prejudices about what causes child abuse. The fact is that any answer to the question "What causes child abuse?" will likely fail, based on the statistical evidence adduced for that factor alone, to persuade those who disagree. The combinations of various answers, however, is another story. But why focus on corporal punishment? In combination with other factors, corporal punishment, say the experts, figures prominently.[7] That is, the statistical tendency of any more socially accepted risk factor for child abuse—parent having been abused as a child, for example—in combination with the use of corporal punishment to lead to child abuse is significantly higher than it is for any factor on its own or any other combination of factors. Therefore, the experts defend the claim that corporal punishment is a significant risk factor for child abuse by showing that more than any other risk factor, when it is associated with one or more of the others, the statistical tendency for occurrences of child abuse becomes significant.

In addition to the role corporal punishment plays in combination with other factors when it comes to the risk of child abuse, the consequences to other children whose parents may not be as stress-free must be considered when one is reflecting on the merits of social policy. While most people who corporally punish their children do not go on to abuse them, is there a certain number of abused children considered a price worth paying for the general privilege of assaulting children for the purpose of disciplining them? This question needs to be addressed by those who argue that because most parents who corporally punish their children do not go on to abuse them, the practice need not be prohibited.

We know that almost all child abusers used corporal punishment of varying degrees (mild to severe) on their children long before they abused them. We know that most parents identified by social welfare agencies as child abusers believed, at the time, that what was judged later by others to be child abuse, fell within the bounds of reasonable corporal punishment. We also know that corporal punishment rarely occurs on its own and that in combination with other risk factors, corporal punishment becomes a significant predictor of child abuse.

We agree that, as a society, we should be doing everything possible to reduce the risks associated with child abuse. We should eliminate spousal abuse, alcohol and drug addiction and unemployment. We should make sure new parents have adequate support networks and childcare education. A tall order. Why not start, advocates of repealing Section 43 say, by making corporal punishment legally unacceptable? Governments, judges, health care professionals, teachers, law enforcement officers and church leaders can tell parents that from now on, in addition to using an approved safety seat when transporting children in a motor vehicle, having their infants inoculated for German measles, turning up with their six year olds at the local school to register them for their education (or registering themselves as approved teachers with their provincial government) and providing their children with the necessaries of physical and mental health until they turn sixteen, they must never hit their children under any circumstances.

It follows from the claims of experts in this area and some rough calculations for Canadian numbers, that statistically, as long as we ignore the risk factor associated with corporal punishment for child abuse, many thousands of children in Canada a year will be victims of a level of corporal punishment which we consider child abuse resulting in grave physical injury, disability or even, in about 2 percent of these cases, death.[8] Expert opinion implies that many if not most of these abuses and deaths would be averted if corporal punishment were no longer considered socially or legally acceptable. As we saw in the case of Sweden, however, improvement would not occur overnight. But the clear message is that it will not occur at all unless corporal punishment is taken off the menu of discretionary disciplinary practices.

Given the much larger number of children who are corporally punished, the number of children who will likely be abused may not sound too worrisome for some. But, it is estimated that among those children who are severely abused, roughly fifty die each year from their injuries.[9] It is safe to say that most Canadians would agree that this is fifty too many.

The evidence which has been amassed by researchers in the field and the experience of countries in which corporal punishment has been banned very strongly indicate that if corporal punishment of children became as socially unacceptable as having sex with them, this number would be dramatically reduced over time. Given the risk of child abuse and even death, and of the many other, much more widely experienced harms even more clearly associated with the use of corporal punishment, the argument for legally permitting it which is based on the belief that, in general, children will be worse off without it, cannot be sustained.

It follows from the reasoning above which relies on numerous studies and expert opinion in the field, that if we consider the group of all parents who have been identified by the state as child abusers and ask, "If these actual people had lived in a society which simply did not permit corporal punishment, would most of them have abused their children?" the answer would be "no." When experts claim that corporal punishment is a risk for child abuse, it is fairly clear that they cannot justifiably mean that any parent who uses corporal punishment on his or her child is likely to become a child abuser. They cannot even justifiably mean that there is a fifty-fifty chance this will happen. Nevertheless, they can justifiably claim that if a parent is in the habit of using corporal punishment, approves of its use and sees its use as socially acceptable, and was abused as a child, is either unemployed, mentally unwell, in a violent spousal relationship, poor or uneducated, that there is a much better chance that the corporal punishment will escalate into an abusive episode. That's what the numbers tell us. But what the numbers do not tell us is why this is the case. How is it that stressed parents who use corporal punishment and approve of its use run this unacceptable risk? What, in other words, is the mechanism of conversion from what most people currently consider acceptable corporal punishment—say, a few hard slaps to a three-year-old child's covered buttocks with one's bare hand—to what most people consider unacceptable child abuse—say, several rounds of whipping with an electrical cord across the bare back of that same child? Why is it that some parents who use corporal punishment become child abusers?

The Problem of Escalation

According to those who have studied the question of how corporal punishment becomes child abuse, there are two equally important mechanisms involved in the transition. The first is a parent's state of mind. Is he or she stressed by unemployment, spousal violence, lack of knowledge about successful parenting strategies ("I just didn't know what else to do"), his or her own history of being abused as a child, depression, alcoholism, drug addiction, or chronic poverty? Is the parent angry or frustrated by work-related or relationship problems? All these conditions interfere with judging children's misbehaviour fairly, with accurately gauging the intensity of a punitive assault and with arriving at conclusions about whether non-corporal or moderate corporal punishments have worked based on actual evidence. They also exacerbate the parent's need to release hostile emotion.

The second and not unconnected aspect involved in the transition from mild corporal punishment to child abuse involves the nature of punishment itself. In terms of penalties for offences, the law sees fit to impose harsher and harsher penalties on persons who repeat their crimes with the expectation that if, for example, six months imprisonment or a $500 fine is not enough of a disincentive to break the law, perhaps two years in jail or a $10,000 fine will be. Straus writes, "If corporal punishment is not effective, abusive parents increase the severity of the punishment until the point where a child may be injured."[10] According to Kadushin and Martin, most parents who end up abusing their children started out by punishing them in nonviolent ways (yelling, removal of privileges, grounding, etc.,) and proceeded to use more and more severe forms of corporal punishment which ended in serious injury or death to them.[11]

According to many studies, this happens because the parent perceives the child as noncompliant and is made more and more angry by his or her "willful and disobedient" behaviour. If simply being told or yelled at to stop crying, hitting a sibling, taking money from the cookie jar, failing math, talking back, breaking a neighbour's window and so on is not enough of a disincentive, then maybe being grounded will be. If being grounded fails to elicit compliant behaviour, maybe three quick smacks to a covered buttocks will. If the child continues to disobey (either with respect to the rule broken previously or some new one) or worse, resists this punishment, then the pants come down. That should work. If it doesn't, then perhaps a rod or yardstick should be used. Arguably, what the parent in this scenario is after is not really an honest or kind child; it is a respectful, obedient one.

"When the child does not comply," Murray Straus writes, "or, in the case of older children, hits back and curses the parent, the resulting frustration and rage leads some parents to increase the severity of the physical attack and kick, punch, or hit with an object."[12] Furthermore, this escalation is not limited to parents who end up abusing. Referring to the studies of Marion, Straus writes:

> Corporal punishment creates a false sense of successful discipline because of the temporary end it puts to undesirable behaviour. [Marion] also cites research that shows the corporal punishment tends to *increase* undesirable behaviour in children. So, parents who rely on hitting to control behaviour have to continually increase the intensity. Besides the clinically based conclusions we just mentioned, there has been some research on this increasing intensity, or escalation. Frude and Gross (1980) studied 111 mothers and found that 40 percent were worried that they could possibly hurt their children.[13]

At stake here is a parent's perception of how successful or unsuccessful a particular punishment is and his or her emotional response to what he or she perceives to be willful disobedience. Both, as discussed earlier, may be deeply affected by factors which have nothing to do with the actual behaviour of the child. But the child's behaviour is also a factor. Some children, as I noted in chapter 1, are slow to learn; others quick to learn but extremely adventurous. All children are busy learning and curious. If a parent's expectations are not in line with what it is reasonable to expect based on child development, that parent may well misidentify the normal learning processes of his or her child as willful disobedience. If a parent is excessively stressed, angry or upset, he or she may overreact to behaviour which is actually self-defence (running away, twisting and turning). If the parent has come to rely on external sanctions to control his or her own behaviour, and knows that corporal punishment is socially acceptable, since most corporal punishment takes place in the privacy of the home, there may be little or nothing holding the parent back.

Of special importance here is the parent's perception of what "works." Immediate compliance gives parents the false impression corporal punishment is effective. But two factors contribute to repeat behaviour. The first is the child's developmental level and temperament. Learning how to behave takes time especially when it comes to socially complex behaviours like telling the truth. It may take several months of constant reminding and explanation before a child "gets it." Also, children are different from one another. Some may be slower to learn than others; some may learn best in ways which involve strategies their parents are not familiar with. The second factor which contributes to repeat behaviour is corporal punishment itself. Corporal punishment contributes to increased levels of aggression in some children. This aggression often expresses itself in repetition of the behaviour for which the punishment was administered in the first place.

The escalation of punishment in the case of repeat behaviour or resistance appears to suggest that parents who approve of corporal punishment on the grounds it is effective may do so, in part, because they believe very severe forms of corporal punishment (abusive levels) will be effective in curbing a child's willfulness and hope that the child will comply before it gets to that point. As it happens, child abuse is often very successful in curbing the curiosity of children, their desire to act independently or their need to question authority. So a parent's belief that very severe corporal punishment "works" is not altogether unreasonable — when this is what parents want to teach their children. If a child is explicitly or implicitly warned that this is what awaits, perhaps the mere threat of it will be enough to produce compliance. It seems to me that this warning is what is implied when a parent tells a crying child who has just been corporally punished to stop or he or she will give that child "something to cry about."

I have argued that acting on the desire to produce dull, compliant children is immoral. I have suggested that while few parents would recognize this as desirable, their behaviour and the widespread support of corporal punishment seems to indicate otherwise. Perhaps their behaviour and beliefs are instead simply habitual — habits they would break if they realized the consequences of following them unquestioningly.

Changing the law so that corporal punishment is no longer considered justified does not imply that children should not be disciplined or taught to behave according to certain social expectations which are imposed on all persons who want to live in society with others. Instead, such a change implies the view that if adults are prevented by social norms from hopping the disciplinary "pain train" and not protected by law when they do, a significant proportion of child abuse and murder due to excessive corporal punishment will be averted. Add to this highly valued benefit, the reduction in risk of the many other harms associated with corporal punishment and the moral case for repealing Section 43 is made all the stronger.

Just in case corporal punishment was the only disciplinary strategy available to parents and teachers, we would be forced to weigh the consequences of not disciplining children at all against those of continuing to use it. Perhaps, under such circumstances, we would find ourselves agreeing with Barbara Amiel and James Dobson that hitting children, whatever the harm and whatever the nonsense of doing so, is better than letting them become social deviants, hurt others or damage their property. But corporal punishment is not the only disciplinary strategy available to parents and teachers. Other techniques are always available regardless of the nature of the behavioural problem.

It may have occurred to some of you, as it has to both Amiel and Dobson, that while there are other strategies available, corporal punishment is sometimes the most effective one and so ought to be used in such cases. So long as the goal of corporal punishment is to turn children into caring, law abiding citizens, this impression of the effectiveness of corporal punishment is deceptive. To justify the claim it is effective, one must first ask, "Effective at what?" Looking at its statistically demonstrated consequences, it seems to be effective at increasing levels of aggression in some children, impairing their ability to learn, interfering with the parent-child bond, reducing children's self-esteem, increasing the likelihood of depression in some children and the tendency to become spousal abusers in others. Corporal punishment is effective at achieving these outcomes. But they are not the ones most parents who believe corporal punishment is effective are aiming at.

No matter how far and in which way the procorporal punishment side of the effectiveness debate heads, it encounters serious conceptual and practical obstacles. It may be argued by those who defend the use of corporal punishment against children that the empirical evidence showing it is an ineffective discipline strategy is nevertheless compatible with its continued use. In this case, it might be urged that the point of corporal punishment is not to actually improve the behaviour of children but rather to simply manage or control it. As such, the fact that its only benefit seems to be immediate compliance is sufficient to justify using it. It would not matter to this argument that the use of corporal punishment tends towards an increase in antisocial behaviour or even child abuse since the aim of rearing children would simply be to immediately stop such behaviour, however much of it there is or how frequently it occurs.

This view of the matter is not, however, the one expressed in our law. Section 43 restricts the legal use of corporal punishment to cases where improvement of behaviour is the aim. Further, as I have argued, the view of children which underpins this extreme position is morally untenable. On the other hand, for those who agree with the reasoning behind Section 43 and so support corporal punishment—but only as a means of improving the behaviour of children–there is no empirical evidence to support the belief that it improves behaviour or character and plenty to suggest the opposite. For these supporters of corporal punishment, the fact that it is strongly correlated with increases in antisocial behaviour and that cessation of corporal punishment results in decreases of such behaviour must be taken to refute their position. On either defence, Section 43 is clearly unjustified.

The difficulty we face in light of the proposal to morally and legally condemn corporal punishment is what to do given the putative facts that most parents are not psychologically able to refrain from using corporal punishment; not trained in the use of nonviolent discipline. Barbara Amiel seems to think that this is a good reason for rejecting the call to abandon the practice. Not only are such parents not trained, she argues, but they are untrainable. There seems to be a theme of sorts emerging. If it is true that not only children but their adult counterparts are for the most part "uncivilizable" and the results of studies on the effects of corporal punishment are dispositive, then we are living in the very "state of nature" which Thomas Hobbes argued was long ago replaced by civil society. Canadians reject this conclusion and the more obvious trappings of the culture of violence which it calls to mind. Granting the rational persuasiveness of the studies in question, we must then proceed on the basis that Amiel's claims about parents and teachers as untrainable are false. At the moment, teachers and only those parents caught by the wide and multileveled net of interlocking political and social systems of child welfare, criminal justice and family law tend to find themselves on the threshold of mandatory training in nonviolent discipline. In most though not all cases, damage to children has already occurred. This needs to change and I have recommended David Archard's modest collectivism as a starting point for a much more comprehensive and pre-emptive social and political approach to the all-important matter of parent education in nonviolent discipline techniques. At the very least, children need to begin their education in nonviolent parenting and childcare in their early school years. And clearly, such an education could not be rationally delivered accompanied by the threat of violence for disciplinary breaches.

A Revised Family Statism Argument

While many may worry that additional Government intrusion into the disciplinary practices of parents—especially parents who have given the state no other reason to doubt their skills—will start us off on a slippery slope to totalitarianism, I have argued that such fears and the family statism argument which is based upon them are overblown and incendiary.[14] Nevertheless, the family statism argument is the one relied on by the Law Reform Commission when it concludes that the parental privilege conferred by Section 43 should not be eliminated from the Criminal Code (though it concludes the teacher privilege should be) and is arguably the main support offered in the Ontario Superior Court's denial of the application to have Section 43 declared unconstitutional. While various versions of the family statism argument are clearly weak or unsound (Amiel's and Dobson's for example) there is a version of it which is, I think, more reasonable.

Parents do not have a natural right to be free from state-imposed limits on their treatment of their children. Whenever such limits tend towards the better protection and well-being of children, they are justified. However, parenting is an activity which is largely experimental. Parents make lots of mistakes, even when they have the best interests of their children in clear view, love them, are informed about good parenting practice and support the law's prohibitions and requirements. They may find a particular strategy works well with one child, use it for another then discover it is not right for the second child and so on. But they learn from those mistakes and are capable of redressing them with their children and are motivated to do better. Given the experimental nature of parenting, it is not the sort of activity which has a single "correct procedure" or one which, for that reason, is improved by having someone watching over your shoulder for every error; a higher authority scrutinizing your every move, anxious to jump in and correct you with the least cause. It is not, for example, like learning how to perform neurosurgery. While it is granted that the state must engage in some general monitoring of the welfare of the nation's children and must enforce rules which govern limits on parental behaviour beyond which children are imperilled, any more invasive or closer scrutinizing role on the part of the state would constitute something uncomfortably close to "over your shoulder" surveillance and as such must be rejected as incompatible with the necessary conditions of successful parenting. If Section 43 were repealed, this new and improved version of the family statism argument would insist that the state's role as guardian of the nation's children would be raised to this unacceptable level of surveillance. As such, this family statism argument could conclude that Section 43 should not be repealed.

In brief, this more reasonable version of the family statism argument against repeal characterizes the debate in terms of two competing interests: the interest of the parent, given the experimental nature of parenting, to exercise his or her parental authority autonomously and confidently and with a certain amount of discretion versus the interest of the child in his or her security of the person. As stated, this conflict of interests would not last long in a court of law. This is because when it comes to conflicts of interest or rights which involve the welfare of children, Canadian law places the interests of children first and foremost.

To bolster this argument against repeal, a countermove could be made. This move involves redefining the parental interest noted above in terms of the interests of children. The result is a redescription of the conflict where the interests in competition are both those of children. As such, the conflict is not so easily dismissed as the one between the interests of children and adults. The redefined version of the conflict is one between a child's interest in having a parent who is autonomous and confident of his or her parental authority rather than one who sees him or herself as a mere agent of someone else's authority versus a child's interest in his or her security of the person.

A child's interest in having a parent who sees him or herself as the primary source of authority in that child's life cannot be denied. Arguably, a child's sense of stability, values and generally speaking, his or her identity are no doubt bound up to an important degree in the extent to which the parent acts and feels like he or she is in charge. The best version of the family statism argument against repeal assumes that this interest is greater than the child's interest in security of the person. Unfortunately, for that argument, this assumption cannot be supported.

I have already argued that everyone's interest but perhaps especially children's interest in security of the person is unequivocally essential to their sense of well-being. Without full security of the person, no human being can flourish. It is a Canadian "super-value." While a child's interest in having a confident parent is real, however, it is unlikely, for the following reasons, that it is unequivocally essential to their well-being. The sense of confidence implied by the argument above entails the notion that parents must have no or very few or weak doubts as to their primary authority in order to benefit their children — that any reduction or interruption of their parents' confidence would have harmful effects on them which would be worse than those risked by violating a child's security of the person. But if there are any parents of young children who have the degree of confidence implied by the argument, there are very few. The majority of parents of young children experience many doubts as to their authority and these doubts sometimes — perhaps even often — culminate in crises of confidence which lead them to confide in others or even to seek expert guidance. In addition, one might point to certain tribal cultures in which the authority of the individual parent is an unknown concept — where the authority of anyone identified by a child as "parent" is clearly derived from the authority of the group or tribe of which both child and parent are members. It follows that the interest children have in being parented by adults who are certain of their authority cannot be as fundamental to their well-being as is their security of the person.

So, even when the interests to be balanced are both interests of children, and even when it is admitted that all the interests involved are indeed relevant to children's welfare, the best version of the family statism argument fails to justify its conclusion that Section 43 should not be repealed. It fails in this task because its success relies on the claim that a child's interest in having an autonomous, confident parent is greater than his or her interest in security of the person — that a child will suffer a greater harm from violations of the first interest than he or she will from violations of the second. This claim is dubious at best; false at worst. There are other problems with the best version of the family statism argument — many of which have already been discussed. One of these was the unlikelihood, based on the experiences of other countries, that repealing Section 43 would, in fact, result in a "Big Brother" level of state surveillance of and intrusion into family life. My aim here, however, has been to argue that even if this did happen, it would still fail to justify the conclusion Section 43 should not be repealed.

In his decision rejecting the application by the Canadian Foundation for Children, Youth and the Law to have Section 43 declared unconstitutional, Justice McCombs, referring to the position of one of the respondents, The Coalition for Family Autonomy, wrote that:

> The Family Coalition does not claim that corporal punishment is an effective method of childrearing. Instead, its focus is on the importance of preserving the autonomy of the family as the most important environmental factor in child development. Indeed, the Coalition agrees that the time has come when it should no longer be considered reasonable by the courts to use objects for corporal punishment, nor to apply any force to the head. The Coalition also concedes that it is not a reasonable use of force to apply corporal punishment to teenagers or very young children. The Coalition concedes that these acts do not deserve protection under s.43. Its position, in summary, is that s.43, properly construed, is constitutional. By creating a protected sphere of activity permitting the use of reasonable force for correction, s.43 protects children [sic], yet recognizes the importance of the family as the central influence in child-rearing.[15]

McCombs himself concluded that:

> Parliament's purpose in maintaining s.43 is to recognize that parents and teachers require reasonable latitude in carrying out the responsibility imposed by law to provide for their children, to nurture them, and to educate them. That responsibility, Parliament has decided, cannot be carried out unless parents and teachers have a protected sphere of authority within which to fulfill their responsibilities. That sphere of authority is

intended to allow a defense to assault within a limited domain
of physical discipline, while at the same time ensuring that
children are protected from child abuse.[16]

Advocates of repeal agree with their opponents that parents
should have "a protected sphere of authority within which to fulfill
their responsibilities." But in the context of the above decision, this
phrase may simply be a euphemism for something advocates of repeal
deny — that parents require the privilege to assault their children for
their education as long as such assaults do not result in or risk serious
injury or death. Alternatively, the privilege to assault may be seen to
directly follow from the more general principle. Clearly, the reasoning
in the second case is spurious and in the first, there is no reasoning at
all; simply assertion. It seems that, in this case only, it is no business of
the law whether such assaults pose a risk of serious injury or death nor
whether they result in noninjurious harms or the risk of such harms.
McCombs counters that on its own, there is no strong evidence that
corporal punishment poses any such risks granting that, in combination with other factors, it may indeed do so. As I have argued, those
other factors include stresses which virtually no parent in this day and
age can avoid at all times. For all intents and purposes then, adding
corporal punishment to the normal conditions of being a parent is
indeed a risk factor for harms and injuries to children.

When we consider the use of safety seats for children in vehicles or
the use of helmets on bicycles, we see the law at work preventing us
from taking chances not only with the lives of others but indeed with
our own where there are only statistical risks of harms and injuries.[17]
In the case of safety seats, for example, no one would argue that not
being in such a seat ever caused a child to sustain a fatal head injury. A
car crash does that. What we say is that if the injured or dead child had
not been thrown around inside the vehicle or through the windshield,
he or she would probably not have died. This seems to be a good
enough reason to require the use of safety seats for all young children.
In a sense, the same can be said here. Even if it was granted for the sake
of argument that corporal punishment on its own might not cause serious harms to children, given the children who have been seriously
harmed, it seems safe to say they would not have been if they had
never been corporally punished. We decided that "a protected sphere

of authority within which to fulfill their responsibilities" did not entail or support the claim that parents should have the privilege of not putting their children in safety seats. The Supreme Court may find that this widely accepted view is no reason for it to reject the family statism argument in favour of Section 43 since it has never had to rule on the constitutionality of the safety seat requirement. But the fact that the latter rule is widely accepted in Canadian society is good evidence that Canadian parents and lawmakers do not regard the principle of parental autonomy as having nearly as much weight or scope as do the Family Coalition and Justice McCombs.

In addition to the moral and broad political issues surrounding the use of corporal punishment, are the strictly legal ones. According to the law as it stands, every act of corporal punishment is an act of assault. As such, every act of corporal punishment is prima facie illegal. However, two considerations currently in law serve to block the likelihood of criminal prosecution in the event of its moderate use. The first is Section 43.[18] This defence does not necessarily apply in every case of corporal punishment. As we have seen, for instance, the use of force must be reasonable. While reasonableness is supposed to be determined by the court relative to societal norms, the beliefs of defendants about reasonableness often seem to take precedence in actual cases. In addition, when it comes to cases of corporal punishment which do not clearly involve what the community agrees is child abuse, there is an absence of clear norms to refer to. Some Canadian courts still interpret reasonable force as including those uses which result in serious physical trauma to children, strongly implying that societal norms indicate the moral acceptability of such harms. As such, prosecution is unlikely in all but the most serious cases of punishment—ones approaching what most people would agree is abusive. But in a recent Ontario case, these norms appear to have dramatically shifted.

A mother charged with assaulting her four-year-old son was found guilty but given a conditional discharge by the judge. In his decision, Judge Saul Nosanchuk narrowed the definition of reasonable force to exclude the use of anything but the hand. Mrs. Klassen, the mother, had spanked her son with "a foot-long pine stick" for failing to stop crying after receiving a hand spanking for failing to come inside from playing and do his home schooling.[19] Judge Nosanchuk considered the second spanking excessive and so found that Mrs. Klassen could not use Section 43 to defend herself. This new legal definition of what counts as reasonable force was relied on in Justice McCombs's decision of the Ontario Superior Court that Section 43 does not violate the Charter of Rights and Freedoms. However, as a new legal definition, the idea that reasonable force does not include the use of weapons such as sticks or belts may yet be challenged or reversed. Whether this definition reflects a change in community standards or imposes one is also an open question but one less easily resolved. Dallas Miller of the Medicine Hat Homeschool Legal Defense Fund is quoted in the *Report* as saying, "This particular judgement does not have the weight of case law on its side" and Darrell Reid, President of Focus on the Family Canada insists the case "still comes down to parents being in the best position to decide how to discipline. Spanking or not spanking remains a parental right."[20]

Until public debate produces a stronger sense of widespread agreement on the norms which indicate when a use of physical force is reasonable, predictability on which ones are informing the courts should not be expected. However, as Miller pointed out, case law still seems to be in favour of incredible tolerance concerning what is considered legally defensible. As such, Section 43 is likely to continue to discourage prosecutions for assault when the assailant is a parent and the victim is that parent's child. If repealed or declared invalid, this constraint on prosecutions would arguably no longer operate. But Section 43 is not the only thing holding back prosecutors.

The second consideration which may block criminal prosecution in the case of moderate corporal punishment is the juridical principle of *de minimis non curat lex*. The interpretation of this general rule of jurisprudence rests upon what a given society considers trivial, unwelcome physical contact. Adult women were long subject to "reasonable" beatings from their husbands and fathers on the grounds that within certain limits, such beatings were of a trivial nature. We have done an about-turn on this question when it comes to women but have yet to embrace the principle of nonviolence in the case of children. Until society changes its views, the *de minimis* rule will continue to be an impediment to legal interest or criminal prosecution in most cases of corporal punishment (since most of them involve spanking only) even if Section 43 is removed from the Criminal Code.

I have argued that spanking must be included in what both my moral argument condemns and my legal argument recommends. While my own view, one which is shared by many childcare experts, is that even spanking risks the sorts of harms which must be avoided on moral grounds, I realize that this position is difficult for many if not most parents and teachers to accept. It is in the spirit of sensitivity to their difficulty and my conviction that spanking should be condemned along with all other forms of corporal punishment that I have raised the logical issue of spanking as a behaviour-improving strategy. Those who defend their spanking behaviour frequently protest that it is not their intention to hurt and that they do not hurt their children. But if there is no pain, then these parents must be asked what they think functions as the improving mechanism in spanking. It may be argued that the improving mechanism is the expression of anger which the action facilitates. But in this case, we are confronted with the consequence of teaching children that the administration of unconsented to physical contact is a legitimate means of expressing anger.

The fact that children are hit with great frequency in our society hardly seems to register on most people's moral radars. Nevertheless, incidences of extreme violence towards children occasionally make front page news. As I noted at the start of my discussion, reports of such violence shock us—compel our attention—and that is the most likely explanation of why it is they make headlines. Not even the most strident defenders of corporal punishment defend acts that aim to or reasonably can be expected to seriously harm or kill children. But those who actively defend corporal punishment insist that it is not violent. If incidences of corporal punishment happen to make front pages, it is usually because of its ties to religious or cultural practice. What the media presume will strike its audiences as shocking is government interference with religious or cultural freedom not the fact that some child was paddled for misbehaviour.

Among those who oppose the use of corporal punishment, there are some experts who also argue that certain forms of it—spanking for example—ought to be distinguished from what we ordinarily imagine as violence or child abuse. The temptation on the part of anti-corporal punishment activists to distinguish spanking from other forms of corporal punishment and take spanking out of the realm of violence towards children is understandable. Few parents at the present time will take arguments which insist on its inclusion seriously. But while I see a place for such technical manoeuvers, I do not agree that they ought to restrict the strategies of the anti-corporal punishment movement. The Swedish experience has shown that any slack granted to the status quo has a tendency to slow reform. In which case, room for the very strong view that all forms of corporal punishment are violent and so must be condemned along with what we ordinarily imagine as child abuse must be preserved. You might say my position occupies this radical space.

Some may find the activism implied in my argument inappropriately dogmatic. Philosophers, they might argue, should be circumspect—even neutral—in their presentation of the pros and cons of moral issues. In response, while there are many moral questions which are truly open and so benefit from long and open-minded study, I can only state that I do not believe the question of whether we ought to be permitted to corporally punish children is one of them. I believe, instead, that this question is more like ones which ask whether anyone ought to be permitted to own slaves or whether husbands ought to be permitted to beat their wives. We do not regard either of these questions as ones which are open; indeed philosophical neutrality on such questions would seem immoral.

In closing, I wish to admit that I hit my own children as youngsters in anger and frustration. I did not do it with the intention of improving their behaviour or character and I know that I did hurt and frighten them. And like most parents who hit their kids, I always felt bad after doing so. As I began my studies in philosophy, the moral wrongness of what I had done became clearer and clearer in my mind. I have discussed this with my children and hope that the effects of my behaviour will be mitigated by my efforts, while they were still young, to be a nonviolent parent and one who acknowledged her wrongdoing. As they now enter full adulthood, I hope as well that the effects of my behaviour will not cause them as much difficulty as it does in so many cases—as my own experiences of childhood violence affected me. I am deeply sorry that I treated them in this manner and hope, with all of my heart and mind, that a long history of harming children in my family has finally come to an end.

Notes

•••••••••••

Chapter 1

The Terms of the Corporal Punishment Debate

1. Ongoing story, *The Montreal Gazette*, 10-28 February 1998 as reported by Lisa Fetterman, Mike King, Irwin Block and Peggy Curran.
2. On 26 February 1998, both parents in this case were found guilty by a jury on seventeen counts of assault, assault with a weapon and assault causing bodily harm. They faced a maximum penalty of fourteen years in prison. On 27 February 1998, Justice Kevin Downs sentenced the father to thirty months in prison and the mother to twenty months in prison.
3. *Tremeears 1986* refers to eight cases under Section 43 (two of which refer to the same events) in which the accused pled his or her innocence on the grounds that because it was intended as correction, the assault in question was justified under law. See *R. v. Imbeault* (1977); *R. v. Ogg-Moss* (1981), leave to appeal to Supreme Court of Canada granted 24 C.R. (3d) 264n, 40 N.R. 440 (S.C.C.); *R. v. Wheaton* (1982); *R. v. Lepage* (1983); *R. v. Nixon* (1984); *R. v. Dupperon* (1985); *Ogg-Moss v. R.* (1984); *R. v. Taylor* (1985).
4. McGillivray (1998) 193-242.
5. *R. v. Robinson* referred to in "Brief to: Minister of Justice and Attorney General," [*R43 Brief*] written and submitted by Corinne Robertshaw, founder of the Repeal 43 Committee and distributed by The Institute for the Prevention of Child Abuse, April 1994. See Appendix B, p. IV.

6. Ibid.
7. McGillivray (1998) 3.
8. Archard (1999) 74-89.
9. The part of this definition set off in quotations is from *The Oxford Concise English Dictionary*, (1995). Joan Durrant, a child clinical psychologist with the University of Manitoba and expert on corporal punishment, has defined it as, "the use of physical force with the intention of causing a child to experience pain but not injury for the purpose of correction or control of the child's behaviour." ("Corporal Punishment: Research Findings and Implications for Practice," *Putting Research Into Practice 1999 Workshops*, BC Council for Families, seminar presentation, 27 October 1999. I have excluded the point: "but not injury" on the grounds that many threats of corporal punishment are in fact threats to injure. "I'll beat you 'till you're black and blue'" or "I'll kill you" for example. Most parents would probably not issue these kinds of threats but it is unlikely that ones who do consider them illegal.
10. Quoted in Feinberg and Gross's introduction to Part 5 "Punishment" In *Philosophy of Law*, 515. The theoretical issues concerning punishment per se in the context of moral philosophy and philosophy of law are much more complex than I treat them here. There are more than two theories of punishment though retributivist and consequentialist theories are the dominant ones in the Western tradition. And while relatively recent attempts to reconcile the conflicting claims of retributivists and consequentialists "seemed to many to make a genuine breakthrough" (Feinberg and Gross, 522), I follow the simpler path of treating the two as opposed. In spite of this opposition, it does not follow that each theory will always come up with opposing conclusions regarding the requirements of just or moral punishment. Both seem to require, for example, that "the punishment fit the crime." Indeed, a full-blown philosophical analysis of corporal punishment of children in light of both historical and more recent twentieth century developments in its area, seems called for.
11. Robertshaw (1994) 7.
12. *Law Reform Commission Working Paper #29* (1982) 139. The popular analogy of the family with a ship at sea whose head requires the same sort and degree of authority that a ship's captain has when her vessel is offshore is poetically evocative but factually barren. What warrants the captain's special powers is the fact that certain acts or omissions by any sailor may cause the drowning of the whole crew and loss of the vessel and its cargo. There is a sense in which life aboard ship is always one step from a state of extreme emergency. The typical family is not situated in this way. Acts or omissions by individual family members with respect to rule following, for example, do not generally threaten the lives of "all aboard." As such, the rationale for exempting sailors at sea from full protection of their secu-

rity of the person rights cannot be sensibly used to deny children these rights against their parents.

13. *Canadian Criminal Code* [CrC] published as *Martin's Annual Criminal Code*, (1999).

14. Moral philosophers who argue from empirical premises — that is who advance "naturalistic" moral theories — sometimes claim that our moral feelings or feelings directed towards the good of others develop out of our early feelings for our own welfare. Hume (1902) is frequently cited as the main proponent of naturalized ethics in the Modern period. He wrote that "No man is absolutely indifferent to the happiness and misery of others. The first has a natural tendency to give pleasure; the second, pain. This every one may find in himself." See §V, part II, n. 19. However, while Hume argued that relishing our own pleasure and despising our own pain may form the foundation of our moral feelings, he and many other empirical moral philosophers did not urge, as did Hobbes (1968) that moral feelings were reducible to self-interest. The connection for Hume et al., between self-interest and moral feeling is made via our capacity for imaginative sympathy with the circumstances of others. We are able to imagine what the other feels like by referring their situation and/or expression to our own experience. If this imaginative exercise produces pleasure in us, we are happy for the other and may be impelled to preserve her happy state. If it produces pain, we seek to comfort her or remove the cause of the difficulty. In the absence of any feeling one way or the other for his or her own welfare, it would be difficult if not impossible on this model, for someone to have either sort of moral impulse.

15. I am relying here on nonexpert self-knowledge and common sense which tells me that as I become familiar with certain pains, they tend to cause me less overt distress and indisposition — that is I get used to them. This process of toughening is, I suspect, a psychologically complicated one. One possible consequence of an intentional regime of pain delivery is a weakening of the moral sentiments. As we come to find certain pains tolerable, we may tend to become intolerant of those who find them unbearable. As our capacity for sympathy with others is diminished, so too is our capacity for moral feeling.

16. Several corporal punishment researchers have explored the issue of "escalation." Escalation is defined according to two parameters: the first, described here, is specific to the tendency of the corporally punishing parent to administer more and more severe punishment as a child re-offends. The second relates to the intergenerational transmission of corporal punishing practice and the tendency for such punishment to become abusive in subsequent generations. In the main, the subjects of studies which establish the escalating pattern have been abusive parents and their children. It is clear from such studies that instances of abuse are, in the major-

ity of cases, escalations from more moderate forms of corporal punishment both in the first and second sense noted above. See chapter 6 of
Straus (1994) and chapter 5 from Kadushin and Martin (1981). See also
Durrant and Rose-Krasnor (1995). I will reconsider the connection
between corporal punishment and child abuse and the argument against
prohibiting the former which denies this connection in greater detail in my
concluding chapter when summing up the "best" arguments against
repealing Section 43 and their flaws.
17. See the case *Canadian Foundation for Children,* etc., (5 July, 2000).
18. *Morgentaler, Smoling and Scott v. The Queen* [1988]. In its 1988 decision, the
    Supreme Court of Canada found that Section 251 of the Criminal Code
    restricting access to abortion violated the Canadian Charter of Rights and
    Freedoms and since it was not saved by Section 1 of the Charter which
    allows such violations under certain circumstances, Section 251 was
    declared invalid.

Chapter 2

A Very Short History of Moral Philosophy

1. While it would appear that philosophers have not, historically speaking,
   devoted any considerable attention to the subject of children and childhood, this seems to be changing. Two well-known historical exceptions are
   Locke (1693) and Jean-Jacques Rousseau's (1991). With respect to contemporary work on the subject, I highly recommend the very thorough
   Bibliographic Essay in Archard (1993). In addition are Matthews (1980,
   1984, 1994) and Purdy (1992). Canadians working in this area include
   Turner (1998), and Brennan and Noggle (1998).
2. Socrates lived in Athens, Greece, and pursued philosophical enquiry
   among his friends, students and acquaintances into a great variety of questions—questions about justice, beauty, religious belief and education
   among others. It is believed he earned his living as a stonemason and,
   according to his pupil Plato, Socrates never accepted any money for his
   philosophical activities. What we know about Socrates's views is determined almost entirely by what Plato wrote about them since Socrates himself never put any of his views to paper. It is generally supposed that Plato
   agreed with most of what Socrates taught.
3. Aristotle, (1953, 1976).
4. The Greek term *eudaimonia* is usually translated into English as "happiness." Yet due to the special sense of happiness which it connotes, the
   term has come to be used in its own right. According to Aristotle,
   eudaimonia is the proper and ultimate end or goal of all human conduct, the fulfillment of our unique nature as rational and feeling creatures and the cosmic purpose of our existence. It is a state of being

achieved through the activity of the rational soul "in accordance with virtue, or if there are more kinds of virtue than one, in accordance with the best and most perfect kind" (Aristotle [1953, 1976] Book One, Part vii, 1098a8). Aristotle also qualifies the achievement of eudaimonia as occurring over "a complete lifetime" (Ibid.). It includes, as the reference to the "rational soul" suggests, a high state of intellectual satisfaction and may be understood as close in meaning to the notion of complete human well-being.

5. Alasdair MacIntyre (1981) is noted as a leading contemporary virtue ethicist though more, perhaps, in the tradition of Aquinas than of Aristotle. He attempted via a critique of the moral theorizing of the Modern Era (late seventeenth century to early twentieth century), to bring the virtue approach back into vogue. In both the old and new versions, the concept of the "self" is necessarily encumbered by and integrated within a social web of roles and relationships. Unlike the "self-sufficient" individualist ideal of the Modern period, the integrated ideal of the self identifies virtues of character in terms of their tendency to enhance sharing and devotion to the good of one's community. Less communitarian versions of virtue ethics theories have been advanced by liberal theorists such as Raz (1986) Annas (Fall 1989).

6. Aristotle (1953, 1976) Book Three, xii, 1119b4-18.

7. In ancient Greece and for a very long time after and elsewhere, it was thought there was no point to educating female children. This was not because females were, as it happened, destined to a life a servitude. Rather, it was generally believed by males that all females were congenitally incapable of rationality and so education was wasted on them. It was thought that because they could not be educated females were fated to always serve and never lead. Male slaves were treated in the same manner. Aristotle (1958) did indicate however that his view of the relationship between husbands and wives was somewhat different from that between masters and slaves.

8. For a thorough analysis of Aristotle's opinions concerning children, see McGowan Tress "Aristotle's Child: Development through *Genesis, Oikos* and *Polis,*" *Ancient Philosophy* 17 (1997): 63-84; reprinted in Turner and Matthews (1998).

9. Aristotle (1953, 1976) Book Five, Part v, 1132b28-1133a13. It is curious that in this passage, Aristotle distinguishes between striking a subordinate for his violent act and punishing him for it. Presumably, punishment in this case involves a further penalty for the infraction but I am uncertain why Aristotle did not consider the beating in itself a punishment.

10. Rawls (1972) chap. 8: §69-70. The twentieth-century philosopher of justice lays out a version of the virtue of quietude. Interestingly, he discusses them under the category of the virtues of childhood.

11. Moral requirements generally follow from a particular moral theory in the form of explicit moral rules: "Do This," "Don't Do That." Your moral theory might be: "Whatever God Says to Do is What must Be Done" in which case you must regard the Ten Commandments as moral requirements. If you fail to observe the rule, then you are acting immorally. Moral permissions, on the other hand, generally arise in the absence of such rules. If a particular moral theory has nothing whatsoever to say about how human fetuses ought to be treated, for example, then one may argue that such a moral theory permits abortion. If you have an abortion, since you are not, according to that theory, breaking a moral rule against it, you are not acting immorally. The distinction between moral requirement and moral permission suggests that the distinction between moral (required) and immoral (prohibited) is not exhaustive. Aristotle promises to discuss what he calls the management of wives and children by grown men in the context of a long commentary on the management of household slaves but either failed to deliver or what was written on the subject has been lost. However, when considering the education of children, he states that "the superintendents of education must exercise a general control over the way in which children pass their time." (Aristotle [1958] Book 7, D, chap. 17, §7). He is especially concerned that the young not pick up the habit of bad language from slaves. "Those who are guilty, in spite of all prohibitions, of talking or acting indecently must be punished accordingly. The younger freemen, who are not yet allowed to recline at the common tables, should be subjected to corporal punishment and other indignities." (Ibid.). As such, we know of one instance at least, in which Aristotle viewed corporal punishment of children as morally required.

12. St. Thomas Aquinas is most well-known for his *Summa Theologica* — a work which was lengthy but unfinished when he died. In it, he discusses in disputational or argumentative form, the many dogmas of the Roman Catholic Church including the existence of God, the nature of sin and the afterlife.

13. Aquinas (1960) 181.

14. Ibid. 192.

15. Suicide, since it was the worst sin, could not be used to avoid committing other sins.

16. Aquinas, 217.

17. Natural law theory holds that due to basic and "natural" features of human beings, certain rules follow necessarily for human conduct. These rules constitute the moral framework within which all human beings must arrange their lives and so determine, for example, which laws ought to govern their political and social interactions. Aquinas had a Christian conception of human nature — it included, for example, the existence of a divinely created soul. His morality was justified by this conception and his

position on social and political arrangements was justified in turn by his moral views. Not all natural law theories are theologically based, however. Yet they all begin and are determined by conceptions of human nature. See Finnis (1994).

18. Aquinas, 253.

19. Ibid. The connection is made based on the belief that husbands "contained" their wives bodies, metaphorically in the present, according to Genesis in the Old Testament, and actually at the dawn of human existence.

20. Ibid.

21. As was the case in ancient Greece, women were regarded as irrational creatures in the Medieval Era.

22. See Greven (1991) for a thought-provoking discussion on the Protestant tradition of using pain to drive out "Satanic" impulses in children. The Catholic tradition must be seen as somewhat distinct since it regards pain and suffering as also potentially valuable in themselves.

23. The schism between Christians that occurred during the Reformation was largely fueled by Martin Luther's conviction that intimacy with God was available to and ought to be pursued by all individuals and did not require the mediation of Church officials. One consequence of the Roman Catholic Church's hierarchical approach to personal salvation was that the Catholic laity was discouraged from reading Holy Scripture. Luther reversed this policy and encouraged all of his followers to study the "good book."

24. Kant (1997) argues that human reason is eminently practical; that given the context in which it operates—the world of sense experience or "phenomena"—it can direct us regarding ultimate ends as well as to the means of their realization. Hume had argued earlier in the eighteenth century that human reason was impotent when it came to setting ultimate ends but Kant found this moral view very unsatisfactory. He argued that human beings were unavoidably teleological (or goal oriented) and that only human reason could reveal the ultimate purpose of human activity—that is what Kant called "the highest good." In addition, he said, human reason determines which of our subsidiary goals conform to our ultimate one and selects the means we ought to employ in pursuit of our practical moral ends.

25. The problem which Kant attempted to solve with his notion of the *synthetic a priori* was created by the belief, on the one hand, that we could only be absolutely certain of analytic truths such as "a=a" and the belief, on the other hand, that there must be absolute moral truths. Presumably absolute moral truths would tell us how we ought to act in the world. But analytic truths—the only absolute ones—tell us nothing substantive about the terms they relate. Was it possible to be absolutely certain (*a priori* or prior to experience) of a moral truth (an *a posteriori* or a synthetic proposition

known through or in conjunction with experience? Kant purported to demonstrate that it was using mathematical models. He argued that analytic truths were not the only ones of which we could be absolutely certain. See Kant (1989) Introduction, Parts 4, 5, 6.

26. The term "transcendental" in this context refers to Kant's view that in order to be securely grounded, his moral theory would have to be connected in some way to a reality which existed beyond the world of sense experience. This was because everything in the "phenomenal" world was transitory and uncertain. Kant saw the connection in the activity of human reason as it moved between experience and intuition.

27. See Kant (1964) Chapter II, (specifically) The Formula of the Law of Nature.

28. From chap. 1: "Corporal punishment is the administration by a recognized authority figure upon a recognized subordinate of some level of physical pain for the purpose of 'causing the latter to suffer for an offense' or 'inflicting a penalty for an offense.' Further, it will be supposed that punishment, in the context of corporal punishment, has a morally, legally and politically acceptable purpose: to get the offender to avoid engaging in 'bad' behaviour."

29. Even if children's behaviour was not effectively improved by a hands off approach, the intention to change it in this way would not be contradicted by everyone following this policy. The consequence of everyone following it might be that children were in general ill-behaved but undesired consequences are not relevant, according to Kant, to whether or not one's intention, act or policy is moral.

30. Kant (1995) 83-94.

31. Ibid.

32. To fully comprehend Kant's moral theory, its implications and applications, you—or so many Kant scholars contend—must first master his *Critique of Pure Reason* (1989). That work is generally considered at times to be near to impenetrable even among philosophers. A writer of popular cosmology writes that Kant "had earned his bachelor's degree (paying his tuition out of his earnings from gambling at billiards and cards) but five more years would pass before he was awarded his doctorate. He had not yet ruined his writing style by trying to satisfy the formal requirements established by the philosophy faculty at the University of Konigsberg, where, at the age of forty-six, he would finally be appointed professor of logic and metaphysics." See Ferris (1988) 144-45.

33. Among the early utilitarians were Jeremy Bentham and his close friend, James Mill, Mill's son, John Stuart Mill, and later in the nineteenth century, Henry Sidgwick.

34. These empiricists based their theories of knowledge and morality on the belief that since human beings were restricted to experience and observa-

tion when it came to learning about the world and since experience and observation were sometimes unreliable, everything which they came to know about the world and themselves was susceptible to doubt. The strongest attitude which we can have towards our beliefs is therefore one of confidence. Their methods for coming to know the world with confidence followed those of science. Rationalists, on the hand, begin from the intuition that certain things are known by human beings with absolute certainty (*a priori*) and work back to the conclusion that human reason is in a position to supply the grounds of this ultimately imperturbable certitude in some of our beliefs.

35. Kant's point is well taken if you agree with his overall assessment of moral conduct. If it is true that when acting, I am aware that certain desires I have to make myself happy or satisfy myself in some way are playing into my intentions, then it will be impossible for me to tell whether I would have acted the same way in the absence of such desires or an expectation that my act might satisfy them. If I cannot tell that, then I cannot say for sure that I am acting purely out of a sense of moral duty and if I am not, then my act cannot be considered moral. However, this did not mean, according to Kant, that my act was immoral.

36. See Scarre (1996) 5n, 210. "I suggest that the variations in the conceptions [of happiness] of different people are far less considerable than those who speak of a fragmentation (or degeneration) of values in the modern world would have us believe."

37. See Bentham (1973). John Stuart Mill sought to refine Bentham's somewhat crude method for determining moral utilities by introducing a distinction among the kinds of pleasures and pains different creatures could experience. Mill argued, for example, that in addition to being sentient creatures (ones which could experience physical pain and pleasure), human beings were also cognitive ones and as such, their pleasures and pains could be qualitatively different from those of strictly sentient animals. In fact, Mill argued, the intellectual pleasures of which humans were capable were superior to the "lower" pleasures in most respects — so much so that Mill insisted that were any intelligent human being given a choice between being "Socrates dissatisfied" and "a fool satisfied," she would always choose wisdom over comfort. See Mill's essay "Utilitarianism," vol. 10, 1963. "Mill believed that the happy person is someone who pays close attention to his self-development, who works hard to hone his talents, refine his tastes and increase his sympathies — in short a person who desires 'for its own sake, the conformity of his own character to his standard of excellence.'" Scarre [1996] 5).

38. In addition to introducing the distinction between higher and lower pleasures into Bentham's "classical" formulation of utilitarian moral theory, Mill also foreshadowed a distinction between "rule" and "act" utilitarian-

ism which has yet to settle into a firm conceptual cleft. According to classical utilitarianism, the moral agent appears to be called upon to weigh the consequences of every single instance of her actions. So, even though, for instance, you have a pretty good idea of how your sister gets when you borrow her clothes without asking (since you've done it many times), you must rehearse all of the same data plus what happened the last time on this current occasion of wearing her things before deciding whether it would be all right or not all right to do so. In "Utilitarianism" (vol. 10, 1963), Mill faced the objection that such a requirement went squarely against what seemed intuitively obvious to most people, namely that certain acts were simply contrary to duty regardless of the consequences — stealing for example. Mill attempted to reconcile this intuition with the apparent requirements of utilitarianism by suggesting that over time and experience, human beings develop rules for acting which account for that experience. Nevertheless, Mill saw the ongoing observance of such rules as justified by its benefits to overall utility. In the twentieth century, this suggestion of Mill's was given clearer expression. According to Scarre (1996) 122, "(R.F. Harrod) proposed that utilitarianism should judge actions to be right or wrong, not on the basis of their individual impact on the public utility, but by reference to the utility of the general performance of actions of their kind." As such, if the tendency of using corporal punishment is to produce consequences which go against public utility, a moral rule against it would be called for.

39. See Durrant and Rose-Krasnor (1995) vii. The authors write that "although corporal punishment has been used by the majority of Canadian parents, its justifiability is increasingly being called into question as research consistently reveals that it not only lacks effectiveness but that it carries significant risks for children's development outcomes. Of a large body of research on human learning, child development, and child abuse not a single study has demonstrated beneficial effects of this practice."

40. To adequately support an empirical claim, it is not necessary to provide evidence sufficient to removing any logical doubt about its truth. Rather, one needs to adduce evidence sufficient to remove all reasonable doubt. The concept of reasonable doubt is subtle and one which is often misunderstood in the context of criminal guilt. Those who stand in judgement must be confident of someone's guilt based on the evidence and not, as one often hears, certain of it "beyond a shadow of a doubt."

41. See Sidgwick (1981) Schneewind (1977).

42. For Plato, this "postmodern" difficulty is represented by what has come to be known as "the Euthyphro problem" (named after the title character of one of Plato's dialogues) where the question arises in the course of considering God as the source of all morality whether an act is good because He says it is or whether He says the act is good because it is good accord-

ing to some independent criterion. Both avenues of reasoning lead away from God as a source of the moral. In the case of Kant's duty-based moral system, the difficulty arises in the context of formulating maxims for testing by the categorical imperative. If you want to steal a car and your maxim "Steal a car whenever you feel like a joyride" fails the test, just try again. "Borrow a car bringing it back in original condition whenever the car will not be missed by the owner." Perfectly universalizable but not something which most people would accept as a moral duty or even as morally permissible.

43. Cf. 10n.

44. While the veil of ignorance conceals particular information about each of the participants from themselves and one another, the epistemic (knowledge) situation in the original position does not exclude general information about human beings nor about the world or societies in which they live. This may include information about the various social and political arrangements humans have experimented with. See Rawls (1972) §4 (The Original Position) and §24 (The Veil of Ignorance).

45. What Kant claimed to have done was show how an objective principle of morality could be abstracted from familiar substantive moral rules or practices such as "Honour thy Father and thy Mother" and then applied independently of those rules in all situations calling for a moral decision. The objective moral rule or moral law had the advantage under the condition of religious and cultural pluralism, or so Kant thought, of not having any obvious affiliation with any particular religious, ethnic or cultural doctrine. As such, members of all such groups could give their rational allegiance to the moral law without sacrificing, or more importantly, being seen to sacrifice, their substantive moral commitments. Rawls (1972) makes a similar move. But instead of focusing on the issue of morality, Rawls focuses on the issue of justice arguing that it is our conception of justice rather than our conception of morality which occupies the highest level of abstraction. Even in the face of disagreement over philosophical moral principles, we are able, or so Rawls thinks, to endorse a principle of "justice as fairness" which may be seen as compatible with almost any of our competing moral systems.

46. Alan Gewirth (1978) is perhaps the best known of those philosophers who have worked on the project of updating Kant's rationalist moral perspective for the twentieth century. Gewirth, like Kant, argues that the basis of moral action is unconditioned practical rationality detached from normative beliefs. Charles Larmore (1996) may also be cited as a twentieth-century proponent of the rationalist moral perspective. Larmore criticizes Kant's metaphysics but embraces his notion of moral duty where it is agreed by all that there are some things we ought to do or ought not to do regardless of the feelings which either produce.

47. Mill, (1963) 10, 250. Wayne Sumner, (1987) a Canadian philosopher, has written extensively on consequentialist rights theories — one of these being utilitarian. Sumner argues that contrary to most received views, not only can a consequentialist moral theory provide such a foundation, it is the only sort of moral theory that can do so. In short, Sumner argues that in order to morally ground a theory of rights, one requires a substantive and realistic goal in virtue of which the consequences of human conduct (and institutions) can be evaluated. He argues further that within such a framework, rights take on the role of constraining the individual and collective pursuit of that goal (and its various components) with an eye to maximizing its realization under the imperfect and at times, messy, circumstances of day to day living. "The case which we have made for rights as goal-based constraints, both on the individual and social level, rests heavily on the imperfections of our own nature and of our decision-making environment...the imperfections of our world, while doubtless regrettable, seem [as] unalterable [as the allure of "theories of rights tied less closely to human imperfections"]....In that case, we need not fear that a consequentialist foundation of rights will easily become inapplicable or obsolete."

Chapter 3

Morality and Culture: When Values Collide

1. Canada faces this difficulty squarely every time the subject of group rights comes up in the context of constitutional debate. Recently, for example, The Government of British Columbia signed a treaty with the Nisga'a Nation over land entitlements. While the signing of the Nisga'a Treaty marks an important development in the efforts of Native Peoples to secure their position in Canadian social and political culture, it met with resistance among non-Native British Columbians concerned that this is but a small step on the road to losing their property rights because of their ethnic origin. The problem here is that in order for the Nisga'a Nation to try to preserve their culture — something they are clearly entitled to do under the Canadian Constitution, they must protect their ties to the land upon which they have lived and worked according to their cultural traditions. Property rights, in the language of British North American politics, have become part and parcel of Native culture. Yet the British North American tradition of property rights does not understand them as intimately connected with culture per se. The tension thereby created causes deep divisions between Natives and non-Natives. The suggestion seems to be that bringing the two together threatens to place the values of a particular culture ahead of the so-called culturally neutral rights of all — a consequence which appears, at least on the surface, to contradict the liberal value of neutrality on ideas of "the good life." There is much work to be done on

reconciling the understandings of both groups. See Webber (1994) and Kymlicka (1998).

2. The model of the twelve Apostles of Christ was determinative of the Christian mission for centuries and continues to hold sway among some sects. The Apostles were instructed by Christ to venture forth and spread the word; that recruiting "soldiers of Christ" was their most important task. Greven (1991) 59-60 recounts the experiences in the 1930s of Lester Sumrall in this vein. After having a terrible vision of the pains of hellfire, Sumrall reported that God told him he "was responsible for those who are lost." Greven writes, "His life mission became clear and the twenty-year-old man became an evangelist to the world, intent upon saving souls while remaining haunted by this terrifying vision of hell."

3. The activities of the American Ku Klux Klan in Skokie demonstrate this problem. The KKK's plan to parade down main street in full view of the town's sizable black population prevailed on the grounds of their First Amendment right to free speech. But clearly, their parade would cause serious anxiety if not terror among their African American neighbours — indeed, this may have been its intention. Unfortunately, First Amendment rights are so powerful in the United States that fear is not sufficient to override them. The effect was the continued terrorization of a minority population justified under law. Living together in peace sometimes requires withholding expression of feeling and belief — anyone who lives in an intimate grouping with others knows this. The reason is that such expression may provoke extreme reaction calling for extreme reaction in turn. This process of escalating hostilities almost invariably leads to someone getting seriously hurt. So we "hold our tongues." The right to free speech seems in practice to subvert the normal influence of prudence but clearly cannot be foregone in a liberal democratic society. Canada seems to have worked out a much more sensible understanding of free expression on this score. See MacKinnon (1987) as well as Justice Dickson's reasoning in the Supreme Court of Canada's ruling on *R. v. Keegstra* (1990).

4. Clearly, not all of those who emigrate to Canada are fleeing persecution in their homelands. But Canada is rather unique in the world when it comes to its immigration policies. Even when times have been tough here, we have been a more open society than most. See Kymlicka (1998) especially its Introduction. Its policies have not, however, been without serious problems. See Galloway (1997).

5. Events in Vancouver (APEC) and Quebec City (FTAA) among others stand as a serious challenge to this rosy picture of Canadian freedom.

6. I am indebted to Matthew Stephens for this way of talking about one version of liberalism.

7. In his famous essay entitled "Two Concepts of Liberty" Berlin (1969) distinguishes between "positive" and "negative" liberty. Positive liberty is

the freedom to do something, negative liberty is the freedom from interference. Even though I may be secure in my knowledge that no one may
interfere with my plan to purchase a car, I may still not be free to buy a car.
I may not have the money or there may be no one from whom a car can be
purchased. If I live in a society where I also have positive liberty to buy a
car, then things like lack of money or inefficient distribution of this "good"
will not be allowed to stand in the way of my acquiring it. See also
Galipeau (1994) chap. 4.

8. See Ihde (1990) for an elucidation of the meaning of "life world" borrowed
from Jürgen Habermas.

9. Japanese Canadians did not, as it happened, present any real threat to
Canadian national security. Rather, they presented an imagined threat to
it—one blindly indulged instead of critically assessed—just what one
ought to expect from prejudice based thinking. In fact, many Japanese
Canadians fought for Canada in the Second World War. Normally, the
sorts of irrational and racist fears which prompted the Internment would
not be allowed to direct law or government policy. All fears of threat must
be independently substantiated. But when the worst excesses of racial
hatred occur in the halls of government and justice themselves, everyone
is in trouble. One may argue that wartime presents a special case; that in
wartime one must err on the side of caution. Even if that were true, it says
nothing about which concerns ought to be brought forward in the first
place for consideration. And it is very hard to believe that every such concern is acted on to the extent of this one. A selection process thus occurs
and one would expect that process to proceed rationally. When it does
not, we all have reason to fear for our safety and security. Of course, placing an internal and reasoned limit on what can count as a basis for excluding or prohibiting certain ways of life does not guarantee that the consequences of acting on that limit will not be the exclusion of a certain
group—people of colour and women have clearly suffered from "systematic" discrimination. All such results need to be severely scrutinized, the
procedures which produce them critically evaluated. Our reasoning on
this question has concluded that race, gender, sexual orientation, age and
physical ability should not characterize such exclusions. However, it has
also concluded that political ideology might as in, for example, the case
of neo-Nazism.

10. Even groups such the Amish, Hutterites and Mennonites are feeling the
pressure to integrate somewhat. With each passing generation, some tradition or other is eroded or weakened, splinter groups form. And unless
such groups have no need to buy from or sell to the outside, they will feel
the pressure to adapt to the commercial and technological pressures of the
societies in which they function.

11. See Hinman (1998) 61.

12. Rorty (1989) 46 quoting Joseph Schumpeter expresses the moral pluralist's primary commitment, though in somewhat anachronistic language: "To realize the relative validity of one's convictions and yet stand for them unflinchingly, is what distinguishes a civilized man from a barbarian."

13. Solipsism is a commitment to being all alone in the world — either actually or for all intents and purposes. The slope from moral relativism to solipsism passes through moral subjectivism where no person can know the mind or interests of any other person and has no cause to direct their behaviour in any way. The particular consequences of realizing such a norm are unthinkable to most people unless each person can be given their own world — either actually or virtually — and no two worlds interact in any way.

14. Here, we would have, for example, a case where the residents of the neighbourhood are moral pluralists even though the neighbourhood itself is not morally pluralistic. In Galipeau (1994), Isaiah Berlin's view on Moral Pluralism is reviewed. For the most part, Berlin's was a descriptive theory which set out those features of moral values and ways of life that made monistic or dogmatic moral views unintelligible — their realization politically and socially problematic. Nevertheless, according to Galipeau, Berlin believed that "pluralism has its limits" (64) and that "his preference for moderation, prudence, and toleration lead him easily to claim that the best political order is one that accommodates numerous virtues, a plurality of values, or most of the dispositions which specific cultures, peoples, individuals will hold to be valuable" (67).

15. For example, we are born with several physical reflexes which disappear as we get older. Neither the sucking and rooting impulse prompted by cheek stroking nor the strong gripping reflex of a baby's hand are present by the child's first birthday.

16. As we will see in chap. 9, this directive contained within the Charter often forces the courts outside of the realm of legal precedent when interpreting the law to consider the actual circumstances of moral and cultural life for Canadians.

17. When the language of "superior" and "subordinate" values appears, we have reason to think that some sort of value hierarchy is at work. In general, liberal analyses of social and cultural values follow the "basic" and "nonbasic" goods system. Basic goods are those without which nonbasic goods cannot be pursued and as such are given primary value. For example, the good of free expression cannot be enjoyed unless those to whom it is offered already have the good of security of the person. This way of categorizing values is not, however, entirely straightforward. We may also want to distinguish between human, political and social values. In the political realm, the good of free expression may be basic. Without it, the good of voting would be difficult to realize. In liberal democratic societies,

security of the person is the most fundamental right though it may share this spot with a few others.

18. The theme of "breaking the child's will" is a dominant one in the Christian tradition of parenting. Assuming that a child's will has a strong tendency towards self-interest or sin, this tendency must be "broken" by the wills of adults who aim to train the child's will towards the path of self-sacrifice or righteousness. In effect, the adult aims to replace the child's will with his or her own, at least until such time that the child is able to will itself toward self-sacrifice. Unquestioning obedience to the will of the parent (or other adult caregiver) is therefore considered a primary virtue of childhood and is spectacularly evidenced in Jesus Christ's words as described in the New Testament just prior to his arrest, conviction and execution for sedition. "Abba, Father, all things are possible unto thee; take this cup from me: nevertheless not what I will, but what thou wilt." (St. Mark, 14:36)

19. Aristotle (1953, 1976) Book Three, 1119b4-18.

20. H.L.A. Hart has argued that while in the past, general acceptance and observance of the divine command theory of moral authority supported the command theory of legal and political authority, this aspect of the rule of law can no longer be endorsed. "It is wrong to think of a legislature (and *a forteriori* an electorate) with a changing membership as a group of persons who must be habitually obeyed: this simple idea is suited only to a monarch sufficiently long-lived for the "habit" to grow up." See Hart in "Positivism and the Separation of Law and Morals" (1983) reprinted in Dyzenhaus and Ripstein (1996) 32. While a family may be closer to the monarchy model than the legislature model this often tends not to be the case. Family breakups and reorganizations are common occurrences today. Further is the problem of preparing children for life in our and not some past society.

21. This runs contrary to Rawls (1972) Cf. chap. 1, 10n.

22. The popular children's television program *Sesame Street* celebrated its thirtieth anniversary in 1999. It has been part of its educative goal to teach children about their emotions. I recall one segment on anger that had me somewhat concerned at the time. My children were avid fans and were especially impressed by a cartoon goat who sang to them that "It ain't baaad to get maaad." Thankfully the message was always sandwiched between other characters learning to express their anger in nondamaging and constructive ways.

23. It is clear from studies conducted in Sweden since that country banned the use of corporal punishment in 1979 that almost all children are being raised there without its use. Statistical evidence on adjusted crime rates as well as social service interventions show significant declines in both areas since the "no spanking" law was passed. The combination of these two

measures alone implies that children in liberal societies can be raised properly without the use of corporal punishment. In addition to these sorts of statistics, there is also plenty of anecdotal evidence that corporal punishment is not necessary for raising healthy, well-adjusted children. If this claim were false, one would have to conclude from the fact that if someone was never hit as a child he is morally maladjusted. Such an inference, in the absence of independent evidence, is intuitively unjustified, strongly suggesting that freedom from corporal punishment is not a causal factor in moral maladjustment. It is sometimes argued that while most children will do fine without corporal punishment, certain children need it in order to learn. I will address this issue in greater detail later on. For the time being, it should be noted that such claims have never been adequately substantiated. See Durrant (1999) 435-48.

24. See Martha Minow (1987) for her discussion of "the politics of difference."
25. Cf. chap. 1, 42n.
26. For example, Bitensky (1998) 353-474 writes, in the course of examining Article 19 of the General Assembly of the United Nations' Convention on the Rights of the Child (1989) that "If the slap is administered by a parent to his or her child, pure logic would seem to require that the inherent nature of the act does not change from violent to nonviolent simply because the victim is smaller, less powerful, and the aggressor's own flesh and blood" (394). The same may, of course, be said when the victim is distinguished by race or gender from the aggressor.
27. Taylor (1989) 7 writes for example, that "skin colour or physical traits have nothing to do with that in virtue of which humans command our respect."
28. Ibid. 7. "Stepping outside these limits would be tantamount to stepping outside what we would recognize as integral, that is, undamaged human personhood."
29. In my Ph.D. dissertation, I explore this issue. See Turner (1995) chap. 8.
30. One important aspect of doing all one can do to teach children to act in their best interests is to make your home less of a minefield. Without quite as many "traps" for them to fall into, one's parenting skills may be more devoted to observing children at play in their environment than to policing their every movement with warnings and threats. Serious childproofing has characterized the Swedish experience since that country banned all corporal punishment (Bitensky 367).
31. It may seem obvious to some that by the term "reasonable" when it comes to physical interference and punishment, we just mean "the minimum amount necessary to effect the purpose." As we will see in chap. 9 when we look at legal cases, the matter is very far from obvious to the courts. Rather, reasonable in a legal context refers to what community standards will bear. It is clear that at the present time, community standards bear a lot more than physical restraint or removal. The question then is: what is

the minimum amount of corporal punishment required to effect a corrective purpose? Clearly, the answer to this question must at least take into account the particulars of every disciplinary situation. As such, no objective or policy answer can be given to it. That leaves the determination of reasonableness up to individual parents. And it is at that point that both the moral and legal issues surrounding corporal punishment break down. Unless we are prepared to grant that no parental or teacher corporal punishment episode is of any moral or legal account, the tendency to accept that there is such a thing as reasonable physical punishment ought to be avoided.

32. This line is from the 1981 Louis Malle film *My Dinner With André* starring André Gregory and Wallace Shawn.

Chapter 4

Philosophical Morality: Happiness and Harm

1. During the course of the twentieth century, several of the moral philosophies surveyed in chap. 2 have competed against one another for allegiance among moral philosophers. Deontology and utilitarianism are still generally considered the main contenders as most Introduction to Moral Philosophy curricula will attest. But there are "old faithfuls" and newcomers as well. In particular, communitarianism and other virtue ethics theories have gained momentum. My discussion of the postmodern turn in philosophy presented all these theories as equally viable or nonviable as the case may be. As such, postmodernism is not really a moral theory at all but rather an "attitude" toward the justification of moral theories. My discussion of this attitude also suggested that what appears to be a new openness may in fact be a transitional phase—a period during which uncertainty prevails and the search is on for a better way of securing our moral intuitions than those currently on offer. I have decided to proceed with a utilitarian analysis of the moral issues surrounding corporal punishment because I believe that especially in the realm of social reform, utilitarianism, despite its theoretical flaws, still offers the best framework for assessing our social goals and strategies in moral terms. For an excellent discussion of those flaws, various attempts to remedy them and an argument to the conclusion that despite the problems which remain, utilitarianism is a powerful moral theory and better than its competitors, see Scarre (1996). Using utilitarian theory to chart a course through this issue is nevertheless open to criticism from those who reject social utility as the fundamental basis of moral justification, and I leave it to them to work out the details of an alternative and superior moral analysis. In particular will be those that argue that one must include a rights theory in contemporary moral discussion and that consequentialist theories such as utilitarianism

cannot support rights theories. In support of the claim that they can, see Sumner (1987).

2. The presence of an amending formula in any constitutional document is key to that document's ability to garner universal acceptance by the parties to it. "Amending formulas...balance the importance of constitutional protections against the need to permit amendments" (Webber [1994] 82). The need to permit amendments is generated by the reasonable expectation that our social and political circumstances may change dramatically — so dramatically that protections based on previous conditions may have to be adjusted to suit the new ones. This expectation expresses the liberal belief that even the greatest possible confidence in our current values and norms is open to future doubt; our values and norms subject to future revision. This belief is the one at the heart of moral pluralism. See also Kymlicka (1989) chap. 2.

3. Scarre (1996) 141.

4. Ibid. 142.

5. As I have indicated, the terms "happiness" and "pleasure" are often used synonymously in utilitarian writing. The classical utilitarianism of Jeremy Bentham implies that what we mean by happiness is the accumulation and preservation of sensually pleasurable experiences. John Stuart Mill disagreed in part, arguing that humans were capable of non-sensual pleasures — "higher" pleasures or ones derived from thoughtful reflection and that these were crucial to human happiness. When I use the term pleasure interchangeably with happiness, I mean to imply the Millian conception of the former as including both higher and lower pleasures.

6. Cf. chap. 2.

7. The use of the term "bottom line" evokes the feel of moral "calculation" and the business term "cash flow." In fact, early attempts to simplify utilitarian moral reasoning procedures appropriated the methods of general business accounting to moral judgements. But, as Scarre (1996) points out, "the philosophical sophistication of a concept of utility and its susceptibility to quantitative treatment are generally in inverse proportion to one another" (8). While utilitarian calculations of utility seemed possible in the area of welfare economics, "the idea of a calculus of utilities able to generate solutions to all moral problems is likely to remain a philosopher's pipe-dream" (9). Nevertheless, the notion of "sum-ranking" utilities is not altogether useless outside of the economic sphere. "Utilitarians rightly point out that rough and ready probability judgements and orderings of our preferences, or states of satisfaction, are often sufficient to make utilitarian calculation possible" (15). It is this somewhat "rough and ready" sense of evaluating the relative utilities of options for acting that I presume throughout my discussion.

8. For a more in-depth consideration of the historical background to the issue of child welfare and abuse, see Piper (1999). My discussion here is based on my previous one in Turner (1998). With respect to the history of child welfare in Canada specifically, see Sutherland (2000). In this work, he notes on several occasions the deep agreement most English-Canadians had throughout the twentieth century with the use of corporal punishment as a strategy against what was considered children's tendency towards "delinquent" behaviour.

9. See Robson and Robson (1994) 92-98.

10. Ibid. 95.

11. In Mill's "Autobiography" (1963-1991) 1, he declared that his wife Harriet Taylor Mill was an equal partner in many of his writings and indeed the main author in certain of "his" most important works. It is reasonable to infer that especially his writings on women and children bear her stamp. Nevertheless, those works are published under his name and I shall observe the convention of referring them to him alone in what follows. Mill was, I think, sensitive to the difficulty future scholars would face and so took every opportunity to remind his readers that while the work bore his name, it was a joint effort.

12. Robson and Robson, 95.

13. See Mill's "Punishment of Children," (1963-1991) 25, 1177-78.

14. Mill's thinking on the psychological features of the corporal punishment episode are of course pre-Freudian. Freud provided a way of understanding the mechanism of "repression" where, in this context, the memory of the pain of being corporally punished would be repressed then expressed in inappropriate ways later in life. Mill's comments suggest that the brutalized adult has simply forgotten what it is like to be beaten and needs reminding and that once reminded, he will cease his brutalizing behaviour. We now know that things are much more complicated than this — that it is the beating episode itself and not the forgetting of it which is strongly correlated with future aggression. See Durrant and Rose-Krasnor (1995) Section 2.1.1-2.1.3; Greven (1991), Part IV; Bitensky (1998), Section III A and Hyman (1997) chap. 3.

15. In 1972, legal protection for those accused of assaulting convicted persons was removed from the Canadian Criminal Code. See *R43 Brief*, 7.

16. Mill, (1963-1991) 18, 294.

17. Right-wing extremists in the Canadian Alliance Party have expressed the desire to see more severity used in our treatment of convicted persons. But even within the ranks of Alliance members, this tendency has been opposed by more moderate factions. My conclusion that only a small minority of Canadians would favour the return of corporal punishment to prisons is thus based on the fact that only a minority of those representing a very conservative minority of Canadians feel this way.

18. In their 1995 report on corporal punishment, Durrant and Rose-Krasnor (1995) write that "corporal punishment is used by 70 to 75 percent of Canadian parents." They also report that in a survey conducted in Toronto and Winnipeg, parents surveyed tended to approve the prohibition of corporal punishment if it could be demonstrated that it caused children more harm than good. The authors optimistically conclude that this result indicates that a program of bringing existing data to public attention would likely have the effect of reducing the use of corporal punishment and increasing support for legislative reform on this question. While their optimism may be reasonable — it may be the case that few parents who corporally punish their children are aware of this data — one must account for the fact that many parents and policy-makers who are aware of it continue to defend the use of corporal punishment. In an article reported in *The Ottawa Citizen*, "Should Parents Be Allowed to Spank?" (*The Ottawa Citizen*, 12 February 1997), Jim Bronskill wrote, "Jim Scalter, vice-president of Focus on the Family. an evangelical family support organization, said that there are few, if any cases in Canada where courts have dismissed charges where there was real evidence of abuse....'We still affirm the idea that there are defiant children, children who manifest dangerous bravado, and parents need more in their arsenal than telling them to take time out in a corner.'" Scalter's conclusion depends upon it being true first, that corporal punishment is the only addition to the parent's "arsenal" that will moderate "defiant" behaviour and "dangerous bravado" and second, on the assumption that corporal punishment does in fact eliminate or significantly reduce such behaviour. Of all the studies which have been conducted to determine the truth or falsity of the second claim, the majority (90 percent) show that it is false while the remainder are inconclusive (see Durrant "Corporal Punishment: Research Findings and Implications for Practice," presented at BC Council for Families Conference, October 1999). With one very narrow exception in the area of immediate short-term compliance, there is as yet no scientific basis to Scalter's argument. It is therefore telling that Scalter chooses to affirm the idea that parents must be permitted to use corporal punishment rather than justify it.

19. Recall Mill's comments on the effects of corporal punishment on "the naturally sensitive boy" (1963-1991) 25, 1177-78. The idea here is that beating a child with a timid or sensitive character risks making him or her even more withdrawn and sullen than he or she already is. This effect is what we today refer to as depression. "For many people," Philip Greven writes, "buried anger becomes the basic source of aggression against the self. The most common form of this self-aggression takes in America, past and present, is the emotional experience of depression" (Greven [1991] 131). The depressed child or adult may pose no danger to others. Nevertheless, the danger they pose to themselves is of considerable moral concern.

20. See Durrant and Rose-Krasnor (1995) Section 2.0.0. According to Durrant (1999), out of eight studies specifically conducted to investigate whether there are correlations between corporal punishment and later adult aggression, seven showed there was and one was inconclusive. Out of five studies conducted to determine whether there were correlations between corporal punishment and later spousal abuse, all concluded there were. Durrant steps back from this accumulation of results and concludes that there is adequate empirical evidence for the claim that corporal punishment is a decided risk factor for these and other undesirable outcomes. Critics of her position tend to argue that the evidence gathered from such studies is "inconclusive." Benatar (1998) 246 argues that "Although Murray Straus's study suggests that there is a correlation between rare corporal punishment and increased violence, the study has some significant defects...and the significance of his studies has been questioned in the light of other studies." The other studies Benatar refers to are from Robert E. Larzelere (of Father Flanagan's Boys' Home, Boys Town, Nebraska) who has conducted several such studies on behalf of the pro-corporal punishment side of the debate. Larzelere's work has been roundly criticized by Durrant and others who point out that Larzelere draws his conclusions based on the finding that twenty-five percent of the thirty-five studies looked at showed that immediate compliance levels were somewhat increased for a very narrow range of children. According to the very data he relies on however, close reading shows that thirty-four percent of these studies show both short- and long-term detrimental effects to the child and the parent-child relationship from this use of corporal punishment. Further, as Durrant points out, nowhere does Larzelere provide any evidence that there are other benefits. In short, Benatar's and others' criticism that studies from which researchers conclude there are causal correlations between corporal punishment and increased levels of aggression (and other undesirable outcomes) are inadequate seem to be based on a criterion of adequacy which is either a secret or, if it is the one usually relied by the social science community, one that their own findings also fail to satisfy. See Larzelere (1993, 1996). These issues will be discussed in greater detail in chap. 7.

21. Durrant and Rose-Krasnor (1995) Section 2.2.4. "Another way of establishing causal direction is through the use of experimental and quasi-experimental treatment studies. Forgatch (1988) conducted such a treatment study among parents of antisocial boys referred for treatment. Her study demonstrated that a reduction in harsh discipline is accompanied by significant reductions in child aggression."

22. I will examine Barbara Amiel's use of this argument strategy in detail in chap. 7. An article published 27 April 1998 in *The Ottawa Citizen*, "When Spanking Can't Be Beaten" Barbara Lerner, used the same strategy.

Commenting on the results of expert studies on the harmful effects of corporal punishment, Lerner writes "Whenever I hear this sort of nonsense, I think of my friend Donald's grandfather....Donald's grandfather overheard him [Donald was a "boy" at the time] calling the other boy "nigger"...[he] hauled off and struck Donald with his fist, hitting him square on the jaw, hard enough to knock him down, then turned away sharply on his heel and walked away, leaving his grandson sprawled in the dirt, more shocked than hurt....Donald got the message....If, on rare occasions, it takes a whipping to make [the distinction between good and evil] really sink in, forget the chorus of contemporary experts and remember Donald's grandfather...."As we will see later on, such arguments rely on dubious premises ("more shocked than hurt"), slight of hand ("Donald got the message") as well as the fallacy of reasoning which here says that Donald never called anyone a "nigger" again because his grandfather assaulted him. But the worst aspect of this sort of argument from a philosophical point of view is that it asks us to behave irrationally by ignoring carefully researched findings which produce valid and reliable indices of risk for corporal punishment and instead relying for our assessment of its effects on a single case reported by someone who obviously favours its use.

23. Cf., 19n.
24. See Durrant and Rose-Krasnor (1995). There is, however, a body of data from Sweden that is frequently used by supporters of corporal punishment to show that banning its use is worse for children. Larzelere, for example, cites Gelles and Edfeldt, "Gelles and Edfeldt (1986) found that, one year after abolishing spanking, the Swedish rate of beating up a child or threatening to use or using a weapon against them was two to four times as large as the United States rate" (Larzelere [1993] 145). Several things must be noted about this statement. First, one might very well expect very incomplete compliance in the first year following the ban. Second, Larzelere uses the terms "beating up" and "weapon" prejudicially. What counted as child assault before the ban and after had changed dramatically. Even a light spanking with slipper could now be reported as an instance of "beating up with a weapon" while American statistics reflect instances in which child abuse charges occurred. Such charges, in the current North American climate, would not likely be leveled unless the use of corporal punishment resulted in a serious or life-threatening injury to the victim. With these considerations in mind, it is surprising the reported assault rate in Sweden was not higher than it was for that year.
25. Greven writes that if we have reason to fear for this outcome, it is the use of corporal punishment and not its disuse which tends towards it. Greven refers to the work of Alice Miller in this regard. Miller is a psychologist who has studied the effects of corporal punishment on children in Germany and has concluded that its widespread use contributed to the

ease with which Adolf Hitler came to power. "She believes," writes Greven, "that the harsh discipline these people experienced as children prepared them well for the absolute obedience sought by the totalitarian leader they obeyed" (Greven [1991] 199). Also, quoting the Reverend Jack Hyles on disciplining females, Greven reveals the propagandistic intentions behind the use of disciplinary violence on a female child: "Obedience is far more important to her, for someday she must transfer it from her parents to her husband. This means that she should never be allowed to argue at all. She should become submissive and obedient."

26. Scarre (1996) chap. 7.

27. See Mill's, "Utilitarianism" (1963-1999) 10, 231.

28. See Mill's, "Three Essays on Religion" (1963-1991) 10, 294. Mill referred to this sentiment as a species of egoism under the term *"egoism a deux ou a trois ou a quartre."*

29. See Mill's, "On Liberty" (1963-1991) 28, passim. I have examined the interested and disinterested sentimental bases of Mill's moral philosophy at length in my Ph.D. Dissertation. See Turner (1995).

30. See Robertshaw (1994) 19. "The Law Reform Commission proposed that no one be liable for an offense if, as parent or guardian, he or she touches, hurts or confines a child in the reasonable exercise of authority over the child."

31. See Hart in Dyzenhaus and Ripstein, (1996) 36 for a discussion of his use of the term "penumbral." Penumbral cases are ones which do not obviously fall into one single interpretative framework or whose elements do not fit neatly under this or that definition. This "fuzziness" gives rise to disagreements on how to treat them often prompting a search for higher-level interpretive frameworks within which they can be accommodated.

32. I do not mean to suggest the sort of metaphysical difference between the mind and the body which thinkers such as Descartes argued for—concluding that the mind was an "immaterial substance" and the body a "material substance." Rather, I adopt the convention of roughly distinguishing between cognitive and noncognitive human experience in terms of the mental in the first case and the physical in the second. Both types of experience may be, and I assume are, compatible with the rejection of Descartes's metaphysical dualism. For Descartes's arguments, see his *Meditations* (1984).

33. Joan Durrant in a presentation for the BC Council of Families, October 1999. Elizabeth Thompson Gershoff of Arizona State University, in her manuscript "Corporal Punishment by Parents and Associated Child Outcomes: A Meta-Analytic and Theoretical Review" gives the following details on this research topic. "The potential for parents' use of corporal punishment to disrupt the parent-child relationship is thought to be a main disadvantage of its use (Azrin et al., 1965; Azrin & Holtz, 1966). The

tendency for pain to cause a recipient to attempt to escape the offending stimulus can cause children who experience painful corporal punishment to withdraw from or avoid their parents (Aronfreed, 1969; Azrin et al., 1965, Parke, 1977). Parents whose children repeatedly flee out of fear of possible corporal punishment may eventually lose the ability to affect their children at all (Newsom et al., 1983). In addition, the anger and pain evoked by corporal punishment, if frequent and persistent, can weaken the parent-child relationship (Van Houten, 1983). After frequent spankings, children may learn to associate their parents with painful punishments; subsequently, parents may over time become associated with painful corporal punishments and elicit aggression from children (Berkowitz, 1983). Children who view their parents as dispensers of painful stimuli may fear and resent them, feelings that may slowly erode bonds of trust and closeness established between parents and children in early childhood. In an experimental demonstration of this idea, adults who were negative and punishing toward children were most effective at generating immediate compliance but were avoided in a later play situation and were rated by the children as least preferred (Redd, Morris, and Martin, 1975). A positive relationship between parent and child can thus be sacrificed inadvertently for the salient goal of behavioural compliance" (Thompson Gersoff [in press, 2001]).

34. The Criminal Code of Canada describes certain types of "threats" as offences. (Sections 17, 264.1, 346, 423 [1] [b]) Curiously, it was at one time no offence to threaten someone face-to-face with bodily harm or even death. Yet, if such a threat was transmitted via telephone or mail then it was against the law. The Criminal Code now states that threats to seriously physically or psychologically harm the person of anyone, regardless of the manner of their transmission, are contrary to law (Section 331). The mental requirement for guilt is either intention or recklessness — the defendant must have, in any case, acted "knowingly." The test is therefore whether the words used by the defendant would have caused "a reasonable person" to fear for their safety and not whether this in fact occurred in the circumstances. It is, nevertheless, no crime to cause someone to feel fear per se. What the law acknowledges is that certain fears are clearly debilitating: the fear of immanent death and the fear of immanent and serious physical injury. In both cases, however, the bodily harm caused is not physical but psychological though as such, it may have physical ramifications. This state of the law raises the question whether a parent who has uttered a threat in this vein to a child may defend him or herself under Section 43 of the Criminal Code which justifies the use of reasonable force in the course of correcting a child's behaviour. It would seem that since Section 43 does act to deflect criminal liability in cases of actual assault, it may, *a fortiori*, do the same here. But it may be argued that since "reason-

able force" never includes life- or safety-threatening uses of it, Section 43 could not be applied in cases where threats of death or serious bodily harm are issued by the parent.

35. See Durrant and Rose-Krasnor (1995) passim. To these harms may be added those of the deterioration of parent-child relationships, decreased internalization of moral values, poor child and adult mental health (Durrant [1999] Thompson Gershoff [1999]).

36. See among others, Durrant and Rose-Krasnor 1995, passim; Straus, passim; Greven, passim; Hyman, passim; Bitensky, passim.

37. See Mill's "Utilitarianism" (1963-1991) 10, 250.

38. One may indeed argue that here, utilitarian moral reasoning either overlaps with or illegitimately appropriates deontological moral reasoning. For the conflict between one's end and the results of one's attempt to achieve it appears germane to the sense of incorrectness which characterizes the act. At worst, I would say that utilitarian moral reasoning might overlap here with deontology. Both approaches in this case involve criticizing the fit between one's intentions and something else. However, I do not believe that the overlap is philosophically problematic or even, for that matter, very interesting. What we have under the utilitarian analysis is merely a description of instrumental reasoning. One is rationally obliged, as a cognitive being, to aim at ends in a way which tends to their realization. One is further obliged, as a moral cognitive being, to aims at ends which will promote the greatest happiness for the greatest number. The emphasis here is still on the consequences of one's strategies.

39. Robson and Robson (1994) 26.

40. Ibid. 154-55.

41. Ibid.

42. Cf., chap. 4, 21n.

43. This particular foundation for action is examined in thought-provoking detail by Kierkegaard (1843). There, Kierkegaard explores Abraham's dilemma when God asks him to sacrifice his son Isaac to prove Abraham's devotion. The problem of basing moral knowledge on God's will is also explored in Plato's dialogue *Euthyphro*. In this work, Socrates engages in conversation with his friend Euthyphro the theologian on the topic of piety asking the question: Is the "good" whatever the gods say it is or is it determined independently of their say so? Robert Larzelere also uses biblical injunctions to justify the use of corporal punishment. See Larzelere (1993).

44. In effect, what we have here is the internal limit on toleration inherent within moral pluralism that is respect for bodily security. That limit acts on what may be considered acceptable in the practice of one's customary morality. For example, while the practice of clitorechtomy is part of certain cultures, since it violates the bodily security of female children, it is pro-

hibited in Canada. If the followers of those cultures which include it were to insist that their way of life could not be pursued without the practice, then they would be correct in assuming the limit implied that their customary morality could not be pursued in Canada.

45. Catherine MacKinnon and Andrea Dworkin have argued that this reasoning is indeed what the American Civil Liberties defence of pornographic expression amounts to. See MacKinnon (1987).

46. While a complete exposition of libertarian thinking is impossible here, it will suffice to say that libertarians hold to the view that the combined and cumulative effects on most individuals of all individuals freely acting on their innate competitive impulses and instinct for pleasure will always result in a state of affairs which each would prefer, all things considered. Given this preference, government should be restricted to a sort of "traffic cop" agency and simply and strictly uphold the exclusively individual right to enjoy a maximum amount of liberty. All other human activities should be completely left to private market forces. Libertarianism is usually grounded in a notion of social contract where parties to a proposed social arrangement negotiate then settle on the rules by which they will be governed. Typically, the parameters of such contracts disallow "incompetent" persons from negotiating and "incompetence" is identified as an inability or a lack of desire to be completely self-sufficient. See Robert Nozick (1974).

Chapter 5
Human Adults and Human Children

1. Sutherland (2000) 6.
2. See discussion of "basic goods," chap. 3, 17n.
3. While this description may also fit certain adults, the presumption here is in favour of their having overcome these natural deficits of childhood as compared to adulthood. One might speculate, for example, that the proportion of adults who fall short to adults who do not is roughly the same as the proportion of children who exhibit competence in these areas to children who do not. In any case, what is needed at the policy level are general rules. Interestingly, adults who do not fit the general description benefit from rules designed for the majority who do, and children who do not fit the general description of children lose according to the rules designed for children who do.
4. Sutherland (2000) 11, 17, 18, 241.
5. Matthews (1994).
6. Spock (1968).
7. Matthews (1994) 229.
8. Ibid.
9. Ibid. 26-27.

10. Ibid.
11. Ibid.
12. Fundamentalist religious persons frequently attempt to explain the appearance of what we recognize as a fully human being by way of special creation. But even the more scientifically minded are not immune from the temptation to think in such dramatic terms. The so-called "missing link" theory of hominid development was popular when I was a child. The idea was that according to the available fossil record, it was impossible to trace a continuous developmental line from known "prehistoric" examples of human-like beings to modern or living forms. Unless a linking specimen could be found, science might have to conclude that the appearance of the modern human form was spontaneous and not in any way related to the prehistoric. The hunt was then on among the evolutionary minded for the missing link. In its absence, the conclusion that the older evidence was not evidence of human life at all could follow. The debate within the archaeological community raged for several decades and even produced a fraudulent attempt to link the two developmental stories (Piltdown man).
13. One of the most well-known examples of this theme in literature is William Golding's *Lord of the Flies*.
14. Ariès (1962).
15. Archard (1993).
16. Ibid. 18. Archard writes, "Heroard's diary is a single document telling the story of an exceptional child, the heir to the throne. There is no reason to think the upbringing of Louis XIII representative. Contrary to Ariès's claims there is evidence from legal documents, medical writings and church chronicles for the view that the child's "particular nature" was recognized in the Middle Ages."
17. Blake (1971).
18. Ibid. 11.
19. For a detailed account of the history of medieval views of childhood in the context of infanticide, see Boetzskes, Turner and Sobstyl, (1990) For a more general review of Protestant views in the Modern Era, see Greven (1991) Part 3.
20. Jean-Jacques Rousseau is famous for his utopian vision of prehistory as well as childhood. He begins his best known work, *The Social Contract* (1938), with the powerful claim that "Man is born free; and everywhere he is in chains" (Book I, Chapter I). In his lesser known work *Emile* (1991), Rousseau lays out, in narrative form, a plan for the complete education of a boy on his way to manhood. It was Rousseau's view in both works that the fetters of civilization, convention and taste were anathemic to the natural tendency towards the good which each human being possessed. Only if left completely free to explore and arrange the world, would "man"

develop "his" innate impulses for good. Henry David Thoreau is also noted for this extremely beneficent view of human being in its natural "uncivilized" state. See Simon (1998).

21. The dichotomy alluded to here is the age-old Apollonian v. Dionysian one. The Apollonian represents "formalism": the logical, dry, neat and orderly world of the superior intellect which tends to be identified with the so-called authoritative elements in society (males, adults, whites) while the Dionysian represents formlessness: the sensual, wet and chaotic world of the flesh and tends to be identified with the so-called subordinate or slavish elements in society (women, children, persons of colour). Apollo was the Greek god of reason and Dionysius was the Greek god of pleasure.

22. The term *"telos"* is from the Ancient Greek and refers to the preset goal or purpose for which an object or organism was intended. Artifacts such as hammers realize their *telos* as long as they perform well at the function for which they were designed — that is pounding nails into hard materials. Natural objects such as trees and human beings realize theirs in similar fashion. According to Aristotle, as we have seen, the *telos* of the human being was *eudaimonia*. Cf. chap. 2, 4n.

23. The postmodern turn, discussed in chap. 2, is not as intolerant of logical contradictions as the rest of philosophical history has been. This greater tolerance, however, has been expressed philosophically in stronger and weaker forms. In the weak vein are those logicians who work on "deviant" and paraconsistent logics. In the stronger, are those, most notably in the field of comparative literature, who embrace the logical contradiction as itself significant of the human condition and so as ultimately meaningful. While there may be room for considerable tolerance of contradiction in the arts, I follow the path of my philosophical ancestors when it comes to building arguments for and against suggestions for practical social and political policy.

24. Sutherland (2000) 11, 17.

25. See Mill's "Utilitarianism" (1963-1991) 10, 233, where he uses "moral blank" to describe a person who laid out "their course of life on the plan of paying no regard to others except so far as their own private interest compels." See Mill's "Civilization" (1963-1991) 18, 122, where he writes: "The savage cannot bear to sacrifice, for any purpose, the satisfaction of his individual will. His social cannot even temporarily prevail over his selfish feelings, nor his impulses bend to his calculations" (122). This characterization of the "primitive" is anachronistic at best. Since Mill's time, we have come to realize that so-called primitive peoples may be as sophisticated in their social feeling as so-called civilized peoples, if not more so.

26. Hobbes is noted for his theory of human nature as psychologically egoistic. In his *Leviathan* (1968), Hobbes declared that human beings were basically self-interested. "He thinks that children are born concerned only with

themselves but that with appropriate education and training they may come to be concerned with others and with acting in a morally acceptable way. He thinks that, unfortunately, most children are not provided with such training. Thus he holds that most people care primarily for themselves and their families, and that very few are strongly motivated by a more general concern for other people" (Bernard Gert, *Oxford Companion to Philosophy*, ed. Ted Honderich, Oxford University Press 1995)). See also King (1998) 65-84. Hobbes developed a defence of the monarchy out of his belief that the instinctive drive to self-interest would nevertheless propel warring and mutually suspicious human beings towards a negotiated settlement for rights and protections against one another which involved handing the administrative power over the distribution of such rights and protections to a single agreed-upon sovereign. Once this handover had occurred, Hobbes claimed, human society became "civilized." Prior to the securing of this arrangement, human life was, from Hobbes's point of view, "nasty, brutish and short."

27. I will not wade into the difficult moral issues surrounding the treatment of nonhuman animals. I realize that many of those who are especially concerned about animal rights, for example, will wince at the suggestion that children ought not to be treated according to the norms by which we treat nonhuman animals. I also realize that my argument for treating human children more like human adults is based on principles which might be used to justify animal rights as well. Until such time, however, that nonhuman animals are accorded these rights, I see a danger for both groups in failing to make the distinctions between them and children which I am making here.

28. Matthews (1994) 27, 29.

29. Archard (1993) 28.

30. According to Sutherland (2000), the nineteenth- and early-twentieth-century history of adult views towards children is obsessed with youth crime and juvenile delinquency. But the obsession is not of course confined to this demographic. As Christine Piper (1999) also argues, Victorian England was similarly caught up in the same concerns. Going further back or further afield, it is not difficult to find numerous examples of the same adult fear throughout literature and other types of writing, especially of the religious sort.

31. Rates of violent youth crime, like other such statistics, are difficult if not impossible to understand as figures which go up or down over time. As such, our general impressions of whether they are on the increase or decrease are largely unreliable. For example, Statistics Canada reports that charges for violent crime among youth (12-17) went down 1% in 1998 for the third year in a row. However, the number of youths charged in 1998 was still 77% higher than it was in 1988 (*Juristat* Vol. 19, no.13, "Youth violent crime, 1999). Based on such statistics, one cannot clearly say that the

youth crime rate is increasing or decreasing. Furthermore, our impressions of youth violence are often based on or confirmed by the number of charges laid by authorities and not necessarily on the number of violent acts committed by youth. It is possible that while the number of charges laid in 1998 is 77% higher than the number in 1988, the actual number of violent acts committed has not actually increased by that percentage. In which case, it is hard to say just what such impressions correspond to in the real world. A "get tough" attitude in 1988 towards youth violence based on something other than an actual increase in youth violence may have produced an increase in charges which in turn fueled the view that youth are much more violent today than they were ten years ago and so deserve the "get tough" approach. Critics of Sweden's ban on corporal punishment are quick to point out that rates of assault among Sweden's youth are up dramatically since the ban took effect. However, as Joan Durrant points out, these numbers reflect a new zero tolerance in Swedish society for all forms of schoolyard bullying including verbal harassment. Every such incident discovered by school authorities must be reported to the police and so are now counted in general assault statistics (Durrant, 1999). It may be that armed violent crime among black youth in the United States is an exception to the rule that generalizations are difficult to make since it has definitely been on the increase since the 1960s. But here one must ask where such youth are getting their guns? An episode of the American CBS TV program *48 Hours* with Ed Bradley suggested that the Mafia is responsible for "delivering" boxcars full of guns and ammunition to rail yards in poor African-American neighbourhoods and seeing to it that the open cars are left there, unsupervised. The issues here are much more complex than those who point the finger at "today's youth" or worse, "today's black youth" would have us believe. It is also highly unlikely that a failure to corporally punish is in any way a cause of black youth violence since as a population, black parents are very likely, for various culturally historical reasons, to use it. See Bitensky (1998) 422-23.

32. Opinion makers in the media are quick to defend their story choices whenever it is suggested that these choices contribute to increasing public tolerance and even thirst for violence by claiming that they are just giving the public what it wants. This defence is highly problematic for two reasons. Firstly, it removes the media from the high ground it likes to occupy when it senses threats to its freedom of expression. That high ground puts the media in the role of "informer" and "interpreter" when it comes to those events and comings and goings that have serious social and political consequences. The public gives the media privileged access to the halls of government, for example, entrusting them with the responsibility of reporting back what goes on there. If the media is in fact in the same business as say, Coca Cola, this privilege seems undeserved. Secondly, the defense seems to

assume that the media have no moral obligations whatsoever to the public it serves. Even if the defence might be said to acknowledge the public's autonomy in moral matters, it ignores the fact upon which the media's raison d'être is based: the public lacks the information it requires to make informed moral judgements, among others. In which case, they have a moral obligation to present balanced stories. Americans may not want to hear, for instance, that the Mafia is in large part responsible for the proliferation of arms among black youth—this really complicates what otherwise seems like such a simple problem—but this information, if correct, would be crucial to building an informed picture of where the fault lies with respect to escalation of violent crime among black youth.

33. James (1992) 6.
34. Ibid. 98.
35. Hobbes (1968) 183-88.
36. Sutherland (2000) 17.
37. Joseph Kunkel (1991) has argued against the moral acceptability of using violence in self-defense.
38. Cf. chap. 4, n. 17. Also, Primo Levi (1996) wrote extensively from his own experience on the human personality and psychology of the concentration camp inmate. Ultimately, systemic violence of all kinds against the body and mind succeed in turning already obedient persons into empty automata; what Levi referred to as "musselmen." "To sink is the easiest of matters; it is enough to carry out all the orders one receives, to eat only the ration, to observe the discipline of the work and the camp. Experience showed that only exceptionally could one survive more than three months in this way."
39. Case details will be discussed in chap. 9.

Chapter 6

The Paradox of Child Protection

1. This criticism of the strict self-interest argument may also be made against deontological arguments which ignore the "greatest good" and discount the moral significance of children where they are considered pre- or non-rational. I would nevertheless argue, though not here, that deontological moral theories have other features which save them from the criticism that they are not theories about morality at all.

2. There may, of course, be other ways of refuting arguments for corporal punishment or a way to save the case for it on alternate philosophical moral grounds. Again, I leave it to the proponents of other moral theories to work out the details.

3. See chap. 7.

4. Samantha Brennan of the University of Western Ontario has written and co-written numerous articles in this area. See Brennan and Noggle (1998).

5. Plato (1973). In chaps. 6 and 7, Socrates discusses his theory of the state with his companions. His theory is based on his understanding of the organization of the human "soul" or what we today would call human psychology.

6. Ibid. chaps. 12, 13 and 14.

7. Several experiments of the sort Plato envisioned have in fact been tried with greater and lesser success. The Israeli *kibbutz* is modeled on the principle of communal parenting and one might argue that the Communist regime implemented a similar system in the former USSR though in a somewhat moderated form. There are many other examples of limited communal parenting at the local level such as babysitting co-operatives. While these smaller scale efforts can prove very effective, it is unlikely that anything like what Plato had in mind will ever dominate human strategies for childcare in large states. See Archard (1993) Chapter 11.

8. John Locke (1993) raised his concerns and offered recommendations in his *Treatises of Government*.

9. See Durrant and Rose-Krasnor (1995) Section 3.0.0. "Almost one-third of all child victims of homicide were killed before they reached the age of one; over seventy percent were killed before they were five years old (Statistics Canada 1991)...physical abuse is responsible for more than ninety-five percent of serious intracranial injuries during the first year of life (Manitoba Family Services 1993)."

10. Turner (1994).

11. Archard (1993) 166, 170.

12. David Archard has argued that the notion of familial privacy is suspect when it concerns the rights of parents over their children, though not when it concerns the affairs of consenting adults. Ibid. 123-29.

13. Bradbury (1969).

14. Ibid. 154-55.

15. The scapular I have in mind here was a small metal or cloth amulet which depicted a scene from the New Testament or a portrait of a saint or member of the Holy Family. The one I wore was made of black felt — I no longer recall the depiction. It hung around my neck by a string and I wore it under my clothing. The scapular's purpose is to protect the wearer from harm and identify her as a Roman Catholic. I also recall being made to carry a small camphor tablet in the pocket of my school jumper which was alleged to ward off germs. My mother had all the bases covered.

16. Hobbes (1949) Part 2, chap. 8.

17. The difficulty here lies in the deep tendency to regard our children as our private property and so to regard the children of others as theirs. On this model, we would no more consider interfering without invitation in the childcare conduct of others than we would in our neighbour's rough usage, for instance, of her winter coat. Even when we grant that parents

do not "privately own" their children and adopt the "custodial" model of the relationship between parent and child, trouble lingers. If your neighbour is the "custodian" of her children then while she does not have complete title over them, she does have sole responsibility for their care. I have incomplete entitlement to the use of a section of garden attached to the home in which I live. No one but me and my landlord may use it and as long as I am using it, I have sole responsibility for its maintenance. If my downstairs neighbour thinks I am abusing my privilege in some way, he may ask my landlord to interfere. According to the custodial model then, we may complain about a neighbour's childcare behaviour to the authorities and see direct involvement as inappropriate if not illegal. To justify direct interference even if only in certain cases, we therefore require a third way of modeling the parent-child relationship. See Archard (1993) Part 3.

18. We need not and ought not to go beyond the sort of "modest collectivism" proposed by Archard since a stronger version of it would come into direct conflict with the parent-centred model of childrearing which our society embraces. Archard has also argued that there are good reasons for maintaining this model — reasons independent of the fact that it is the one we have followed since our country was formed. See Ibid. 115-21. On 18 October 1997, the *Globe and Mail's* Jane Gadd reported on a Hawaiian program designed to improve its child welfare situation. The Healthy Start program "is the program that leading pediatricians and child-welfare workers in Canada point to as the one that the country must duplicate if it is to attack the roots of delinquency, crime, domestic violence, welfare dependency and wasted human potential." With the knowledge that "vital neural links governing emotions and the ability to learn and communicate are formed in the first three years of life...child psychiatrists, pediatricians and child-welfare workers have been able to mount a powerful lobby to overcome cultural reluctance to interfere with the privacy of families and push for programs that improve bad parenting" (Ibid.). The program involves the weekly visit of a family support worker whose job it is to gently lead the parents towards positive parenting practices — ones which omit, for example, the use of physical punishment.

19. This is especially true according to libertarianism and may be said to characterize the United States much more strongly than it does Canada.

20. Archard (1993) 114.

21. This may be less true of women living in rural areas but even such women have a history of collective life.

22. Rosenberg (1987).

23. Recall that Mill's conception of "happiness" as he understands it in the context of the "greatest happiness for the greatest number" necessarily involves the sense of wellbeing humans experience as a consequence of satisfying what he called their "social feeling." Mill defines social feeling

as "the desire to be in unity with our fellow creatures" and argues that it "is already a powerful principle in human nature" (Mill [1963-1991] 10, 231). Mill intended by "fellow creatures" human beings (or other sentient creatures) at large and reserved another sort of sentiment for familiars and intimates. His theory implies that if one is in any way deprived of the ability to satisfy one's social feeling then even if one has satisfying relationships with family members, one will experience a certain unhappiness. To develop most fully, human beings need, in Mill's view, to realistically feel a part of a wider community. Parenting in a vacuum deprives adults of opportunities to satisfy this need; deprives them of the opportunity to be truly happy human beings.

24. Jeremy Bentham, employing the *double entendre* to full effect, argued in *Introduction to the Principles of Morals and Legislation* that the husband/father must be the sole authority in the family — that more than one such authority would dissolve into familial anarchy. "The man would have the meat roasted, the woman boiled: shall they both fast till the judge comes to dress it for them? The woman would have the child dressed in green, the man, in blue: shall the child go naked till the judge come and clothe it?...How can [the legislator] do so well as by placing the legal power in the same hands which are beyond comparison the more likely to be in possession of the physical?" (Bentham [1789] chap. XVI, Section XL, 1n.). While Bentham's argument has been subjected to repeated criticism and with good reason, the importance of parental solidarity and consistency continues to dominate childcare literature.

25. Along with its ban on the use of corporal punishment, Sweden instituted a far-reaching and comprehensive program of parent education. See Durrant and Olsen (1997) 443-61.

26. In his book *The Case Against Spanking*, Hyman (1997) chaps. 4-9 lays out what may best be described as the curriculum for such an education. It may be argued that television and especially public television, serves the need for parenting education discussed here. Documentaries on child development and rearing are common and often excellent. But the presentation of such programming does not reach the majority of parents who need it most.

27. There is a difference, however, between today's "aftershocks" and those of twenty years ago. When one of my daughters attempts to raise questions of a "feminist" nature in her classes, she is reminded by the other young women in the room that the battle has already been won and so there is no need to discuss the matter any further. Doing so only makes the males present feel uncomfortable and unnecessarily guilty. A male teacher told her that she was engaging in "reverse discrimination" and was being overly subjective by not considering the harmful effects on men of policies such as affirmative action.

28. Michel Foucault (1980) wrote that the tendency for government to increase the surveillance of its citizens was consistent with the practice of jailing or committing them and ought to be resisted at all costs as long as individual freedom of action and thought was valued. Megill (1985) 241 writes of Foucault's vision in this work that "its central contention...is that the social role of the prison was not to repress delinquency but to create it. By thus manufacturing a threat to social stability, the prison provided a rationale for the construction of the vast apparatus of control and discipline that now dominates bourgeois society." It may indeed be the case that Foucault would have preferred a violent, chaotic but "free" society to a peaceful, well-ordered but slave society. But I presume that he would not have endorsed complete privacy for children. Children require complete though gradually decreasing levels of observation because they lack a lot of what they need to know about being safe in the world. As long as our observation of them is accompanied by the aim of teaching them to do with less of it, the act of observation itself need not have the effects which Foucault writes it does. It seems reasonable to suppose that the same would hold for the educative observation of parents by the state. The point of such observation is to ensure the safety of children and to teach parents how to take care of their children in ways which will not result in more drastic state intervention down the road. See Archard (1993) 123-32.

Chapter 7

Corporal Punishment: Its Defenders

1. Dobson (1970, 1992). Philip Greven writes that *Dare* and *The New Dare* "have sold over a million copies" and "have been enormously successful among evangelical Christians." Greven (1991) 80.
2. Benatar (1998).
3. Dobson, 12-13.
4. Ibid.
5. Ibid. 63-65.
6. Ibid. 62.
7. Ibid. 63.
8. Ibid. 66.
9. Ibid. 65.
10. Ibid. 64.
11. Ibid.
12. Ibid. 15.
13. Ibid. 27.
14. *The Yearling* (1946) MGM was directed by Clarence Brown and starred Gregory Peck, Jane Wyman and Claude Jarman Jr. It is the story of a young

boy who captures a young dear and tries unsuccessfully and largely against his parents wishes, to raise it as a pet.

15. *Fanny and Alexander* (1982) AB Cinematograph/Swedish Film Institute/Swedish TV One/Gaument was directed by Ingmar Bergman. Philip Greven writes that "*Fanny and Alexander* centers on the calm, deliberate and harsh beating of a ten-year-old boy by his stepfather, a Protestant bishop" (Greven [1991] 150-55). One difference between Bergmann's depiction and that in *The Yearling* is that in the latter, the father is presented as a sympathetic character and in the former, he is not.

16. Philip Greven discusses what Dobson seems to accept as nonabusive punishment. See Greven, 78-79. Also, Irwin Hyman distinguishes between corporal punishment which is "abusive" and that which is "subabusive." While he is not prepared to categorize "a few light smacks on the behind" as child abuse, he states that "the crucible of child abuse is the belief that it is all right to use discipline based on the intent to inflict a degree of pain, any degree of pain. While it may be below the point of abuse, it is still on that continuum." He concludes, however, that "because we know that whenever any group is given the power to inflict pain on others, that power will invariably be misused, why are we even debating the issue?" (Hyman [1997] 36).

17. Dobson (1970, 1992) 61.

18. This theory of child learning is the one Jean-Jacques Rousseau deploys in *Emile*. Cf. chap. 5, 20n.

19. The problem of distinguishing between "disobedience" and "willful disobedience" in Dobson's work is discussed later. Being able to tell the difference is crucial since only willful disobedience merits corporal punishment, according to Dobson.

20. Dobson, 66.

21. Ibid. 61.

22. Ibid.

23. Greven writes that "The language of warfare is invoked at times in these treatises on will-breaking and punishment. Dobson, for example, uses the imagery of battles in his books such as *Dare to Discipline*" (Greven [1991] 68-69).

24. Dobson, 60.

25. Ibid.

26. Ibid. 62.

27. From the point of view of philosophical argument, an age-old problem rears its head here. It rests on the "is/ought" fallacy of reasoning. David Hume is most frequently cited as the philosopher to bring this problem to our attention but Immanuel Kant also made hay of it. Hume argued that it was illogical to proceed from a claim about "facts" or the way things were or are to one about "values" or how things ought to be. In this case,

what is "natural" is considered the way things are (Book Three Part I Section I). Dobson seems to argue that because learning sometimes does in fact proceed in response to painful consequences, this is how all childhood learning ought to or indeed must proceed. Brief reflection on this style of argument quickly shows that the conclusion does not follow from the premise. One might just as well argue that because human beings happen to kill one another from time to time, that they ought to or must do so. We can all accept the premise but few of us would accept the conclusion. That just means that the "is" reason is not a good one for accepting the "ought" conclusion. Dobson's claim, therefore, that children happen to learn things via pain does not support his conclusion that they ought to do so.

28. Dobson (1970-1992) 62.
29. Ibid. 64.
30. Ibid.
31. Ms. Amiel's "family statism" piece appeared in the *Edmonton Sun* (29 August 1993).
32. Here, once again, we find the "super-value" of security of the person directly contradicted. The reason why security of the person is so highly prized in our social and political culture is that we know from experience that freedom from the fear which physical threats and violence occasion is necessary (though not sufficient) for a human being to learn what she needs to know, make the plans she needs to make and freely execute those she chooses to execute. Without such knowledge, plans and activities, no human being can thrive. What we have then, in the case of the authoritarian family is a school of human maladjustment.
33. Monty Roberts has successfully domesticated wild horses solely through the use of nonviolent gestures developed on the basis of horse behaviour which he has observed in the field. See his *The Man Who Listens to Horses* (Random House 1997). In interviews, Roberts, who with his wife has raised 47 foster children plus their own, has argued that his methods are transferable, *mutatis mutandis*, to caring for children.
34. See Archard (1993) 122-32.
35. It has to be possible for parents to raise well-adjusted children without hitting them if the moral principle that we ought not to do so is to make any sense. If and only if it is impossible then parents may choose to abandon their childcare duties or to hit their children in the course of raising them. Whether they "ought" to do one or the other depends, from a moral point of view, on which option will produce, in this case, the least harmful consequences. On that basis, it is likely that parents will conclude they ought to hit their children. Since it is possible, however, to raise children without hitting them, the force of the moral obligation to refrain from using corporal punishment remains intact. The force of all "ought" statements is in what philosophers call their "action-guidingness." If the action or con-

straint on action called for is generally impossible to observe, such statements have no moral force. Philosophers have debated this issue at length. For example, if it is not possible for me to save a drowning child because I cannot swim, that does not mean I have no moral obligation to save drowning children. This matter has been resolved, for the most part, by the idea that as long as saving is possible — generally speaking — the moral obligation to do so remains in force. My particular circumstances may provide me with an excuse for failing to meet it on this or that occasion. But such excuses can wear thin rather quickly. Even if it is true, then, that some parents are unaware that they can raise children without hitting them and for that "reason" may be excused for hitting them on some occasion, unless it can be demonstrated that it is impossible for parents to do so, they must change their behaviour in the future.

36. Amiel (1998).
37. Dobson (1970, 1992) 64.
38. George Orwell is best known as the author of the futuristic novel *1984*.
39. *Post hoc ergo propter hoc* is Latin for "after which therefore because of which." Whenever we argue that the reason for or cause of some event is one that preceded it solely on that basis, we commit this fallacy of reasoning. Examples abound which demonstrate the problem. Say, for instance, a neo-Nazi would like to see Black Canadians denied the right to vote. He might point to the rise in crime in African American neighbourhoods and argue that it has been on the increase ever since the time they were given the right. He might then try and claim that being given the right to vote is the reason for the crime wave and as such, Blacks shouldn't be allowed to vote. Clearly such an argument is not rationally persuasive. You may simply want to reject the conclusion out of hand, but there is a logical reason for doing so. The neo-Nazi has made the mistake of assuming that because being given the right to vote chronologically preceded the crime rise, it is responsible for the increase. Unless he can show that no other factors were at work and that being given the right to vote always or nearly always leads to criminal behaviour, he has no argument. It is highly unlikely he would be able to show either of these things and typically, neo-Nazis and their ilk do not attempt to do so.
40. I recently had occasion to explore this sort of problem with an acquaintance. We were discussing the merits of public transit over car travel. Finally he said that public transit was a lot more trouble for him since he could not make sense of the bus schedules. I pointed out to him that the schedules were written so that anyone who knew their numbers and could tell time could figure out how to use them. He immediately realized that his "reason" was a bad one — that being unfamiliar with how the schedule worked was no excuse for not trying to figure it out and that his real reason — equally bad — for not wanting to use public transit

was that he had never used public transit. I believe that most parents who defend the use of corporal punishment do so because they have never experienced a society or family life in which its use was not permitted. However, while this might be a good explanation of such defences, it is not a good reason for them. In their report, Durrant and Rose-Krasnor (1995) viii write that "approval of corporal punishment is a strong predictor of its use and of the intensity with which it is administered. Approval of this disciplinary method is a function of the normative beliefs and practices of the culture at large. Cultural legitimization of the use of physical force with children contributes to stereotypes of parents and teachers as doing what is necessary and of children as deserving punishment."

41. On 25 March 1998, the British Parliament "voted overwhelmingly to ban corporal punishment in all schools, ending a centuries-old practice abhorred by liberal critics who said beating children scarred bodies and minds." (*Toronto Star* 26 March 1998). But no move has even been suggested to deny parents the right to assault their children. Many opponents of Parliament's action in Britain have, echoing Dobson and Amiel, expressed worries that the country is now on a slippery slope to a ban on all corporal punishment. Conservative MP Peter Luff, for example, is reported as saying "I think this is a travesty of parental rights. What I do fear is that the next step will be to ban parents from disciplining their children…I think parents should decide what's good for their children, not Parliament" (Ibid.).

42. Benatar (1998).

43. Ibid. 237.

44. Ibid. 240-48.

45. Ibid. 238, 242, 254.

46. Ibid. 238.

47. Ibid.

48. Ibid. 242.

49. Larzelere (1993) 144.

50. Benatar (1998) 257.

51. Ibid. 256.

52. Ibid.

53. Ibid.

54. Ibid.

55. Ibid.

56. Ibid. 257.

57. Ibid. 246.

58. Ibid. 242.

59. Ibid. 243.

60. Straus, Sugarman and Giles-Sims (1997). Also available at http://www.unh.frl/cp24art.htm.

61. "Ethical and practical problems prevent experimental studies with random assignment to a spanking condition" (Straus, Sugarman and Giles-Sims [1997] 2).
62. Durrant and Rose Krasnor (1995) 4.
63. Larzelere (1993) 143.
64. Ibid.
65. Durrant, personal communication.

Chapter 8
Corporal Punishment and Special Defences in the Law

1. Susan Bitensky (1998) 441, commenting on both the Swedish ban on corporal punishment and Irish proposals to follow suit writes, "Apparently, the ISPCC [Irish Society for the Prevention of Cruelty to Children] and the Swedish Government concluded that law has a crucial role to play in ending corporal punishment of children. In this way they are joined by six other nations, in addition to Sweden, that have adopted legal measures explicitly aimed at forbidding such punishment. In fact, law can play a pedagogical role that enhances public awareness in decisive ways."
2. Former Justice Minister Alan Rock was reported by the *Ottawa Citizen* as having said that "the Government has no intention of repealing the provision or making changes."
3. Hohfeld (1919) 35-64.
4. Blackstone (1803) Book I, chap. 16, s. 2, 453.
5. Boswell (1980) 249.
6. Some explanation is in order here of where our Criminal Law fits into the overall Canadian legal picture. This one will be extremely brief. Most of Canada is legally governed by what is called The Common Law system. This system originated in England and emphasizes the rule of precedent. The Province of Quebec is legally governed by The Civil Law system. This system originated in France and emphasizes the rule of codified law. Under The Common Law system, a great deal of attention is paid by courts to what is called "jurisprudence" or the interpretation of law as it occurs and has occurred in judicial reasoning on specific cases and in other judicial writings. This system has a somewhat conservative effect on how laws are applied to specific cases. Under The Civil Law system, greater weight is given to laws as they are written down leaving judges free to interpret their meaning in light of current circumstances. The lower case term "common law" refers to whatever counts as written "law" in a given jurisdiction. In Canada as a whole, the common law or "law" is made up of Statutory (or codified) Law and jurisprudential law. In Quebec, the common law or "law" is comprised of Statutory Law alone. The provi-

sions or sections of the Criminal Code together with countless legislated
regulations and policies comprise Statutory Law. In Canada as a whole,
this includes civil law legislation (not to be confused with The Civil Law
system) which deals with torts (or damage claims) and contracts.
Published versions of The Criminal Code either include the jurisprudential law which has evolved for each section or are accompanied by a supplement which provides it by section number. Judges in the Common Law
system are bound by this jurisprudence. Finally, the Criminal Code has
many parts: The General Part (Sections 3-45) which deals with defences
among other things and more specific parts—"Offenses Against Rights of
Property" for example.

7. The definitive Canadian case on the defence of necessity is currently *Perka
    et al. v. The Queen*, (1984) 13 D.L.R. (4th). In *Perka*, Dickson, J interpreted the
    defence of necessity within the context of the defence of justification. I
    have chosen to treat it separately since on its face, the act taken on grounds
    of necessity may have in fact been the greater of two evils. It need only be
    the case that the accused believed it to be the lesser. Nevertheless, Dickson
    insists that such a belief may only act in the accused's defence if it is con-
    sonant with a "right or duty recognized by law" (Ibid. 37). A belief based
    on mere force of conscience or the perception that on the occasion, the act
    would maximize "social utility" would be insufficient. One may argue
    that here, Dickson is revealing the Supreme Court's rejection of utilitari-
    anism as a basis for interpreting law. But in response, a utilitarian may
    argue that either, he is just being an exclusive legal positivist (someone
    who does not see any place at all in the interpretation of law for morality)
    or that he is implicitly relying on the principles of rule utilitarianism. Rule
    utilitarianism marks a distinction within utilitarianism proper between
    those who argue that the principle of promoting the greatest happiness of
    the greatest number must be applied to each and every act and those who
    argue that it must instead be applied to the formulation and interpretation
    of each and every rule for acting. The latter is rule and the former is act
    utilitarianism. Rule utilitarianism is a response to the criticism that con-
    stant calculation of the harms and benefits of acts would itself be socially
    disutile. This is the sort of criticism implied by Dickson, J's remark.
    Instead, we formulate and apply rules with the understanding that every-
    one will follow them and calculate the effects of that on social utility. In
    which case, the moral principle of the greatest happiness for the greatest
    number instructs us to choose those rules and policies that will have the
    best overall effect. See Scarre (1996) 122-32.

8. See LRCC *Working Paper #29*, "Liability and Defenses," 91-97.

9. "Essentially, (the doctrine of necessity) involves two factors....The first is
    a utilitarian principle to the effect that, within certain limits, it is justifiable
    in an emergency to break the letter of the law if breaking the law will avoid

a greater harm than obeying it" (LRCC *Working Paper* #29, p. 93). The Commission takes a philosophically interesting stand on the matter of what it calls "'life for life'" cases. It reasons that since the value of one person's life cannot in principle outweigh the value of any other's, a person who saves his or her own life at the cost of another's cannot properly avail themselves of a necessity defence. "This, however, would not preclude prosecutors, courts, juries and cabinets from exercising their discretion and making concessions in appropriate cases on the basis that, in extreme emergency, loss of the accused's own life may well have seemed to him to outweigh the loss of someone else's. The use of such discretion, although derogating from the rule of law, seems to be the most appropriate way of dealing with the most difficult of such rare cases." The sense in which such a "weighing" of the circumstances "derogates" from the rule of law is in its prioritizing of the subjective point of view. For it is only from the point of view of the accused that one life, namely his or hers, could rightfully be seen as of greater value than someone else's. The rule of law dictates that those who stand in judgement maintain the objective point of view from which no life is worth more or less than any other. Yet there must be some room made for this sort of choice. Rather than formalize this room, however, the LRCC recommends it be discretionary.

10. Recall the discussion of the argument from forgiveness in chap. 4. There, I examined the claim that a parent who, acting on an uncontrollable impulse caused by some extreme provocation by the child, hits that child, ought not to be punished for the act. Instead, he or she ought to be forgiven. Historically, excusatory defences have included provocation under the familiar term "crime de passion." But no such excusatory defence exists in Canadian law. Rather, the defence of provocation is available to accused persons only under the sort of circumstances that characterize self-defence situations and is considered a "justificatory" defence rather than an excusatory one. Independently of provoking causes, one may nonetheless argue that the parent's state of mind was "disturbed" to such an extent that he or she lost self-control. In this case, the defence is clearly excusatory.

11. *Criminal Code of Canada*, Section 403.

12. LRCC *Working Paper* #29, *"Liability and Defenses,"* 98.

13. Ibid.

14. Ibid. 105.

15. Ibid. 111.

16. In the Recodification Subcommittee's report to the Solicitor General in 1993, it was stated that "The Law Reform Commission proposed that no one be liable for an offense if, as a parent or guardian, he or she touches, hurts or confines a child in the reasonable exercise of authority over the child" (*R43 Brief* Appendix F). This is a significant departure from Section

43's current wording bringing it into line with the wording of Section 45. I believe this change in wording would imply a change from the current justificatory defence to one of necessity in which case corporal punishment would be regarded as the "lesser evil" when comparing it to losing authority over children.

17. LRCC, *Working Paper #29*, "Liability and Defenses," 98.
18. The LRCC *Working Paper #38* "Assault" (40). The Commission recommended that Section 44 of the Canadian Criminal Code be repealed on the grounds that the protection is "otiose" and that no such privilege is conferred on the captains of aircraft.
19. See Criminal Code sections under "Protection of Persons Administering and Enforcing the Law" (Sections 25-34).
20. Lafollette (1980). In this piece, Lafollette argues that parents ought to be subject to at least the same level of regulation as sport fishers and hunters.
21. LRCC *Working Paper #29*, "Liability and Defenses," 1982.
22. LRCC *Working Paper #38*, "Assault," 1984, 41. Note here, the Commission seems to assume the privilege of teachers and other non-parental caregivers to hit children is derived from the privilege parents have. This is not the case according to the wording of Section 43.
23. Ibid. 42.
24. Ibid. 43.
25. Ibid.
26. Ibid.
27. Ibid. 44.
28. Ibid.
29. Ibid.
30. Ibid. 45.
31. Ibid.
32. Ibid. 46.
33. Again, the issue here is what may a parent do in the exercise of what Susan Bitensky (1998) 453 refers to in the American context as their "substantive due process right to rear children as they see fit," their right to freedom of religion and their right to familial privacy. The issue of privacy is not as constitutionally salient in a Canadian context as it is in the American one, but the worry referred to is certainly common as we saw in the discussion of Amiel. It may be argued that the law already limits any right of parents to rear their children as they "see fit," rear them according to their religious beliefs or under the cover of familial privacy. Parents may not, for example, raise their children as practitioners of sibling incest, teach their children about God's view of sexual matters by engaging in sexual relations with them, impose dangerously strict diets on them, deny them life-saving medical treatment, or kill them to end their physical suffering and so on. In spite of these and numerous other restrictions, parents in general

do not feel intruded upon by the state because few parents do or endorse such practices. It is only when something which most parents have traditionally done in the course of their childrearing is questioned or condemned that they claim such intrusion. There is of course a sense in which the state is "intruding" in the family when it imposes laws against certain child care practices. But this sense of intruding carries with it no obvious evaluative connotation. The question then is, is the intrusion in the interest of children and families? I have argued throughout that the intrusion of the state into the family when it comes to the use of corporal punishment is indeed in the interests of children and families. Corporal punishment must be regarded as a denial of children's basic needs — in this case the need for a sense of security of the person — and not like the denial of their pleas for the latest style in running shoes.

34. Section 1 of the Charter places a limit on the extent to which individual rights and freedoms may be protected in Canada. The limit defines the conditions necessary for democracy and freedom to flourish and has been worked out in detail by the courts. It was in *R. v. Oakes* (1986) that the Supreme Court first set out a formal procedure for determining the constitutional validity of laws which are in prima facie violation of the Charter. For example, when Jim Keegstra appealed his guilty verdict for the crime of disseminating hate propaganda to Eckville students to the Supreme Court, the court found that while his freedom of expression was violated by the law against Hate Propaganda, this limit on his freedom to disseminate his opinions on the Jews in his classrooms was judged to be necessary in a free and democratic society.

Chapter 9
The Legal Challenge For Section 43

1. Boswell (1980) 171.
2. Blackstone (1803) Book I, chap. 16, s. 2, 453.
3. Ibid. 452.
4. Ibid.
5. Boswell 171.
6. Greene (1998) Part I 288-317, (1999) Part II 463-84.
7. It was in *R. v. Oakes* [1986] that the Supreme Court first set out this formal procedure for determining the constitutional validity of laws which are in prima facie violation of Charter rights or freedoms.
8. Greene, Part II, 465.
9. Ibid. 471.
10. *Canadian Foundation for Children, Youth and Justice* (Applicant) etc., (5 July 1999) 16.
11. Ibid. 473.

12. Ibid. Part I, 301.
13. Ibid. 293. Reference to *Ogg-Moss v. R.* (1984).
14. *R. v. Dupperon* (1985).
15. Waluchow (1991), reprinted in Dyzenhaus and Ripstein (1996) 156.
16. To attract the law, cases of assault must involve the use of intentional force. There are a great many unwelcome contacts (excluding sexual ones) which would fall beneath such a threshold. I discuss this issue in greater detail in chap. 10. For each degree of assault, there are additional criteria to be met. For example, in order to lay a charge of "aggravated assault" the authorities must be satisfied that the effect of the assault was to wound, maim, disfigure or endanger the life of the victim. See Criminal Code Section 268.

Chapter 10

What About Spanking?

1. It certainly is possible under such circumstances for a court to introduce a new interpretive extension to Section 43 by defining the notion of "reasonable force" to exclude all forms of corporal punishment. This would leave, for example, the use of physical restraint in place. The Court might well see the use of such restraint as reasonable under the circumstances of parental discipline even though it might not be in other kinds of circumstances. In other circumstances where physical restraint is used in a prima facie unlawful manner, to defend himself, the accused may invoke, for instance, the common law defence of necessity. But given the stringent criteria that must be satisfied for such a defence to work, it is unlikely that many parents would find it successful.
2. In almost every successful Section 43 case cited by the Repeal 43 Committee in their brief to the Federal Government, the punishment in question involved striking the child either with the hand or with some object. In one case, the act in question involved grabbing and shaking only. In *Ogg-Moss v. R.*, the Court stated that Section 43 "does not deal with the protection of persons using physical force in response to violent or dangerous behaviour" and that it "deprives an individual, or a group, of the protection normally offered by the criminal law, namely, the right to be free from unconsented invasions of physical security or dignity" (Tremeears [1986] 165). The historical pedigree of Section 43 also shows that it follows from a line of special defences intended to protect persons in authority from being found guilty of assault when they strike a subordinate. In the past, the *de minimis* rule has operated to exclude, for the most part, cases in which the assault in question did not involve the causation of harm. The *de minimis* rule will be discussed in greater detail later. From all this, we may infer that Section 43 is specifically intended to refer to cor-

poral punishment even though it may include other uses of physical force in its protective ambit.

3. According to Joan Durrant and Murray Straus (in correspondence), the effects on children of witnessing the corporal punishment of other children, especially their siblings, has not yet been explored. In Durrant and Rose-Krasnor, for instance, a distinction is made between adult respondents who experienced corporal punishment themselves and those that did not. But there is no indication of whether those who did not ever witness others being punished in this way. I suspect that even witnessing corporal punishment especially of siblings would have some if not all of the effects that being corporally punished has. It would, in any case, have the effect of instilling fear in the child and so causing both silence and the developmental problems associated with this state of mind. I am reminded of the situation brought to our attention by feminists such as Catharine MacKinnon (1987) where even those women who are not themselves victims of spousal violence are constantly on alert due to the fact that many women are, since before these victims were assaulted the first time, they too were not direct victims of it. See also Wallach (1993). In general, the reporting of teacher violence has been met in the past by parents either with proprietary indignation ("If Johnny has misbehaved then I will be the one to beat him") or deference to teacherly authority ("if Teacher has beaten you [or whoever] then you [or whoever] must have deserved it"). Neither outcome supported children in the reporting of such violence. In the case of the latter outcome, parents may be less uncertain of their authority today.

4. It is not surprising that the "Canadian Teachers Federation has taken a stand in opposition to the repeal of Section 43" since "it is concerned that teachers will lose their right to self-defence or to restraining children who are causing harm to themselves or others" (Durrant [1996] 110). But as noted earlier (cf.fn 2), according to case law, Section 43 is not intended for use in cases where an individual uses physical force in defending him or herself or someone else from threat or other danger. The CTF's argument for retention is therefore unpersuasive. In spite of its unpersuasiveness, it was used again in defence of maintaining Section 43 in the recent application to the Ontario Supreme Court to have the section declared unconstitutional.

5. *Q. v. Robinson* (1899) cited in *R43 Brief* Appendix B.

6. Ibid. *K. V. Zink* (1910).

7. Ibid. *R. v. Metcalfe* (1927).

8. Ibid. *R. v. Corkum* (1937).

9. It is not clear just what may be inferred from the tendency of lower courts to convict in such cases. It may be that they are expressing a sensitivity which higher courts do not to a natural rights distinction between the entitlements of parents on the one hand and those of teachers on the other,

tending to side with the parents in their thinking that teachers are traversing on parental territory when they hit students. Or it may be that they are more sensitive than are the higher courts to the moral unacceptability of corporal punishment. I suspect that it is the former, though only a thorough analysis of the complete decisions in each case would settle the matter.

10. In *R. v. Dupperon*, a father was accused of assault causing bodily harm for strapping his emotionally disturbed 13-year-old son on the buttocks "about 10 times" with a leather belt (*R. v. Dupperon* [1985]). The father was convicted at trial but appealed to the Saskatchewan Court of Appeal. On appeal, the charge was overturned and replaced with a conviction for common assault. "The trial Judge erred in finding that the strapping was not for the purpose of correction. However, evidence established that the force was excessive under the circumstances. The accused was therefore not entitled to the protection of Section 43 of the Code. Furthermore assault causing bodily harm was not proved since there was no evidence that the bruises caused by strapping were more than transitory or trifling in nature" (Tremeears [1986] 165). The reason then, that Section 43 was unsuccessfully invoked was that the punishment was excessive. But even though it was excessive enough to disentitle the father to a Section 43 defence, it was not excessive enough to justify a conviction for assault causing bodily harm. For, according to the Court of Appeal, the assault did not cause bodily harm. This, in spite of the fact that the beating left bruises on the boy's body.

11. *Campeau v. The King* [1951].

12. Tony Major, "Horrifying Codified Cruelty: Report to Parliament and People (Aids to Thinking and Feeling)," unpublished manuscript 1996, 43.

13. *R43 Brief* Appendix B.

14. *R. v. S. et al* (1992) unreported, (Ontario); *R43 Brief* Appendix B; Durrant (1996) 109.

15. Tremeears (1986) 165.

16. Ibid.

17. *R43 Brief* Appendix C.

18. The American Academy of Pediatrics definition of spanking is the: "use of an opened hand on the extremities or buttocks that is physically noninjurious" (Hyman [1997] 58). I prefer to use the term "spanking" more restrictively to refer to the buttocks only, since the terms "slapping" or "smacking" seem more appropriate when describing blows of this sort to other body parts. For example, it sounds odd to say that I "spanked the back of his head" or "I got spanked on my arm" even though the terms "slap" or "smack" are used interchangeably with "spank" when it comes to the buttocks. If it is specifically "spanking" that parents are concerned about, then I think it best to adopt the more narrow meaning. I also use the term more broadly to include uses of implements such as belts, paddles, shoes, rulers

or yardsticks. Spankings with the use of such weapons may be classified as "severe" spankings especially when they are administered to a bare buttocks.

19. Hyman (1997) xii.
20. Ibid. 4.
21. Cf., chap. 2, 1n.
22. Ibid. 186.
23. *R. v. Taylor* (1985) noted in *Tremeears* (1986) 166.
24. Ibid.
25. Straus, Sugarman and Giles-Sims (1997). Also available on the Internet at http://www.unh.edu/frl/cp24art.htm. In their reporting of results, the authors state that "Forty-four percent of the mothers reported spanking their children during the week prior to the study and they spanked them an average of 2.1 times that week. The more spanking at the start of the period, the higher the level of ASB (anti-social behaviour) 2 years later. The change is unlikely to be owing to the child's tendency toward ASB or to confounding with demographic characteristics or with parental deficiency in other key aspects of socialization because those variables were statistically controlled" (1). The authors then conclude that "When parents use corporal punishment to reduce ASB, the long-term effect tends to be the opposite. The findings suggest that if parents replace corporal punishment with nonviolent modes of discipline, it could reduce the risk of ASB among children and reduce the level of violence in American society" (Ibid.). The authors argue that these results are more reliable that those drawn from longitudinal studies in the past because children's ASB levels prior to the commencement of the study (among other factors) were strictly controlled for.
26. John Stuart Mill referred to two forms of behavioural control when he discussed the problems of getting adults to act in a moral manner: internal and external control. External sanctions include the threat of and actual physical punishment. The ultimate internal sanction of moral behaviour is conscience which is "a feeling in our own mind; a pain, more or less intense, attendant on a violation of duty, which in properly cultivated moral natures rises, in the more serious cases, into shrinking from it as an impossibility" and is itself an "outgrowth" of our feelings for the well-being of others (Mill [1963-1991] 10, 229). Irwin Hyman writes in the same vein that "Democratic discipline in the home requires that children should be taught to do the right thing because it is the right thing to do. This is called moral persuasion, as opposed to moral coercion, which is based on fear of punishment....Discipline that is based on moral persuasion involves discussion, praise for correct behaviour, negotiation, and parental modeling of good behaviour" (Hyman [1997] 7).
27. See Hyman (1997) on spanking as "sub-abuse," 33-40.

28. *R43 Brief,* Appendices B and D.

29. Typically, schools and universities have mechanisms for dealing with these sorts of allegations at the local level. Various tribunals and boards of inquiry are set up to hear complaints and render judgements and penalties. Depending upon the outcomes of these hearings, a complainant or defendant may elect to pursue the matter outside of the institution in the courts. Or it may happen that the allegations are considered serious enough at the outset to warrant legal action. Courts, in any case, have tended to be intolerant of complainants whose accusations do not involve the causing of "harm" seeing these as falling below the threshold for assault set by the *de minimis* rule.

30. Susan Bitensky notes that Italy's more punitive approach to corporal punishers is in part explained by its desire to sever its historical links to fascism. The use of physical pain and its attendant climate of terror was an essential feature of Benito Mussolini's World War II military dictatorship known for its extreme right-wing nationalism and authoritarianism. The term "fascism" comes from the old Roman word *fasces* which means "a bundle of rods with a projecting axe-blade, carried by a lictor as a symbol of a magistrate's power" (*Concise Oxford English Dictionary*). The Italian courts seem particularly sensitive to the country's past as characterized by this period of its history and concerned to represent its rejection of all the trappings of the fascist era. Bitensky writes that "Judge Ippolito noted that as Italy moved away from fascism, it also moved away from the concept of the authoritarian father" (Bitensky [1998] 383).

31. Will Kymlicka asks whether "we have any right" to deny the cultural expression of values which contradict those we have enshrined in our Charter of Rights and Freedoms given the "'logic' of multiculturalism" (Kymlicka [1998] 65-66). He notes that certain commentators argue that "the limits we now draw in accommodating diversity are arbitrary and ad hoc, and that the "logic" of multiculturalism will drive us towards accepting such illiberal practices" (Ibid.). Kymlicka responds, "That is not true. Such oppressive practices are not the "logical" extension of current multiculturalism policies....It is perfectly logical to accept that aim while denying that groups are entitled to continue practices that violate individual rights, or to impose practices on members who do not wish to maintain them....The line that has been drawn in Canada...is neither arbitrary nor ad hoc. It is just what one would expect in a liberal democracy" (Ibid.).

32. Hyman writes, for example, that "If no child were spanked, none would be spanked severely, thereby reducing deaths of children in their homes" and that "threatening with a gun should have the same type of deterrence value as threatening with a spanking. That is, both convey to potential victims that if they don't behave in a certain way they will receive pain. The less they comply, the more the potential for pain and harm. This is the type

of thinking that occurs when some parents beat their children to death"(Hyman [1997] 31). Greven, relying on the work in this area of psychologist Alice Miller, states that "Physical pain and abuse originating in discipline are consistent progenitors of authoritarianism....The polarities of order and disorder, obedience and rebelliousness—always present in authoritarians—are among the most enduring legacies of corporal punishments" (Greven [1991] 199).

33. *Cambria*, Supreme Court of Cassation, 6th Penal Section, 18 March 1996.
34. Bitensky 380.
35. Ibid. 382.
36. On 20 November 1989, the General Assembly of the United Nations adopted the *Convention on the Rights of the Child* to which Canada (with the exception of the province of Alberta) was a signatory. Insofar as it was a signatory, the Government of Canada agreed to abide by all of the terms set out in that Convention and as such, agreed to abide by Article 19.1 of the document which states the following: "States Parties shall take all appropriate legislative, administrative, social and educational measures to protect children from all forms of physical or mental violence, injury or abuse, neglect or negligent treatment, maltreatment or exploitation, including sexual abuse, while in the care of parent(s), legal guardian(s) or any other person who has the care of the child." Italy takes it signatory status far more seriously than Canada appears to, citing it as one of the prime reasons for changing its laws on the issue of corporal punishment. In addition to a child's right to be free from physical or mental violence, the Convention also grants children the rights to freedom of expression, thought, conscience and religion and to freedom of association and peaceful assembly in conformity with laws aimed at preserving "democratic society," "the interests of national security," "public safety, public order, the protection of public health or morals or the protection of the rights and freedoms of others" (Articles 12, 13, 14 and 15). See Durrant, (1994) 129-36.
37. See Durrant and Olsen (1997) and Bitensky (1998) 362-67.
38. Durrant and Olsen (1997) 444.
39. Ibid. 445.
40. Ibid.
41. Durrant (Winter 1993-1994) 2-6.
42. Ibid. 5.
43. Moira Welsh and Kevin Donovan of *The Toronto Star* reported on 1 March 1998 that "after relying for decades on American studies, the federal government is spending a half a million dollars to research the causes and effects of child maltreatment from British Columbia to Newfoundland." The three-month study only considers those cases of child abuse which are "reported" however, and as such, will only produce "tip of the iceberg" results. It is also assumed by those involved that the study is the first part

of an ongoing process of determining the state of child abuse and neglect in Canada which will involve at least two further studies. University of Toronto Professor Nico Trocme was awarded the study grant from the Child Maltreatment Division of the Federal Health Division through a competition and has called the study the "Canadian Incidence Study of Child Abuse and Neglect."

44. Two such groups are the *Evangelical Fellowship* (Bruce Clemenger, director) and the Vancouver-based *Focus on the Family* (Cindy Silver, legal analyst).

Chapter 11
Child Abuse and Family Statism Revisited

1. Tremeears (1986) 165.
2. Mill (1963-1991) 10, 250.
3. See Kadushin and Martin (1981), chap. 5 and Durrant and Rose-Krasnor (1995) 12-14.
4. *The Canadian Incidence Study of Child Abuse and Neglect* was commissioned by the Child Maltreatment division of Health Canada in 1998 to collect nation wide data on child abuse in Canada. The study is headed by Dr. Nico Trocme of the University of Toronto. The study website is located at www.hc-sc.gc.ca/hpb/lcdc/brch/maltreat/result_e.html
5. See Straus (1994) chap. 6, especially 81-97.
6. Ibid. 87.
7. Ibid. chap. 6.
8. In the context of American estimates of the numbers here, Kadushin and Martin note that such figures are very difficult to determine. But if only substantiated cases of abuse are counted, the most conservative estimate based on U.S. nationwide studies is around 25,000 per year (Kadushin and Martin [1981] 7-9). A rough estimate of substantiated cases of severely abused children based on the results of the Canadian Incidence Study suggest a figure for Canada at around 10,000 (Corinne Robertshaw, personal communication).
9. This figure is taken from Durrant and Rose-Krasnor (1995) 11, who base it on information from the Institute for the Prevention of Child Abuse.
10. Straus (1994) 85.
11. Kadushin and Martin (1981) chap. 5.
12. Straus 85.
13. Ibid.
14. Some may argue that the specific intrusion into parent disciplining practices and the difficulties this presents is the least of the problems with a legal ban on the use of corporal punishment or the removal of special protections for parents who wish to use this childrearing strategy. Far more serious, they might argue, is the fact that a key threshold is crossed when

government agencies take it upon themselves to make what goes on in the private households of their citizens a matter of public concern. Loudest among those who make these sorts of complaints is the far right—those who uphold the values of libertarian individualism and state minimalism. For them, the private/public divide is sacrosanct and every encroachment upon it by state institutions represents a threat to individual freedom and well-being. I do not want to be seen as dismissive of the worry that government surveillance can become a serious problem. While checks and balances are in place to ensure things do not get out of hand, the effectiveness of those checks and balances depends largely upon the integrity of our government officials and the good sense of the citizenry—two things which appear to be in short supply from time to time. But while I share the worry to some extent, my worries for children take precedence. Where children are concerned we have far to go before there is too much monitoring of their care. Until such time as that care can be generally relied upon to be nonviolent, I believe we must simply bear the cost to our privacy which stepped-up government efforts to monitor it will entail. Finally, the removal of Section 43 from the Criminal Code does not in any way imply the sorts of monitoring I am speaking about here. And so the complaints about privacy in the face of calls to remove it are premature.

15. *Canadian Foundation for Children, Youth and the Law* (Applicant) etc. (5 July 2000) 9.
16. Ibid. 11.
17. My thanks to Joan Durrant for the "safety seat" example.
18. The issue of just what merits correction when we speak about children is one which gets some though insufficient attention in the literature. Much is made of the trivial nature of many of the behaviours children are punished for. For example, Irwin Hyman, commenting on deaths that have resulted from corporal punishment, writes, "What were the horrendous misbehaviours that ended in death? Some toddlers soiled or wet themselves after many warnings and previous spankings for behaviour that was so inconvenient to the caretakers. Some caretakers claimed that the children were 'out of control,' and others said that children just 'wouldn't behave.' Some other misbehaviours that carried the death penalty included stealing, 'blocking my view of the TV,' and refusal to take out the trash. One victim ate an unauthorized piece of cake; another 'wouldn't eat her dinner.' One caretaker, explaining why the child was murdered, was quoted as saying, 'she was annoying me'" (Hyman [1997] 32). But there are other reasons children are physically punished. They are physically punished for using "swear words" even when they have picked up the words from adults and have no idea of what the words mean. They are physically punished for being "weak"—crying or complaining about their situation. They are physically punished for being "disrespectful" where a

look or a tone of voice is taken violent offence to. In their research, Kadushin and Martin (1981) decided to focus on the interactive context of child abuse and their findings are relevant to corporal punishment. They conclude that while children are not equal players in the discipline routine and should not be blamed for their victimization, their dispositions and behaviours are typically what their parents identify as the principle cause of the abuse incident, and as such must be taken into account by social welfare workers when family interventions are necessary due to the occurrence of child abuse.

19. This information about the case is taken from a story entitled "Changing the Rules: A Mother 'Crosses' the Hazy Line between Corporal Punishment and Illegal Abuse" by Marnie Ko in *Report* (Alberta Edition), 01 January 2001, 28. The decision in the case was rendered on 28 November 2000.

20. Ibid.

Bibliography

• • • • • • • • • • • •

The following bibliography contains the titles of books, articles, essays, government documents and other sources used in this book as well as a number of other relevant titles. A selected list of legal cases appears at the end.

Amiel, Barbara. "Beware the Sinister Arm of Family Statism." *Edmonton Sun*, 29 August 1993.

_____. "The Case for Corporal Punishment." *Montreal Gazette*, 28 March 1998.

Annas, Julia. "MacIntyre on Traditions." *Philosophy and Public Affairs* 18 (fall 1989).

Aquinas, St. Thomas. *Pocket Aquinas: Selections from the Writings of St. Thomas*. Ed.Vernon Burke. New York: Washington Square Press, 1960.

Archard, David. *Children: Rights and Childhood*. London: Routledge, 1993.

_____. "Can Child Abuse Be Defined?" Chap. 5 in *Moral Agendas for Children's Welfare*, edited by Michael King. London: Routledge, 1999.

Ariès, Philippe. *Centuries of Childhood*. Trans. Robert Baldrick. London: Jonathan Cape, 1962. Originally published as *L'Enfant et la vie familiale sous l'ancien régime* (Paris: Librairie Plon, 1960).

Aristotle. *Nicomachean Ethics*. Trans. J.A.K. Thomson. New York: Penguin Classics, 1953, 1976.

_____. *Politics*. Ed. and trans. Ernest Barker. London: Oxford University Press, 1958.

Atwood, Margaret. *The Blind Assassin*. Toronto: McClelland and Stewart, 2000.

Benatar, David. "Corporal Punishment." *Social Theory and Practice* 24 (summer 1998).

Bentham, Jeremy. *A Fragment on Government*. Ed. F.C. Montague. London: Oxford University Press, 1931.

_____. *The Principles of Morals and Legislation*. Ed. Lawrence Lafleur. New York: Hafner Press, 1973.

Berlin, Isaiah. *Four Essays on Liberty*. Oxford: Oxford University Press, 1969.

Bitensky, Susan H. "Spare the Rod, Embrace Our Humanity: Toward a New Legal Regime Prohibiting Corporal Punishment of Children." *University of Michigan Journal of Law Reform* 31 (winter 1998).

Blackstone's Commentaries on the Laws of England. 14th Edition, 1803.

Blake, William. *Songs of Innocence and Experience: A Great English Poetic Work*. Ed. Ruth Everett. New York: Bard Books Avon, 1971.

Boetzskes, Elizabeth, Susan Turner (Guerin), and Edrie Sobstyl. "Women, Madness and Special Defenses in the Law." *Journal of Social Philosophy* 21 (fall and winter 1990).

Boswell, James. *Everybody's Boswell: Being the Life of Samuel Johnson abridged from James Boswell's complete text*. London: Bell and Hyman Limited, 1980.

Bradbury, Ray. *I Sing the Body Electric*. New York: Bantam, 1969.

Brennan, Samantha and Robert Noggle. "John Rawls's Children." In *The Philosopher's Child: Critical Perspectives in the Western Tradition*, edited by S.M. Turner and G.B. Matthews. Rochester: University of Rochester Press, 1998.

Bronskill, Jim. "Right to Use Force Must End, Senator Argues: Should Parents be Allowed to Spank?" *The Ottawa Citizen*, 12 February 1997.

Canada. Charter of Rights and Freedoms. Enacted by the *Canada Act 1982* (U.K.) c.11. Proclaimed in force 17 April 1982.

Canada. Health Canada. Population and Public Health Branch. Child Maltreatment Division-Publications. *The Canadian Incidence Study of Reported Child Abuse and Neglect*, by Nico Trocmé, Bruce Mac Laurin, Barbara Fallon et al. Ottawa, ON: 20 March 2001.

Canada. The House of Commons of Canada, Second Session, Thirty-Fifth Parliament, 45 Elizabeth II. Bill C-305. "An Act to amend the Criminal Code (protection of children)." Submitted by The Right Honourable Member of Parliament Mr. Svend Robinson. First Reading 12 June 1996.

Canada. Law Reform Commission of Canada. Working Paper #29 *Liability and Defenses*. Ottawa, 1982.

_____. Working Paper #33 *Homicide*. Ottawa, 1984.

_____. Working Paper #38 *Assault*. Ottawa, 1985.

Canada. The Senate of Canada, Second Session, Thirty-Fifth Parliament, 45 Elizabeth II. Bill S-14. "An Act to Amend the Criminal Code and the Department of Health Act (security of the child)." Submitted by The Honorable Senator Sharon Carstairs. First reading 12 December 1996.

Canada. Statistics Canada. "Youth violent crime." *Juristat* 19: 1998.

Descartes, René. *Meditations*. In *The Philosophical Writings of Descartes*. Vol. 2. Eds. and trans. John Cottingham, Robert Stoothoff and Dugald Murdoch. Cambridge: Cambridge University Press, 1984.

Dobson, Dr. James. *The New Dare to Discipline*. 2nd ed. Wheaton Ill.: Tyndale House Publishers, 1992.

Durrant, Joan. "Sparing the Rod: Manitobans' Attitudes Toward the Abolition of Physical Discipline and Implications for Policy Change." *Canada's Mental Health* (winter 1993-1994).

_____. "The Abolition of Corporal Punishment in Canada: Parents' versus Children's Rights." *The International Journal of Children's Rights* 2 (1994): 129-136.

_____. "Public Attitudes Towards Corporal Punishment in Canada." In *Family Violence Against Children: A Challenge for Society*, edited by Detlev Frehsee, Wiebke Horn and Kai-D. Bussman. Berlin: Walter de Gruyter, 1996.

_____. "Culture, Corporal Punishment and Child Abuse." In *Readings in Child Development: A Canadian Perspective*, edited. By K. Covell. Toronto: Nelson: 1995.

_____."Corporal Punishment: Research Findings and Implications for Practice." *Putting Research Into Practice 1999 Workshops*, BC Council for Families, seminar presentation, 27 October 1999.

_____. "Evaluating the Success of Sweden's Corporal Punishment Ban." *Pergamon* 23 (1999): 435-48.

_____. "Trends in Youth Crime and Well-Being Since the Abolition of Corporal Punishment in Sweden." *Youth and Society* 31 (2000): 437-55.

Durrant, Joan and Linda Rose-Krasnor. "Corporal Punishment: Research Review and Policy Recommendations." Family Violence Prevention Division of Health Canada and the Department of Justice, 1995.

Durrant, Joan and Gregg M. Olson. "Parenting and public policy: contextualizing the Swedish corporal punishment ban." *Journal of Social Welfare and Family Law* 19 (1997): 443-61.

Dworkin, Ronald. *Law's Empire*. Cambridge: Harvard University Press, 1986.

_____. "The Law's Ambitions for Itself." *Virginia Law Review* 71 (1985): 173-87.

Dyzenhaus, David and Arthur Ripstein, eds. *Law and Morality: Readings in Legal Philosophy*. Toronto: University of Toronto Press, 1996.

Feinberg, Joel and Hymen Gross, eds. *Philosophy of Law*. 2nd ed. Belmont, Cal: Wadsworth, 1980.

Ferris, Timothy. *Coming of Age in the Milky Way*. New York: William Morrow and Company, 1988.

Finnis, John. 1994. Natural Law and Legal Reasoning. In *Natural Law Theory: Contemporary Essays*, edited by Robert P. George, Oxford: Oxford University Press. Selections reprinted in Dyzenhaus and Ripstein, 1996.

Foucault, Michel. *Discipline and Punish: The Birth of the Prison*. Trans. Alan Sheridan. New York: Random House Pantheon Books, 1980.

Frehsee, Detlev, Wiebke Horn, and Kai-D. Bussman, eds. *Family Violence Against Children: A Challenge for Society*. Berlin: Walter de Gruyter, 1996.

Fuller, Lon. *The Morality of Law*. New Haven: Yale University Press, 1969.

Galipeau, Claude J. *Isaiah Berlin's Liberalism*. Oxford: Oxford Clarendon Press, 1994.

Galloway, Donald. *Immigration Law*. Concord, ON.: Irwin Law, 1997.

General Assembly of The United Nations. *Convention on the Rights of the Child*. 20 November 1989.

Gewirth, Alan. *Reason and Morality*. Chicago: University of Chicago Press, 1978.

Golding, William. *Lord of the Flies*. Harmondsworth: Penguin Books, 1962.

Gert, Bernard. s.v. "Thomas Hobbes." *Oxford Companion to Philosophy*. Ed. Ted Honderich. Oxford: Oxford University Press, 1995.

Greene, Sharon. "The Unconstitutionality of Section 43." *Criminal Law Quarterly* 41 (1998) Part I: 288-317; 42 (1999) Part II: 463-84.

Greven, Philip. *Spare the Child: The Religious Roots of Punishment and the Psychological Impact of Physical Abuse*. New York: Knopf, 1991.

Hart, H.L.A. *The Concept of Law*. Oxford: Oxford University Press, 1961.

_____. *Essays in Jurisprudence and Philosophy*. Oxford: Oxford University Press, 1983.

Hinman, Lawrence. *Ethics: A Pluralistic Approach to Moral Theory*. Fort Worth: Harcourt, Brace and Company, 1998.

Hobbes, Thomas. *Leviathan*. Ed. C.B. MacPherson. London: Penguin Classics, 1968.

_____. *Thomas Hobbes: De Cive or the Citizen*. Ed. Sterling P. Lamprecht. New York: Appleton-Century-Crofts, 1949.

Hohfeld, Wesley Newcomb. 1919. Rights and Jural Relations. In *Fundamental Legal Conceptions*, edited by W. Wheeler Cook, New Haven and London: Yale University Press.

Honderich, Ted, ed. *Oxford Companion to Philosophy*. Oxford: Oxford University Press, 1995

Hume, David. *Hume's Treatise of Human Nature*. Ed. A.D. Lindsay. London: J.M. Dent and Sons Ltd., 1923.

_____. *Enquiries concerning the Human Understanding and concerning the Principles of Morals*. Ed.L.A. Selby-Bigge, Oxford: Clarendon Press, 1902.

Hyman, Irwin A. *The Case Against Spanking: How to Discipline Your Child Without Hitting*. San Francisco: Jossey-Bass Publishers, 1997.

Ianno, Tony, M.P. Trinity-Spadina. "Ianno Tackles Child Abuse." Press Release 11 March 1998.

Ihde, Don. *Technology and the Lifeworld: from Garden to Earth*. Bloomington: Indiana University Press, 1990.

James, P.D. *The Children of Men*. Toronto: Alfred. A. Knopf Canada, 1992.

Kadushin, Alfred and Judith A. Martin. *Child Abuse: An Interactional Event*. New York: Columbia University Press, 1981.

Kant, Immanuel. *Groundwork of the Metaphysic of Morals*. Ed. and trans. H.J. Paton. New York: Harper and Row Publishers, 1964.

_____. *Critique of Practical Reason*. Trans. Mary J. Gregor. Cambridge: Cambridge University Press, 1997.

_____. *Immanuel Kant's Critique of Pure Reason*. Trans. Norman Kemp Smith. London: MacMillan Education Ltd., 1989.

_____. "Education". Trans. Annette Churton. Ann Arbor: University of Michigan Press, 1960. In *Philosophical Foundations of Education*. 6th ed.. Eds. Howard Ozman and Samuel Craver. Up Saddle River, N.J.: Merrill, 1995.

Kierkegaard, Sören. "Eulogy on Abraham." In *Fear and Trembling, Repitition,* edited by Howard V. Hong and Edna H. Hong, Princeton: Princeton University Press, 1983.

King, Michael, ed. *Moral Agendas for Children's' Welfare*. London: Routledge, 1999.

King, Peter O. "Thomas Hobbes's Children." In *The Philosopher's Child: Critical Perspectives in the Western Tradition*, edited by Susan M. Turner and Gareth B. Matthews, Rochester: University of Rochester Press, 1998.

Ko, Marnie. *Report (Alberta Edition)*, 01 January 2001.

Kunkel, Joseph. "Challenging the Domestic Analogy: A Critique of Killing in Self-Defense." In *Ethical Issues: Perspectives for Canadians*, edited by Eldon Soifer. Peterborough, ON: Broadview Press, 1997.

Kymlicka, Will. *Liberalism, Community and Culture*. Oxford: Clarendon Press, 1989.

_____. *Finding Our Way: Rethinking Ethnocultural Relations in Canada*. Don Mills, ON.: Oxford University Press Canada, 1998.

Lafollette, Hugh. "Licensing Parents." *Philosophy and Public Affairs* 9 (1980).

Larmore, Charles. *The Morals of Modernity*. Cambridge: Cambridge University Press, 1996.

Larzelere, Robert. "Response to Oosterhuis: Empirically Justified Uses of Spanking: Toward a Discriminating View of Corporal Punishment." *Journal of Psychology and Theology* 21 (1993).

_____. "A Review of the Outcomes of Parental Use of Nonabusive or Customary Physical Punishment." *Pediatrics* ISSN 0031 4005 (1996).

Lerner, Barbara. "When Spanking Can't be Beaten." *Ottawa Citizen*, 27 April 1998.

Levi, Primo. *Survival in Auschwitz*. New York: Simon and Schuster, 1996.

Locke, John. *Two Treatises of Government*. Ed. Mark Goldie. London: J.M. Dent, 1993.

_____. *Some Thoughts Concerning Education*. Ed. F.W. Goforth. New York: Barron's Educational Series, 1964.

Lovaas, O.I. "Behavioral treatment and normal educational and intellectual functioning in young autistic children." *Journal of Consulting and Clinical Psychology* 55 (1987).

MacIntyre, Alasdair. *After Virtue*. Notre Dame: Notre Dame University Press, 1981.

MacKinnon, Catharine. *Feminism Unmodified: Discourse on Life and Law*. Cambridge: Harvard University Press, 1987.

Major, Tony, "Horrifying Codified Cruelty: Report to Parliament and People (Aids to Thinking and Feeling)." Photocopied manuscript, 1996.

Martin's Annual Criminal Code 1999. Annotations by Edward L. Greenspan and The Honourable Mr. Justice Marc Rosenberg. Aurora, ON.: Canada Law Book Inc., 1999.

Matthews, Gareth B. *Philosophy and the Young Child*. Cambridge: Harvard University Press, 1980.

_____. *Dialogues with Children*. Cambridge: Harvard University Press, 1984.

_____. *The Philosophy of Childhood*. Cambridge: Harvard University Press, 1994.

Megill, Alan. *The Prophets of Extremity*. Berkeley and Los Angeles: University of California Press, 1985.

McGillivray, Anne. "'He'll learn it on his body': Disciplining Childhood in Canadian Law." *International Journal of Children's Rights* 5 (1998).

McGowan Tress, Daryl. "Aristotle's Child: Development through *Genesis, Oikos* and *Polis*." In *The Philosopher's Child: Critical Perspectives in the Western Tradition*, edited by S.M. Turner and Gareth B. Matthews, Rochester: University of Rochester Press, 1998. Originally published in *Ancient Philosophy* 17 (1997): 63-84. 1998.

Mill, John Stuart. *The Collected Works of John Stuart Mill*. 33 Vols. General ed. John Robson. Toronto: University of Toronto Press and Routledge Kegan Paul, 1963-1991.

Minow, Martha. "Foreword: Justice Engendered." 101 *Harvard Law Review* 10 (1987).

Nozick, Robert. *Anarchy, State and Utopia*. New York: Basic Books, 1974.

The Oxford Concise English Dictionary. 9th ed. Ed. Della Thompson. Oxford: Clarendon Press Oxford, 1995.

Piper, Christine. "Moral Campaigns for Children's Welfare in the Nineteenth Century." In *Moral Agendas for Children's Welfare*, edited by Michael King, London: Routledge, 1999.

Plato. *The Republic of Plato*. Ed. and trans. Francis MacDonald Cornford. Oxford: Oxford University Press, 1973.

Purdy, Laura. *In Their Best Interest? The Case Against Equal Rights for Children*. Cornell: Cornell University Press, 1992.

Rawls, John. *A Theory of Justice*. Oxford: Oxford University Press, 1972.

_____. "Two Concepts of Rules." *The Philosophical Review* 64 (1955).

Raz, Joseph. *The Morality of Freedom*. Oxford: Clarendon Press, 1986.

Robertshaw, Corinne. "Brief to: Minister of Justice and Attorney General, Solicitor General, Minister of Health, Secretary of State for the Status of Women and the Standing Committee on Justice and Legal Affairs re: Section 43 of the Criminal Code and the Corporal Punishment of Children." *The Institute for the Prevention of Child Abuse*, April 1994.

Roberts, Monty. *The Man Who Listens to Horses*. New York: Random House, 1997.

Robson, John and Anne Robson, eds. *Sexual Equality: Writings by John Stuart Mill, Harriet Taylor Mill and Helen Taylor*. Toronto: University of Toronto Press, 1994.

Rorty, Richard. *Contingency, Irony and Solidarity*. Cambridge: Cambridge University Press, 1989.

Rosenberg, Harriet. "The Kitchen and the Multi-National Corporation: An Analysis of the Links between the Household and Global Corporations." *Journal of Business Ethics* 6 (1987).

Rousseau, Jean-Jacques. *The Social Contract*. Ed. and trans. G.D.H. Cole. London: J.M. Dent and Sons, 1938.

_____. *Emile, or On Education*. Ed. and trans. Allan Bloom. New York: Basic Books, 1979.

Scarre, Geoffrey. *Utilitarianism*. London: Routledge, 1996.

Schneewind, J.B. *Sidgwick's Ethics and Victorian Moral Philosophy*. Oxford: Oxford University Press, 1977.

Shiner, Roger. "Adjudication, Coherence and Moral Value." In *Legal Theory Meets Legal Practice*, edited by Anne Bayefsky, Edmonton: Academic Printing and Publishing, 1988.

Sidgwick, Henry. *The Methods of Ethics*. Indianapolis: Hackett, 1981.

Simon, Julia. "Jean-Jacques Rousseau's Children" in *The Philosopher's Child: Critical Perspectives in the Western Tradition*, edited by S.M. Turner and Gareth B. Matthews, Rochester: University of Rochester Press, 1998. Originally published under the title "Natural Freedom and Moral Autonomy: Emile as Parent, Teacher and Citizen," in *The History of Political Thought* 16 (spring 1995): 21-36.

Spock, Benjamin. *Baby and Child Care,* 3rd ed. New York: Hawthorne, 1968.

Straus, Murray. *Beating the Devil Out of Them: Corporal Punishment in American Families*. New York: Macmillan, 1994.

Straus, Murray, David Sugarman, and Jean Giles-Sims. "Spanking by Parents and Subsequent Anti-Social Behavior of Children." *Archives of Pediatrics and Adolescents Medicine* (August 1997). Also available at http://www.unh.edu/frl/cp24art.htm

Sumner, Wayne. *The Moral Foundation of Rights*. Oxford: Oxford University Press, 1987.

Sutherland, Neil. *Children in English Canada: Framing the 20th Century Consensus*. Reprinted, with a new foreword by Cynthia Comacchio. Waterloo: Wilfrid Laurier University Press, 2000.

Taylor, Charles. *Sources of the Self*. Cambridge: Harvard University Press, 1989.

Thompson Gershoff, Elizabeth. "Corporal Punishment by Parents and Associated Child Outcomes: A Meta-Analytic and Theoretical Review." *Psychological Bulletin*. In press, 2001.

Tremeears Criminal Annotations 1971-1986. 2nd Permanent Supplement. Ed. Leonard J. Ryan. Carswell, 1986.

Turner, Susan M. "John Stuart Mill's Children." In *The Philosopher's Child: Critical Perspectives in the Western Tradition*, edited by S.M. Turner and Gareth B. Matthews, Rochester: University of Rochester Press, 1998.

_____. "The One Eyed Moral Outlaw." Paper presented at the Northwestern Philosophical Association Conference, November 1993.

_____. "Locke and a Sort of Parental Dominion." Paper presented at the Descartes Conference, University of Toronto, October 1995.

_____. "Conceiving Individualism." Ph.D. diss., University of Alberta, 1995.

Turner, Susan M. and Gareth B. Matthews, eds. *The Philosopher's Child: Critical Essays in the Western Tradition*. Rochester: University of Rochester Press, 1998.

Wallach, Lorraine B. "Helping Children Cope with Violence." *Young Children* (May 1993).

Waluchow, W.J. "Charter Challenges: A Test Case for Theories of Law." *Osgoode Hall Journal* 29 (1991).

Webber, Jeremy. *Reimagining Canada: Language, Culture, Community and the Canadian Constitution*. Kingston: McGill-Queens University Press, 1994.

Selected Legal Cases by Year

The subject of each case is noted in parantheses.

Q. v. Robinson, 7 C.C.C. 52 (1899). (Corporal Punishment)

K. v. Zink, 18 C.C.C. 456 (1910). (Corporal Punishment)

R. v. Metcalfe, 49 C.C.C. 260 (1927). (Corporal Punishment)

R. v. Corkum, 67 C.C.C. 114 (1937). (Corporal Punishment)

Campeau v. The King, 103 C.C.C. 355 (1951). (Corporal Punishment)

R. v. Imbeault, 17 N.B.R. (2d) 234 (1977). (Corporal Punishment)

R. v. Ogg-Moss, 60 C.C.C. (2d) 127, 24 C.R. (3d) 264 (1981). (Corporal Punishment)

R. v. Wheaton, 33 NFLD. & P.E.I.R. 520, 99 A.P.R. 520 (1982). (Corporal Punishment)

R. v. Lepage, R.L. 247 (C.M.Q.) (1983). (Corporal Punishment)

R. v. Nixon. 5 O.A.C. 107, 14 C.C.C. (3d) 257, [1984] 2 S.C.R. 197 (S.C.C.) (1984). (Corporal Punishment)

Ogg-Moss v. R., 41 C.R. (3d) (1984). (Corporal Punishment)

Perka et al. v. The Queen, 13 D.L.R. (4th) (1984). (Necessity)

R. v. Taylor, 19 C.C.C. (3d) 156 (1985). (Corporal Punishment)

R.. v. Dupperon, 16 C.C.C. (3d) 453 (1985). (Corporal Punishment)

Morgentaler, Smoling and Scott v. The Queen, S.C.R. 30 (1988). (Abortion)

R. v. Keegstra, 3 S.C.R. 697 (1990). (Hate Speech)

Lavalee v. R., 555 C.C.C. (3d) 97 (1990). (Self-Defense)

R. v. Butler, 1 S.C.R. 697 (1992). (Obscenity)

Cambria, Supreme Court of Cassation (Italy), 6th Penal Section (1996). (Corporal Punishment)

Canadian Foundation of Children, Youth and Justice (Applicant) and *The Attorney General of Canada* (Respondent) and *The Canadian Teachers' Federation, The Coalition for Family Autonomy*, and the *Ontario Childrens' Aid Society* (Interveners), Ontario Superior Court of Justice, Court File No.: 98-CV-158948 (2000). (Corporal Punishment)

Appendix

•••••••••••

(Taken from document produced
by the Repeal 43 Committee)

"The purpose of this table is to show the kind of assaults on children approved by section 43 of our Criminal Code. It is not to advocate prosecution as the appropriate way to deal with these cases. If in fact s. 43 were repealed as we propose, these criminal prosecutions would be unnecessary because the question of whether such assaults were "reasonable" or for "correction" would no longer be relevent. Repealing the section would give a *clear and unambiguous* message that assaults on children were no longer legal. This would *reduce* the need for these prosecutions. Instead, counselling and education in alternative methods of discipline could be offered to parents and teachers; with criminal prosecution used only as a last resort where this approach fails or where prosecution is warranted by the nature of the assault.

This information on assault charges against parents and teachers is limited because these decisions are rarely included in law reports or newspapers. Where assaults are reported, the information given does not always include the facts needed to complete the table. The table was prepared by the Repeal 43 Committee, July 2001."

Judicial Decisions in which Parental Assaults Held Reasonable under S.43
1990 to 2001

Case Citation	Child's Age & Sex	Child's Misconduct	Punishment	Charge	Trial Decision	Appeal Decision	Judges Comments
1. R. v. Dunfield 1990 103 NBR (2d) 172 New Brunswick	Girl, 9	Did not finish lessons	Struck on arm twice with ruler which broke. Other bruises on body but no proof inflicted by accused.	Common assault foster mother	Guilty	Acquitted	Hyperactive child: difficult to manage
2. R. v. Wheeler unreported Yukon, 1990, Faulkner J. No. 191	Boy, 7	Stealing school lunches	About 12 slaps on wrist with open hand. Bruise on hand and wrist	Common assault foster mother	Acquitted	No appeal	Punishment causing bruises not necessarily excessive
3. R. v. Laframboise, 8 WCB (2d) 202, Merredew, J 1990 Vol 10 T.L.W. NO. 37,12 Ont. Cosgrove, J.	Boy, 13	Boy slammed door after being slapped for being "disruptive"	Slapped and struck on buttocks and legs several times with piece of wood	Common assault father	Guilty conditional discharge	Acquitted	Trial Judge failed to consider the "subjective nature" of S. 43 defence. A strict construction of s.43 is incorrect
4. R. v Olsen 1990 Ont. O.J. 3248 Unreported Loukdelis, J	Boy, teenage	Took mother's car without consent. Had previous conviction for theft	Knocked off bike, punched and kicked "a few times" causing swollen eyes and nose bleed	Assault causing bodily harm by mother's male friend with her consent	Acquitted	Guilty absolute discharge	Trial judge erred in holding assault "reasonable"
5. R. v. Goforth (1992) 98 Sask. R, 26	Boy, 8	No info	A "spanking or whatever you want to call it" causing bruises and discolouration	Common assault father	Acquitted	Upheld	No evidence of community standards needed

6. R. v. L.A.K. (1992) 104 Nfld. and P.E.I. R. 118 NFLD.	Girl, 11	Gestures with "obscene connotation"	Struck once with belt causing bruise on leg	Common assault father	Acquitted	No appeal	No hospitalization or disfigurement resulted. While "perhaps a little distasteful" force is authorized by law
7. R. v. Vivian unreported BC, 1992, Leggatt, J. No. 2190	Girl, no age given	Disagreement during discussion	Grabbed by hair and head pushed into cupboard door	Common assault step-father	Guilty	Acquitted	Trial judge found girl was not "insolent" but step-father had "honest belief" that she was.
8. R. v. K.(M) 1993 16 CR (4th), 121 Manitoba Ct. of Appeal	Boy, 8	Opened bag of seeds contrary to instructions. Seeds caught in baby's throat	Kicked on buttocks, hit on shoulders several times leaving imprint of sweater on skin	Assault bodily harm father	Guilty conditional discharge	Acquitted	"Well within range of generally accepted punishment - mild compared to what I received"
9. R. v. Atkinson (1994) 9 WWR 485, Manitoba	3 children age 2 - 3	No details given	Hit with belt on "diapered bottom" and upper thigh. One child hit on chest with open hand. Evidence of other injuries but no evidence caused by foster mother	Common assault foster mother	Acquitted	No appeal	Belts have potential for injury & child should not be hit on chest but no description of belt. Life and limb not endangered.
10. R. v. V. L. 28 WCB (2d) 476, 1995 Ontario	Boy, 13	Told stepfather to "shut up" during course of argument	Struck in mouth with open hand causing swollen lip	Common assault stepfather	Acquitted	No appeal	Blow to head dangerous but injury doesn't mean force unreasonable. Cases going back to 1899 cited in support.
11. R. v. D.W. 28 WCB (2d) 348, 1995 Alberta	Boy, 4	Child yelling	Slap on face that left imprint of hand while child suffering from ear infection	Common assault father	Acquitted	No appeal	Slap to head not per se excessive force. Hyperactive child.

Case	Age/Sex	Reason	Action	Charge	Verdict	Appeal	Notes
12. R. v. Pickard unreported BC, 1995, de Villiers, J No. 2861	Boy, 15	Annoyed father by intentional noise	Grabbed and wrestled to ground, punched in neck and grabbed by hair. Pain for some days and bruise on forehead.	Assault causing bodily harm father	Acquitted	No appeal	A hard body blow was necessary for a "submissive response" and to correct the boy.
13. R. v. Peterson (1995) 124 DLR (4th) 758 Ontario	Girl, 5	Fighting with younger brother. Shut car door on his hand.	Pants pulled down, put over trunk of car in public parking lot and spanked 6 times.	Common assault father	Acquitted	No appeal	Community standards may not be relevant. S.43 doesn't deal with them. Court is not a court of social justice. Court's job is to apply the law.
14. R. v. M (W.F.) Alberta 1995 41 C.R. (4th), 330 Ct. of Appeal	Girl, 12	Not details given	Ordered to remove slacks and underpants and spanked on bare buttocks	Sexual assault stepfather	Acquitted on basis that spanking was simply discipline	Upheld with one dissent	Dissenting Judge held that forcing 12year old girl to strip for spanking violated her sexual integrity and was a sexual assault
15. R. v. Kootenay Alberta, Reported in The Province Mar. 27 & 29 /95 Wambolt, J. P.	Girl, 11	Burned cheese on stove	Struck on buttocks several times with belt	Common assault triple amputee mother	Acquitted	No appeal	None reported
16. R. v. Mills Alberta, Reported in Ottawa Citizen Dec 30 /96 Abbott, J	Boy, No Info	No info	Hard slap to head in parking lot	Common assault mother	Acquitted	No appeal	Boy like a 'wild Indian'
17. R. v. J. (O) 30 WCB (2d) 199, Ontario	Girl, 6	Refused to go to school	Spanked twice with hand and twice with ruler. Bruising and red marks.	Common assault mother	Acquitted	No appeal	Deliberate disobedience requiring correction. Reasonable standard of force "elusive".
18. R. v. Morton Unreported 1998 Nova Scotia	Girl, No Info	Fighting with siblings	spanked 5 - 10 times with a stick	Common assault father	Acquitted	No Appeal	"Controlled correction"

Case Citation	Child's Age & Sex	Child's Misconduct	Punishment	Charge	Trial Decision	Appeal	Judges Comments
19. R. v. James 38 WCB (2d) 48 Ont. 1998.	Boy, 11	Swore following argument with father	Slapped on face leaving marks	Common assault father	Acquitted	No appeal	No clear test but previous decisions show this is allowed by s. 43
20. R. v. N.S. 1999 OJ 320 Ontario, Karam, J Unreported	Boy and girl under 12	Not given	Strapped with horse harness on at least 2 or 3 occasions leaving welts during childhood in 1970s and 1980s	Assault bodily harm and assault with a weapon laid after children became adults	Acquitted	No Appeal	Raising welts does not amount to bodily harm; bruises "merely transient" In view of s. 43, "insufficient evidence" of assault with weapon where there was "progressive discipline, which included warnings"
21. R. v. Bell 49 WCB (2d) 507, Ontario	Boy, 11	Suspicion he had stolen candy	Struck with belt 2 or 3 times. Bruise on thigh in shape of buckle	Assault with weapon	Guilty	Acquitted	S. 43 does not restrict discipline to what is appropriate or proportional or that it must be a last resort. Pain and a 'trifling' bruise is not unreasonable

Judicial Decisions in which Teacher's Assaults Held Reasonable under S.43 1990 to 2001

Case Citation	Child's Age & Sex	Child's Misconduct	Punishment	Charge	Trial Decision	Appeal Decision	Judges Comments
1. R. v. Harriott (1992) 128 NBR (2d) 155 New Brunswick	Boy, 14	Disruptive	Grabbed by head and shaken, pushed into seat	Common assault	Acquitted	No appeal	"Grave concern" expressed about "corrective action by contact with child's head".
2. R. v. Funder unreported Que. 1993 Ct. of Appeal. No. 238	Boy, 14	Indulging in "horseplay" during lesson	Hit on head with book	Assault causing bodily harm	Guilty	Acquitted	Injuries minor

Case	Victim	Behaviour	Action	Charge	Result	Appeal	Comments
3. R. v. Condon (1993) 102 NFLD & PEI Reports 142 NFLD	Boy, no info	Persisted in calling teacher nickname	Grabbed boy by the shoulder and when boy pushed back, teacher "struck boy in throat area as a reflex"	Common assault	Acquitted	No Appeal	"One blow only- no permanent injury"
4. R. v. Plourde (1994) 140 NBR (2d) 273 New Brunswick	2 boys, 14	Objected to way teacher pushed other student	1 boy pushed out of room causing marks on back and arm, 2nd grabbed and slapped on head	Common assault	Acquitted	No appeal	Insolent behaviour. Respect for authority important.
5. R. v. Bouillon unreported Que. 1993, Decoste, J No. 000493-938	Boy, 15	Talking in class	Grabbed by hair and head pushed onto desk.	Common assault	Acquitted	Upheld	Teacher's action may be disgraceful, but it was not excessive.
6. R. v. Swanson unreported BC, 1993, Gordon, J No. 2945	Boy, 13	Talking in shop class	Hit on head with hammer causing pain and possible small bump	Common assault	Acquitted	No appeal	Head injury benign. No threat to health.
7. R. v. Gallant (1994) 110 NFLD & PEI Reports 174 P.E.I.	Boy, 11	Disruptive behaviour by boy with discipline problem	Slapped in face to get boy "back to reality"	Common assault	Acquitted	No appeal	No risk of injury to head
8. R. v. Whalen (1994) 118 Nfld & PEI R 331, NFLD	Girl, 11	Talking in class "insolent"	Slammed book on child's desk, hitting arm	Common assault	Acquitted	No appeal	Action justified for "cheeky" girl.
9. R. v. Graham (1995) 151 NBR 81, (1995), 39 CR 4th 339 New Brunswick	Girl, 9	Refused to do assignment and argued with teacher	Lifted from seat and struck on buttocks with open hand leaving red mark for 24 hours	Common assault	Acquitted	Upheld	Trial judge's reference to Bible and "trip to woodshed" acceptable; policy documents on punishment irrelevant.
10. R. v. Wetmore New Brunswick 1996, 172 N.B.R. (2d) 224	4 boys, 16 to 18	Rude and disrespectful	Karate chops to shoulder, arm and face	Common assault	Acquitted	Upheld	Instilling respect, even through fear, is acceptable.

Case	Child(ren)	Circumstances	Action	Charge	Verdict	Appeal	Comment
11. R. v. Godin New Brunswick (1996) 172 NBR (2d) 375	2 boys, 10 and 11	Fighting each other	Both hit in face with hand	Common assault	Guilty	Acquitted	No injuries. Decisions dating from 19th century cited with approval.
12. R. v. Spenard unreported Ont., 1996, Donnelly, J	4 boys, 8 to 10	Breach of classroom rules	Slapping, pushing, grabbing over 10 year period	Common assault	Acquitted	No appeal	Discipline develops character. Injured dignity has corrective potential.
13. R. v. Ocampo 36 WCB 479 1997, Ont.	Various pupils about age 9	Disobedience	Pinched nose, Hit leg with pointer Slapped head Slapped face	5 counts common assault	Acquitted	No appeal	Reasonable force. School board policies on corporal punishment do not affect s.43
14. R. v. Park (1999) 178 NFLD & PEI Reports 194, Nfld.	Girl, 9 Mental age of 6	Resisted getting into snowsuit by kicking and screaming	Slapped on leg Whether fingerprint marks caused by slap not proven	Common assault	Guilty	Acquitted on appeal	Slap had a "salutary effect on behaviour"
15. R. v. Holmes Unreported No. 555-01 0267-998 Aug 31, 2000 Que. Lapointe, J	Boy, 13	Fooling around in gym class	Lifted off ground by chin and head in wrestling hold by 260 lb. teacher	Assault causing bodily harm	Acquitted	May be appealed	No objective evidence of actual harm
16. R. v. Skidmore Unreported No. 8414 /99 June 27, 2000 Ontario Nosanchuk, J.	Boy, 13	Ignored instructions not to kick volleyball in gym class and continued "horseplay" contrary to instructions	Grabbed by arm and throat, pushed against wall, accidentally hit on head with clip board	Common assault	Acquitted	No appeal	Teacher showed "incredible restraint" and should not have been prosecuted.

Index

• • • • • • • • • • • •

Sutherland, Neil: on Canadian history of childhood, 94, 103, 107, 256n8, 266n30
Sweden: corporal punishment reforms in, 188, 204, 208–10, 221, 236, 252n23, 253n30, 259n24, 266n31, 271n25, 277n1

Taylor, Charles, 253n27
teachers, 142–43, 163; and protection under Section 43, 171, 190, 211–14, 283nn4, 9
Theory of Justice, A, 37–38, 58
Thomson Gershoff, Elizabeth: parent-child relationship, 260n33, 262n35
tolerance, 43–48, 52, 53. 262n44
trauma. *See* harm; corporal punishment, cases
Trocme, Nico, 287n43
Turner, Susan M., 256n8

United Nations Convention on the Rights of the Child, 208, 253n26
utilitarianism: "act" and "rule," 245n38, 278n7; corporal punishment and, 69–89; moral theory of, 5–6, 39, 65–91; rights

and, 39–40; under Jeremy Bentham and John Stuart Mill, 34–36; Section 43 and, 165

vagueness: as legal flaw, 181–82, 184; in Section 43, 181–82, 184; and security of the person, 52–53
values, 42; Canadian, 5; liberal, 45–52; moral, and relationship to law, 17, 22; moral education, 54–60; parental, 159–60; traditional, 4
veil of ignorance: in John Rawls's *A Theory of Justice*, 37–38, 58
violence, 73–78, 107–108, 266n31; culture of and corporal punishment, 206–207
virtue: according to Aristotle, 27

Wallach, Lorraine, 283n3
Waluchow, Wilfred, 282n15
Webber, Jeremy, 248n1, 255n2
willfulness: defiance, 131–33, 141, 252n18; perceived, as cause of child abuse, 223–24
women: 115–16, 119, 123–24, 243n21; girls, 258n25, 262n44